THE COMPLETE WRITER

Level Three
Workbook for Writing with Ease

INSTRUCTOR SECTION

By

Susan Wise Bauer

WELL-
TRAINED
MIND
PRESS

www.welltrainedmind.com

This workbook is to be used in conjunction with
THE COMPLETE WRITER: WRITING WITH EASE
Strong Fundamentals

ISBN   978-1-933339-77-1

Available at www.welltrainedmind.com or
wherever books are sold

CONTENTS

READING SELECTIONS

Week 1: "The Straw, the Coal, and the Bean" and "Cat and Mouse in Partnership" by Jacob and Wilhelm Grimm

Week 2: *Mr. Revere and I* by Robert Lawson

Week 3: *And Then What Happened, Paul Revere?* by Jean Fritz and *The Many Rides of Paul Revere* by James Cross Giblin

Week 4: *Homer Price* by Robert McCloskey

Week 5: "Jabberwocky" by Lewis Carroll and "Stegosaurus" by Jack Prelutsky

Week 6: *Time Cat* by Lloyd Alexander

Week 7: *The Story of the World, Volume 1: Ancient Times* and *The Story of the World, Volume 2: The Middle Ages* by Susan Wise Bauer

Week 8: *The Lion, the Witch and the Wardrobe* by C. S. Lewis

Week 9: *C. S. Lewis: The Man Behind Narnia* by Beatrice Gormley and *Everyday Life: World War I* by Walter A. Hazen

Week 10: *Farmer Boy* by Laura Ingalls Wilder

Week 11: *Tales of Ancient Egypt* by Roger Lancelyn Green and *The Histories* by Herodotus, trans. by Robin Waterfield

Week 12: "Ali Baba and the Forty Thieves" by Jacob and Wilhelm Grimm

Week 13: *The Four-Story Mistake* by Elizabeth Enright

Week 14: *The Moffats* by Eleanor Estes

Week 15: *The Lemonade Trick* by Scott Corbett

Week 16: *Magic...Naturally! Science Entertainments and Amusements* by Vicki Cobb, and Adapted from *Magic Through Science* by Robert Gardner

Week 17: *Harry Houdini, Young Magician* by Kathryn Kilby Borland and *Harry Houdini: Death-Defying Showman* by Rita Thievon Mullin

Week 18: *Paul Bunyan Swings His Axe* by Dell J. McCormick and *The Story of Canada* by Janet Lunn and Christopher Moore

Week 19: *The Story of the Declaration of Independence* by Norman Richards and *The Young Oxford History of Britain & Ireland* by Mike Corbishley and Kenneth O. Morgan

Week 20: "The Garden of Live Flowers" and "Queen Alice" from *Through the Looking-Glass* by Lewis Carroll

Week 21: "Stopping by Woods on a Snowy Evening" by Robert Frost and "The Listeners" by Walter de la Mare

Week 22: *The Furious Flycycle* by Jan Wahl

Week 23: *Laura Ingalls Wilder, Young Pioneer* by Beatrice Gormley and *Dr. Seuss, Young Author and Artist* by Kathleen Kudlinski

Week 24: *Mrs. Piggle-Wiggle's Magic* by Betty MacDonald

Week 25: *Money, Money, Money: Where It Comes From, How to Save It, Spend It, and Make It* by Eve Drobot and *The Everything Kids' Money Book* by Diane Mayr

Week 26: *Babe: The Gallant Pig* by Dick King-Smith

Week 27: *Hunting and Herding Dogs* by Marie-Therese Miller and *A Dog's World*, edited by Christine Hunsicker

Week 28: *Anne of Green Gables* by Lucy Maud Montgomery and *Pioneers in Canada* by Harry Johnston

Week 29: *The Young Folks' History of England* by Charlotte Yonge

Week 30: *The Black Stallion* by Walter Farley

Week 31: *King Arthur and His Knights of the Round Table* by Roger Lancelyn Green

Week 32: "The Valiant Little Tailor" by Jacob and Wilhelm Grimm

Week 33: *Bambi: A Life in the Woods* by Felix Salten

Week 34: "Prince Wicked and the Grateful Animals" from More *More Jataka Tales* by Ellen Babbitt

Week 35: *The Jungle Book* by Rudyard Kipling

Week 36: *Rabbit Hill* by Robert Lawson

WEEK 1

DAY ONE: Narration Exercise   *Student Pages 1–3*

Focus: *Identifying the central narrative thread in a passage*

Pull out Student Pages 1–2 and Student Page 3. Ask the student to write her name and the date on Student Page 3.

Allow the student to read the story on Student Pages 1–2, either silently or aloud.

This fable is a more difficult narrative than the Level Two narratives. Help the student begin to identify the central elements in the narrative by asking the following questions. She should try to answer these questions without looking back at the story, but if she cannot remember an answer after thinking for a few minutes, allow her to reread. Remind her to answer in complete sentences.

Instructor: How did the bean escape from the old woman?
Student: *It dropped out of the pan.*

Instructor: How did the coal escape from the fire?
Student: *It leaped out.*

Instructor: What else escaped the fire?
Student: *The straw escaped.*

Instructor: What did the bean, the coal, and the straw decide to do together?
Student: *They decided to go on a journey to a foreign country.*

Instructor: What was the first obstacle they ran into?
Student: *They came to a brook with no bridge across it.*

Instructor: What solution did the straw come up with?
Student: *The straw laid herself across the water.*

Instructor: Who tried to cross the straw?
Student: *The coal tried to cross.*

Instructor: What happened then?
Student: *The coal burned through the straw and fell into the water.*

Instructor: How did the bean react?
Student: *She laughed until she split.*

Instructor: Who fixed her?
Student: *A tailor sewed her back together.*

Instructor: This fairy tale is a particular kind of story called a "pourquoi [por-kwa] tale." *Pourquoi* is French for "why," and pourquoi tales give imaginative explanations for *why* something is the way it is. What does this tale try to explain?
Student: *It tries to explain why beans have a black seam.*

Now ask the student the general question, "Can you give me a brief summary of this passage?" The student should answer by summarizing the plot, rather than listing details. Her answer should be no more than three sentences and should resemble one of the following:

"A coal, a straw, and a bean escaped from an old woman. They set out on a journey, but the straw was burnt, the coal fell into water, and the bean split herself laughing. A tailor sewed up the bean with black thread."

"A coal, a straw, and a bean set out on a journey. When they got to a brook, the straw lay down across it as a bridge. The coal went across the straw, but the straw burned, the coal fell into the water, and the bean burst herself laughing."

"A coal, a straw, and a bean came to a brook. The straw tried to become a bridge, but the coal burned the bridge in half and fell in the water. Then the bean split open laughing."

The student will probably attempt to put too much information into the summary. If she has difficulty condensing the story, ask the following three questions:

Who are the three main characters?

What problem did they run into? ["They escaped from an old woman" **OR** "They came to a brook they could not cross" are both acceptable answers.]

What happened to each one?

Then have the student repeat her answers in order; this will form her brief summary. Write down the student's narration on Student Page 3 as she watches.

DAY TWO: Dictation Exercise   *Student Page 4*

Focus: Comma use, capitalization of proper names

Pull out Student Page 4. Ask the student to write her name and the date.
Tell the student that today's dictation sentence is from another one of the Grimms' fairy tales, called "Little Red Cap." It is one of the earliest versions of the story we now know as "Little Red Riding Hood."
Dictate the following sentence to the student two times. Before you read, tell the student that you will pause at the commas. Be sure to indicate the commas in the sentence by pausing significantly at each one.

> The grandmother lived out in the wood, half a mile from the village, and just as Little Red Cap entered the wood, a wolf met her.

Tell the student that since "Little Red Cap" is used as the girl's proper name, all three words should be capitalized. Now ask the student to repeat the sentence back to you before she writes. Remind her to pause, as you did, to indicate the commas. If she cannot remember the entire sentence, you may repeat it additional times.

Watch the student as she writes, and correct her at once if she begins to make a mistake. When she is finished, point out each comma and tell her that these commas are used to avoid misunderstanding. Without the commas, a reader might think that the grandmother lived in a "wood half a mile," or that Little Red Cap "entered the wood a wolf."

DAY THREE: Narration and Dictation *Student Pages 5–7*

Focus: *Identifying the central narrative thread in a passage and writing original sentences from dictation*

Pull out Student Pages 5–6 and 7. Ask the student to write her name and the date on Student Page 7.

Today's exercise will combine narration and dictation. Allow the student to read the story on Student Pages 5–6, either silently or aloud.

If the student is not familiar with the custom of "christening," you may want to explain that this is a church ceremony during which babies are baptized and named.

Help the student begin to identify the central elements in the narrative by asking the following questions. She should try to answer these questions without looking back at the story, but if she cannot remember an answer after thinking for a few minutes, allow her to reread. Remind her to answer in complete sentences.

Instructor: What did the cat and the mouse buy for the winter?
Student: *They bought a pot of bacon fat.*

Instructor: Where did they decide to keep it?
Student: *They kept it in the church.*

Instructor: What excuse did the cat give for going out and eating the fat?
Student: *She said that she had to go to christenings.*

Instructor: How many times did she do this?
Student: *She did it three times.*

Instructor: She told the mouse that the three babies had three strange names. What were they?
Student: *The names were Top-off, Half-done, and All-gone.*

Instructor: When the mouse found out what the cat had done, what happened?
Student: *The cat ate the mouse.*

Instructor: "That is the way of the world" means that the strong will always take advantage of the weak. In what two ways did the cat take advantage of the mouse?
Student: *She ate the bacon fat that they both bought, and then she ate the mouse.*

Now ask the student the general question, "Can you give me a brief summary of this passage?" The student should answer by summarizing the plot, rather than listing details. Her answer should be no more than three sentences and should resemble one of the following:

"A cat and a mouse set up house together. They bought a pot of fat for the winter, but the cat pretended to go to christenings and ate the entire thing. When the mouse found out, the cat ate her."

"A cat and a mouse bought a pot of fat and hid it in a church. The cat told the mouse that she had to go to three christenings. Each time she went out, she ate some of the fat, until it was all gone."

"The cat told the mouse that she was going to the christenings of three babies. She said that they were named Top-off, Half-done, and All-gone. But she had really eaten the pot of fat—first the top, then half, then the rest of it."

If she has difficulty condensing the story, ask the following three questions:

What did the cat and the mouse do together?

In one sentence, how did the cat trick the mouse?

What happened at the end of the story?

Then have the student repeat her answers in order; this will form her brief summary. Write down the student's narration on the lines below, but do not allow her to watch.

_____

_____

_____

_____

Then choose one or two sentences (about 12–15 words) to dictate back to the student. Repeat the sentences twice and ask the student to repeat them back to you before she writes on Student Page 7. If she cannot repeat the sentences, read them again until she is able to keep them in mind.

Give all necessary help in spelling and punctuation.

DAY FOUR: Dictation Exercise

Focus: *Comma and period use*

Pull out Student Page 8. Ask the student to write her name and the date.

Tell the student that today's dictation sentences are from the Grimms' fairy tale called "Hansel and Gretel." In "Hansel and Gretel," two children lost in the wood stumble into a clearing—and see a house all made out of candy and cake. They are so hungry that they decide to taste it!

Dictate the following sentences to the student two times. Before you read, tell the student that you will indicate commas by pausing, and the period by pausing for a longer time. When you read, be sure to let your voice drop to indicate the end of each sentence.

> Hansel broke off a piece of the roof, which was made of cake. Gretel nibbled on a pane of sugar glass.

Ask the student to repeat the sentences back to you before she writes. Remind her to pause at the commas and periods. If she cannot remember the entire selection, you may repeat it additional times.

Watch the student as she writes, and correct her at once if she begins to make a mistake. You may need to help her spell the proper names.

WEEK 2

DAY ONE: Narration Exercise

Focus: *Identifying the central theme in a selection*

Pull out Student Pages 9–10 and 11. Ask the student to write his name and the date on Student Page 11.

Allow the student to read the story on Student Pages 9–10, either silently or aloud. Before he begins, pronounce the name Scheherazade for him (Shu-hair-ah-zahd).

After the student reads, you may want to explain that the names of three of the ships in the story are jokes. Use the following information:

Implacable is a good name for a ship; an "implacable" enemy is an enemy who cannot be soothed or made less hostile. "Placable" comes from the Latin word *placare*, which means "to appease"—to make peace with. You can make peace with a placable enemy, but not with an implacable enemy; adding "im" to "placable" makes the word mean the opposite.

Incapable is a joke. Someone who is "capable" is *able* to do things. If you tell a capable person to clean up the dishes after dinner, the dishes will be washed, dried, and put neatly away. But adding "in," just like adding "im," makes the word mean the opposite. Naming a ship *Incapable* is like naming it "Useless."

If something is "possible," it can be done. Something "impossible" is the opposite—it can't be done.

Plausible means "believable, reasonable, apparently true." An "implausible" story is fanciful and unlikely.

Now help the student begin to identify the central theme in the selection by asking the following questions. He should try to answer these questions without looking back at the story, but if he cannot remember an answer after thinking for a few minutes, allow him to reread. Remind him to answer in complete sentences.

Instructor: Did Scheherazade have a good journey in the hold of the *Glorious*?
Student: *No, it was a very bad journey.*

Instructor: Tell me three things that were terrible about the ship's hold.
Student: *There was no light or air; the hay was moldy and the grain was filled with bugs; the water was bad; rats ate the food and nibbled the horses' hooves; the stalls were never cleaned; the horses were never brushed.*

Instructor: Where did the horses' grooms come from?
Student: *They came from jails and prisons.*

Instructor: Why did the troops (the soldiers) have to be watched carefully when they were allowed to go on deck?
Student: *They tended to jump overboard.*

Instructor: Scheherazade says that by the time the ship anchored, she didn't even care that the journey was over. Why?
Student: *She was too sick and weary.*

Now say to the student, "Try to tell me, in one sentence, what Scheherazade thought of her journey to Boston." The student should respond, "The journey to Boston was horrible," OR "It was a very bad journey," OR "The journey made Scheherazade sick." Prompt the student, if he seems uncertain, by asking the first comprehension question again.

Once the student has come up with this sentence, say, "Now give me two more sentences with specific details in them about *how* the journey was horrible." The purpose of this exercise is to guide the student into stating the central theme of the passage and supporting that theme with specifics.

The answer should resemble one of the following:

"Scheherazade had a horrible journey to Boston. The ship was dark and filled with rats. Her grain and hay were spoiled."

"The journey in the ships was very bad. The horses were never cleaned or brushed, and they weren't properly fed. All of the grooms came from jails and prisons."

"The journey made Scheherazade sick. She didn't have enough food, light, or air. The journey was so awful that some of the soldiers jumped overboard."

Write down the student's narration on Student Page 11 as he watches.

DAY TWO: Dictation Exercise   *Student Page 12*

Focus: *Formation of plural nouns*

Pull out Student Page 12. Ask the student to write his name and the date.

Tell the student that today's dictation sentence is from the book *Mr. Revere and I.* When Scheherazade first comes from England, she believes that the American rebels are simple farmers who aren't very intelligent, and who certainly know nothing about proper fighting.

Before you read the sentence, tell the student that the sentence has a *semicolon* in it. Remind him that a semicolon is used to separate two complete sentences. It acts like a period, but unlike a period, a semicolon tells you that the second sentence will be so closely related to the first sentence that they belong together. The first word that comes after the semicolon isn't capitalized (unlike the first word that comes after a period). Tell the student to listen for the end of the first complete sentence, where you will pause to indicate the semicolon.

As you read, be sure to let your voice fall slightly to indicate the ending of the complete sentence that comes before the semicolon.

Read the sentence twice as the student listens.

> Of course they could shoot; any bumpkins who lived mostly on squirrels, rabbits, deer and wild turkeys would have to be able to shoot.

Ask the student to repeat the sentence back to you.

Then tell the student that you will read the sentence a third time. This time, the student should listen for the commas that separate items in a list. He should raise his hand or tap the table every time you reach a comma.

On this third reading, pause significantly at each comma, but make sure that your pause at the semicolon is *longer*. If the student indicates that he hears a comma after the word "deer," explain that items in a list can be separated *either* by conjunctions (*but, and, or*) or by commas. It is not necessary to use both.

Watch the student as he writes, and correct him at once if he begins to make a mistake.

When he is finished, ask him to point out each plural noun. As he points, tell him the rule that governs each plural.

bumpkins	Most nouns form the plural by adding an *s*
rabbits	Most nouns form the plural by adding an *s*
squirrels	Most nouns form the plural by adding an *s*
deer	Irregular noun; the singular and plural are the same

turkeys

Form the plural of a noun ending in *y* by adding an *s* if the *y* is preceded by a vowel.

DAY THREE: Narration and Dictation

Focus: *Identifying the central emotion in a passage and writing original sentences from dictation*

Pull out Student Pages 13–14 and 15. Ask the student to write his name and the date on Student Page 15.

Today's exercise will combine narration and dictation. Allow the student to read the story on Student Pages 13–14, either silently or aloud.

Help the student recall important details by asking the following questions. He should try to answer these questions without looking back at the story, but if he cannot remember an answer after thinking for a few minutes, allow him to reread. Remind him to answer in complete sentences.

Instructor: What did Scheherazade's cart have in it?
Student: *It was loaded with hoofs and horns.*

Instructor: The passage describes Scheherazade's food with two words; can you remember them?
Student: *Her food was atrocious and scanty. [If necessary, explain that "atrocious" means "of horrible quality" and "scanty" means "not very much."]*

Instructor: What happened to her coat?
Student: *It grew long and matted.*

Instructor: What did the collar do to her skin?
Student: *It rubbed sores.*

Instructor: What was Scheherazade's greatest fear?
Student: *She was afraid that she might see horses from her old regiment.*

Instructor: When she saw the regiment coming, what did she do?
Student: *She ran away.*

Instructor: What two things does Scheherazade say made her feel humiliated?
Student: *Pulling a glue cart and looking shabby and dirty both made her feel humiliated.*

Instructor: Her embarrassment and humiliation were so deep that she decided to do something terrible, if she ever met Ajax and her friends again. What did she mean to do?
Student: *She meant to drown herself in the harbor.*

Now say to the student, "Finish the following thought: 'Scheherazade hoped that she wouldn't see her friends because...'" He may use two or three sentences to complete the thought. His answer should resemble one of the following:

"Scheherazade hoped she wouldn't see her friends because she was embarrassed. She was forced to pull a cart full of bones for making glue. Her coat was long and matted and she had collar sores."

"Scheherazade hoped she wouldn't see her friends because they were still in the regiment and she was not. She was humiliated because no horse of spirit would ever pull a glue cart. She was dirty and shaggy and she had sores."

Encourage the student to use the word "embarrassed" (or "embarrassing") or the word "humiliated" in his answer.

Write down the student's narration on the lines below, but do not allow him to watch.

_____

_____

_____

_____

Then choose one or two sentences (about 12–15 words) to dictate back to the student. Repeat the sentences twice and ask the student to repeat them back to you before he writes on Student Page 15. If he cannot repeat the sentences, read them again until he is able to keep them in mind.

Give all necessary help in spelling and punctuation.

DAY FOUR: Dictation Exercise   *Student Page 16*

Focus: *Plural nouns, exclamations*

Pull out Student Page 16. Ask the student to write his name and the date.

Tell the student that today's dictation sentences are from *Mr. Revere and I.* This is what Scheherazade says, after all of her adventures.

Dictate the following sentences to the student two times. Before you read, tell the student that there is an exclamation point at the end of one of the sentences. Be sure to indicate this with your voice. Pause at the comma in the second sentence.

> How times and fortunes do change! My circumstances are most comfortable, my duties almost none.

Ask the student to repeat the sentences back to you before he writes. Remind him to put the exclamation point in the proper place. If he cannot remember the entire selection, you may repeat it additional times.

Watch the student as he writes, and correct him at once if he begins to make a mistake. Give all necessary spelling help.

When the student is finished writing, tell him that there are four plural nouns in these sentences. Three of them formed the plural by adding an *s*, but the fourth followed another rule. Ask him to find all four nouns and to tell you which three simply added an *s* (times, fortunes, circumstances).

Ask the student to write the singular form of the fourth noun (duty) underneath the plural form (duties). Remind the student that when a noun ends in *y* preceded by a consonant, you form the plural by changing the *y* to *i* and adding *-es*.

WEEK 3

DAY ONE: Narration Exercise   *Student Pages 17–19*

Focus: *Identifying the central details in a description*

Pull out Student Pages 17–18 and Student Page 19. Ask the student to write her name and the date on Student Page 19.

Allow the student to read the story on Student Pages 17–18, either silently or aloud.

Help the student begin to identify the central details in the narrative by asking the following questions. She should try to answer these questions without looking back at the story, but if she cannot remember an answer after thinking for a few minutes, allow her to reread. Remind her to answer in complete sentences.

Instructor: Do you remember one of the two things mentioned in the passage that ships unloaded?
Student: *The ships unloaded turtles and chandeliers.*

Instructor: Do you remember two of the three things that street vendors sold?
Student: *They sold fever pills, hair oil, and oysters.*

Instructor: List three other things that Paul Revere could see in Boston.
Student: *He could see traveling acrobats, performing monkeys, parades, firework displays, fistfights, a pickled pirate's head, and a polar bear.*

Instructor: List five things that Paul Revere made out of silver.
Student: *He made beads, rings, lockets, bracelets, buttons, medals, pitchers, teapots, spoons, sugar basins, cups, ewers, porringers, shoe buckles, candlesticks, and a squirrel collar.*

Instructor: What did Paul Revere do at Christ Church to make extra money?
Student: *He rang the bells.*

Instructor: List four different times or reasons when the bells were rung.
Student: *They were rung on Sundays, three times a day on weekdays [that only counts as one answer!], holidays, anniversaries, fires, emergencies, deaths, good news, bad news.*

Instructor: Paul did six more things to earn extra money. Can you remember at least three?
Student: *He engraved portraits, sold pictures, made picture frames, brought out hymnbooks, and became a dentist.*

Instructor: What did he make false teeth out of?
Student: *He whittled them out of hippopotamus tusk.*

Now ask the student the general question, "Can you give me a brief summary of this passage?" The student should answer by listing details about Paul Revere's busy life. Her answer should be no more than three sentences and should resemble one of the following:

> "Paul Revere was a silversmith who made rings, bracelets, teapots, spoons, and cups. He rang the bells at Christ Church to make extra money. He also sold pictures, made picture frames, and became a dentist."

> "Paul Revere lived in a very busy place—Boston. In Boston, you could always see something exciting going on, like fireworks, a parade, or performing monkeys. Paul Revere was a silversmith, but he also rang church bells, made artificial teeth, and sold pictures."

> "Paul Revere was a silversmith, but that's not all he did. He also rang the Christ Church bells every time there was a special occasion. He made false teeth out of hippopotamus tusks, sold hymnbooks, engraved portraits, and made picture frames."

Write down the student's narration on Student Page 19 as she watches.

DAY TWO: Dictation Exercise   *Student Page 20*

Focus: *Plural nouns*

Pull out Student Page 20. Ask the student to write her name and the date.

Tell the student that today's dictation sentences are from another biography of Paul Revere, *Paul Revere, American Patriot* by JoAnne Grote.

Dictate the following sentences to the student two times. Before you read, tell the student that there are two commas and two periods. Pause briefly at the commas and for a long time at the first period.

> Many huge wooden docks, called wharves, lined the harbor. Paul's family lived on a wharf when he was seven.

Now ask the student to repeat the sentences back to you before she writes. If she cannot remember the entire selection, you may repeat it additional times.

Watch the student as she writes, and correct her at once if she begins to make a mistake. You may need to help her with the spellings "wharf" and "wharves"; also remind her, if necessary, that "Paul's" is a possessive noun, and that it ends with an apostrophe and an *s*.

When she is finished, point out that "wharves" is the plural form of "wharf." To make a plural out of a noun ending in *f*, you often change the *f* to a *v* and add *-es*.

DAY THREE: Narration and Dictation   *Student Pages 21–22*

Focus: *Identifying the central narrative thread in a passage and writing original sentences from dictation*

Pull out Student Pages 21 and 22. Ask the student to write her name and the date on Student Page 22.

Today's exercise will combine narration and dictation. Allow the student to read the story on Student Page 21, either silently or aloud.

Help the student begin to identify the central thread in the narrative by asking the following questions. She should try to answer these questions without looking back at the story, but if she cannot remember an answer after thinking for a few minutes, allow her to reread. Remind her to answer in complete sentences.

Instructor: What kind of cargo were the British ships carrying, as they sailed towards American ports?
Student: *They were carrying tea.*

Instructor: When the *Dartmouth* arrived in Boston, how did the Sons of Liberty keep the owner from unloading the tea?
Student: *They stood guard with muskets and bayonets.*

Instructor: What message did Paul Revere carry to a nearby seaport?
Student: *The message was that British tea ships might try to unload.*

Instructor: How did the Sons of Liberty disguise themselves?
Student: *They dressed like Indians and put soot and lamp black on their faces.*

Instructor: What did they do with the tea?
Student: *They threw the tea into the harbor.*

Now ask the student the general question, "Can you give me a brief summary of this passage?" The student should answer by summarizing the plot, rather than listing details. Her answer should be no more than three sentences and should resemble one of the following:

"British ships filled with tea docked in Boston. The Sons of Liberty refused to let the owners unload the tea. That night, they dressed up like Indians, went on board the ships, and threw the tea into the water."

"The Sons of Liberty refused to let tea ships unload, and sent messages to other seaports so that no ships could unload anywhere else. After dark, they dressed up like Indians and blackened their faces. Then they boarded the ships, broke open the tea chests, and threw the tea into the water."

"The Sons of Liberty decided to keep British tea ships from unloading. Paul Revere helped carry the message to other seaports. Once it was dark, the Sons of Liberty disguised themselves, went aboard the ships, and threw all of the tea into the harbor."

Write down the student's narration on the lines below, but do not allow her to watch.

_____

_____

_____

_____

Then choose one or two sentences (about 12–15 words) to dictate back to the student. Repeat the sentences twice and ask the student to repeat them back to you before she writes on Student Page 22. If she cannot repeat the sentences, read them again until she is able to keep them in mind.

Give all necessary help in spelling and punctuation.

DAY FOUR: Dictation Exercise

Student Page 23

Focus: *Exclamations, plural nouns*

Pull out Student Page 23. Ask the student to write her name and the date.

Tell the student that today's dictation sentences are from a song written to celebrate the Boston Tea Party, when Paul Revere and many others threw tea from England into the Boston Harbor rather than pay taxes on it.

Ask the student if she can decide what punctuation marks come at the end of these sentences. When you read the sentences, use an excited voice.

> Bring out your axes! And tell King George we'll pay no taxes on his foreign tea!

Ask the student to repeat the sentences back to you before she writes. If she cannot remember the entire selection, you may repeat it additional times.

Watch the student as she writes, and correct her at once if she begins to make a mistake. You may need to remind her that "King George" is a proper name, and that both words should be capitalized. You may also need to remind the student that "we'll" is a contraction of "we will," and that the apostrophe shows that the letters *wi* have been left out. If the student needs help spelling "foreign," remind her of the rule: I before E, except after C, or when sounded like A, as in "neighbor" and "weigh." Americans tend to swallow the last syllable of the word "foreign" (so that it sounds like "forn"), but if the student says the second syllable on its own ("reign"), she will hear the A sound.

When the student is finished, ask her to write the singular nouns "ax" and "tax" above or below the plural nouns "axes" and "taxes." Remind that student that nouns ending in *x, sh,* and *ch* form the plural by adding *-es* rather than just *-s.*

WEEK 4

DAY ONE: Narration Exercise   *Student Pages 24–26*

Focus: *Identifying the central narrative thread in a passage*

Pull out Student Pages 24–25 and 26. Ask the student to write his name and the date on Student Page 26.

Allow the student to read the story on Student Pages 24–25, either silently or aloud.

Help the student begin to identify the central thread in the narrative by asking the following questions. He should try to answer these questions without looking back at the story, but if he cannot remember an answer after thinking for a few minutes, allow him to reread. Remind him to answer in complete sentences.

Instructor: What did Homer, Freddy, and Louis see standing in front of the theater?
Student: *They saw the Super-Duper's car.*

Instructor: Tell me two things you remember about the car.
Student: *It was long and red, it had chromium trimmings, it had the Super-Duper's monogram on the side. [You may need to explain that a monogram is a fancy way of writing a person's initials.]*

Instructor: What did Freddy ask the Super-Duper to do?
Student: *He asked the Super-Duper to fly or bend horse shoes.*

Instructor: Did the Super-Duper do either of those things?
Student: *No, he did not.*

Instructor: In the movie about the Super-Duper, what happened when the villain turned the electric ray on the Super-Duper?
Student: *Nothing happened.*

Instructor: How did the Super-Duper get rid of the electric ray machine?
Student: *He threw it over a cliff.*

Instructor: What did the Super-Duper do when he drove up behind old Lucy and the wagon?
Student: *He honked his horn and then he passed the wagon.*

Instructor: What did Homer say about the Super-Duper's driving?
Student: *He said that the Super-Duper was driving too fast.*

Instructor: What did the boys hear at the end of the story?
Student: *They heard a loud crash.*

Now ask the student the general question, "Can you give me a brief summary of this passage?" The student should answer by summarizing the plot, rather than listing details. His answer should be no more than four sentences and should resemble one of the following:

"Freddy, Homer, and Louis went to see a movie about the Super-Duper. The Super-Duper's car was standing outside the movie theater. After they saw the movie, the boys were driving home when the Super-Duper's car passed them. The car was going too fast, and soon the boys heard a loud crash."

"Homer and his friends were fans of the Super-Duper. They got to meet him and see his car. After they left the movie theater, the Super-Duper's car passed them on the way home. Homer said that the Super-Duper was driving too fast. Right away, they heard a crash."

"Homer and Freddy and Freddy's little brother met the Super-Duper when they went to see a movie about him. In the movie, the Super-Duper threw an electric ray machine over a cliff. On the way home, the Super-Duper drove past the boys, going too fast. Next, the boys heard a loud crash."

The student will probably attempt to put too much information into the summary. If he has difficulty condensing the story, ask the following three questions:

Who are the three main characters, and what did they do together for fun?

What did they see?

What happened when they left the movie theater?

Then have the student repeat his answers in order; this will form his brief summary. Write down the student's narration on Student Page 26 as he watches.

DAY TWO: Dictation Exercise   *Student Page 27*

Focus: *Pronouns, exclamations*

Pull out Student Page 27. Ask the student to write his name and the date.

Tell the student that today's dictation sentence is from a book called *The Science of Superheroes* by Lois Gresh and Robert Weinberg. The authors try to find scientific explanations for the powers of imaginary superheroes like Superman and the Super-Duper.

First, the writers tell us that, in the old comic books, "Superman's tremendous strength was the result of being born on a high gravity planet. Earth's gravity was much weaker than that of Krypton, so Superman was able to lift heavy objects due to the difference in gravitational fields." Then they quote from one of those comic books. That quote is today's dictation sentence.

Dictate the following sentence to the student two times. Before you read, tell the student to listen carefully to your tone of voice to decide what the ending punctuation should be. Be sure to use an excited tone of voice to indicate the exclamation point, and pause significantly at the commas. Do not tell the student that you are pausing at the commas; he should now begin to hear these pauses on his own.

> If you were on a world smaller than ours, you could jump over high buildings, lift enormous weights, and thus duplicate some of the feats of the Man of Steel!

Now ask the student to repeat the sentence back to you before he writes. If he cannot remember the entire sentence, you may repeat it additional times.

Watch the student as he writes, and correct him at once if he begins to make a mistake. If he does not put in the commas, stop him and read the sentence again with exaggerated pauses. Ask him what punctuation mark he should use to indicate the pauses.

When he is finished, tell him to point to the words "you" and "ours." Tell him that these are *pronouns*: words that take the place of nouns.

You may also tell the student the book's conclusion: for Superman to be as strong as he is, Krypton would have to be three times as dense as the sun. So far as we know, this isn't possible!

DAY THREE: Narration and Dictation   *Student Pages 28–30*

Focus: *Identifying the central theme in a selection and writing original sentences from dictation*

Today's exercise will combine narration and dictation. Allow the student to read the story on Student Pages 28–29, either silently or aloud.

Help the student begin to identify the central theme in the selection by asking the following questions. He should try to answer these questions without looking back at the story, but if he cannot remember an answer after thinking for a few minutes, allow him to reread. Remind him to answer in complete sentences.

Instructor: Where was the Super-Duper's car?
Student: The car was in a ditch.

Instructor: How did the boys expect the Super-Duper to get the car out?
Student: They expected him to lift it out with one hand.

Instructor: What was the Super-Duper doing?
Student: He was sitting with his head in his hands.

Instructor: The story mentions several of the Super-Duper's superpowers. What did he do to battleships?
Student: He broke them up like toothpicks.

Instructor: What did cannon-balls do to the Super-Duper?
Student: They bounced off his chest.

Instructor: What did the Super-Duper say?
Student: He said "Ouch."

Instructor: Why did he say "Ouch"?
Student: He got caught on a barbed-wire fence.

Instructor: How did they get the car out of the ditch?
Student: Lucy pulled it back onto the road.

Now ask the student the general question, "Can you give me a brief summary of this passage?" The student should answer by summarizing the theme, rather than listing details. His answer should be no more than three sentences and should resemble one of the following:

"The boys thought that the Super-Duper would be able to lift his car out of the ditch with one hand. Instead, he got caught in barbed wire and needed help. They realized that the Super-Duper wasn't really a super-hero."

"Homer and Freddy and Louis saw the Super-Duper's car in a ditch. They thought he would lift it out with one hand. Instead, the Super-Duper got caught in barbed wire and asked the boys to help him find a garage."

"The boys thought that the Super-Duper was so tough that cannon-balls bounced off his chest. But when the Super-Duper's car ran into a ditch, he couldn't even get it out by himself. The old horse had to pull it out instead."

If he has difficulty condensing the story, ask the following three questions:

What did the boys think about the Super-Duper before his car crashed?

What happened to the Super-Duper?

What did the boys think about the Super-Duper after that?

Then have the student repeat his answers in order; this will form his brief summary.

Write down the student's narration on the lines below, but do not allow him to watch.

_____

_____

_____

_____

Then choose one or two sentences (about 12–15 words) to dictate back to the student. Repeat the sentences twice and ask the student to repeat them back to you before he writes on Student Page 30. If he cannot repeat the sentences, read them again until he is able to keep them in mind.

Give all necessary help in spelling and punctuation.

Day Four: Dictation Exercise

Focus: *Pronouns*

Pull out Student Page 31. Ask the student to write his name and the date.

Tell the student that today's dictation sentences are from a book called *Krypton* by Janey Levy. Also tell the student that although Superman is supposed to be tougher than the Super-Duper, one thing can bring him down. Read the student this paragraph from the book *Krypton*: "The word 'krypton' may make you think of Superman. Krypton was the name of his home planet, and kryptonite was the mineral that could drain his superpowers. Given its association with a fictional superhero, it may surprise you to learn there really is a krypton (Kr). It is not a planet, though. It is a chemical element, a gas that belongs to a group of gases called the noble or inert gases."

Now dictate the following sentences to the student two times. Before you read, tell the student that there are three separate sentences in the selection, each ending with a period.

> Krypton looks just like air. It is colorless, odorless, and tasteless. It is also harmless.

Ask the student to repeat the sentences back to you before he writes. If he cannot remember the entire selection, you may repeat it additional times.

Watch the student as he writes, and correct him at once if he begins to make a mistake. You may need to help him with the spelling of "krypton."

When the student is finished writing, ask him to circle the first "it." This is a pronoun. Ask the student to draw an arrow back to the word "it" stands for (krypton). Ask him to do the same with the second "it" (the second arrow should also point back to "krypton").

WEEK 5

DAY ONE: Poetry Exercise   *Student Pages 32–33*

Focus: *Definitions of poetic terms*

Pull out Student Pages 32 and 33.

   Allow the student to read the poem on Student Pages 32–33, either silently or aloud.

   Tell the student that, instead of asking questions about the poem, you are going to discuss it with her.

   Note: It is not necessary for the student to memorize (or even fully understand) everything that follows. This is simply an introduction to poetry; the concepts will be presented again and again so that the student has a chance to master them.

   Look at the poem with the student and point out the following. Definitions are provided on Student Page 33.

1.   This poem is written in "quatrains." A quatrain is a set of four lines that belong together.
2.   You can discover the "rhyme scheme" (the pattern of rhyming words) within each quatrain by finding the words that rhyme with each other and giving each rhyming sound a different letter of the alphabet as its name. Look at the first quatrain of the poem. The word "toves" is at the end of the first line, so we give the ending sound "oves" the letter A as its name. The word "wabe" is at the end of the second line, so we give the ending sound "abe" the letter B as its name. The word "borogoves" is at the end of the third line. It ends with the sound "oves," so we give that sound its name: A. The word "outgrabe" is at the end of the fourth line. It ends with the sound "abe," so we give that sound its name: B.

   The rhyme scheme for the first quatrain is ABAB.

   Now ask the student to fill in the rhyme pattern for the second quatrain. She should come up with ABAB for this quatrain as well; "son" and "shun" are A rhymes, "catch" and "snatch" are B rhymes.

   Look at the third quatrain. We give the rhyming sound "and" (as in hand) the name A. "Ought" (as in "sought") is B. "Tree" ends with a new sound, "ee." Since this doesn't rhyme with either A or B, we have to call it C. The fourth line ends with the "ought" sound again, so the rhyme pattern is ABCB.

   Now ask the student to fill in the rhyme pattern for the next four quatrains. The correct answers are:

Fourth quatrain	ABAB
Fifth quatrain	ABCB (If the student points out that "dead" and "head" rhyme, you may tell her that this is called an "internal rhyme.")
Sixth quatrain	ABCB

Seventh quatrain   ABAB

3.   Tell the student that you are now going to talk about "meter." Before she can understand meter, though, she will have to understand three new words.

The first word is "syllable." This may not be a new word for the student, but if she is unfamiliar with it, explain that a "syllable" is a part of a word containing one vowel sound. Read the following words to the student and ask the student to clap once for each vowel sound:

baseball	base	ball	two syllables
airplane	air	plane	two syllables
drumbeat	drum	beat	two syllables
elephant	el	e	phant	three syllables

The second word is "stress." When you "stress" part of a word, you let your voice emphasize that part of it. Read the words again, this time emphasizing the bolded syllable:

baseball

airplane

drumbeat

elephant

Explain that in each of these words, the stress falls on the first syllable. Read the words again, stressing the last syllable instead, and ask the student whether the words sound right. (The answer should be "no.")

The third word is "foot." In poetry, a "foot" is a certain number of syllables that always fall into the same pattern of stresses. These patterns create rhythms that help make a poem a poem.

Ask the student to read the lines from the poem printed on Student Page 33 aloud, stressing the bolded syllables with her voice. After she reads, point out that the syllables always fall into the same pattern:

unstress   **stress**

unstress   **stress**

unstress   **stress**

In this poem, each "foot" has two syllables, and those syllables always fall into the pattern "unstress **stress**."

Ask the student to circle each foot in the quatrain on Student Page 33. Her quatrain should look like this:

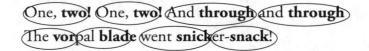

He **left** it **dead**, and **with** its **head**
He **went** galumphing **back**.

Tell her that this pattern (sets of two syllables in the pattern "unstress **stress**") is called **iambic.** Anytime a poem uses this particular rhythm, we say that the meter is iambic. "Meter" is the word we use to refer to the rhythm of a poem.

Optional: for students who are comfortable with identifying parts of speech.

Even though so many words in the poem are made up, you can still tell what part of speech each word is. "Slithy" and "toves" are both made-up words, but if you know that "slithy toves" are "gyring and gimbling," you know that "toves" has to be a noun. The toves are **doing** the verbs in the sentence, so they have to be persons, things, or animals. "Slithy" describes "toves." We know that a word that describes a noun is an adjective, so "slithy" must be an adjective.

DAY TWO: Dictation Exercise

Student Page 34

Focus: *Action verbs*

Pull out Student Page 34. Ask the student to write her name and the date.

Tell the student that today's dictation sentence is also from *Through the Looking-Glass* by Lewis Carroll. In these two sentences, Humpty Dumpty is explaining to Alice what some of the words in "Jabberwocky" mean.

Dictate the following sentences to the student two times. Before you read, tell the student that you will pause significantly at each comma, but that you will pause even longer at the period that separates the two sentences. Also tell the student to listen for the word "they're." Explain that this is the contraction for "they are," not the adverb "there." If necessary, remind the student to put an apostrophe where letters are left out of the contraction.

> Toves are something like badgers, they're something like lizards,
> and they're something like corkscrews. They make their nests under
> sundials and live on cheese.

Now ask the student to repeat the sentences back to you before she writes. If she cannot repeat both sentences, you may repeat them additional times.

Watch the student as she writes, and correct her at once if she begins to make a mistake. When she is finished, point out that there are two different kinds of verbs in these sentences. The verb "are" is a *linking verb*. It links "toves" to "something." The verbs "make" and "live" are *action verbs*.

DAY THREE: Poetry Exercise

Focus: *Definitions of poetic terms*

Pull out Student Page 35.

Allow the student to read the poem on Student Page 35, either silently or aloud.

Tell the student that, instead of asking questions about the poem, you are going to discuss it with her.

This poem is written in sets of four lines. Ask the student if she can remember the name for a set of four lines that belong together. If necessary, remind her that the name is "quatrain." Help her to write "quatrain" on Line 1 below the poem.

Ask the student to give each ending rhyme a letter, as she did for "Jabberwocky." She should write these letters in the blanks at the end of the lines. The pattern is:

A

B

A

B

A

B

A

B

Remind her that this is called a "rhyme scheme."

Now ask the student to read the two lines written below Line 1 out loud, stressing each bolded syllable.

When she is finished, tell her that this is the opposite of iambic meter. Iambic meter falls into this pattern: unstress **stress**. Help the student to write "iambic" on Line 2, after the words "unstress **stress**."

In this poem, each pair of syllables falls into the pattern **stress** unstress. Ask the student to circle each "foot" in the two lines she just read. Remind her that in this poem, each foot is two syllables. Her answer should look like this:

Stego**saur**us **blund**ered **calm**ly **through** the **pre**his**tor**ic **scene,**
never **caus**ing **an**y other **crea**ture **woe.**

This is called "trochaic" meter: a stressed syllable followed by an unstressed syllable. You will probably need to point out to the student that Jack Prelutsky ends each line with a half foot: he drops the second, unstressed syllable in each final foot because it makes the poem sound choppier, like a stegosaurus lumbering and blundering along.

DAY FOUR: Dictation Exercise

Focus: *Poetic form*

Pull out Student Page 36. Ask the student to write her name and the date.

Tell the student that today's dictation exercise is from the poem "The Walrus and the Carpenter," found in Lewis Carroll's book *Through the Looking-Glass.* Begin by reading the first stanza of the poem to the student:

> The sun was shining on the sea,
> Shining with all his might,
> He did his very best to make
> The billows smooth and bright—
> And this was odd, because it was
> The middle of the night.
> The moon was shining sulkily,
> Because she thought the sun
> Had got no business to be there
> After the day was done—
> "It's very rude of him," she said,
> "To come and spoil the fun!"

Now read the first four lines to the student, emphasizing the bolded syllables:

> The **sun** was **shin**ing **on** the **sea**,
>
> Shi**ning** with **all** his **might**,
>
> He **did** his **ver**y **best** to **make**
>
> The **bill**ows **smooth** and **bright**—

Remind her that this is iambic meter; each pair of syllables falls into the pattern "unstress **stress**."

Now remind the student that, in poetry, each line begins directly underneath the previous line, and each line begins with a capital letter. Read these four lines twice more, pausing significantly at the end of each line. Now ask the student to repeat them back to you, reproducing your pauses. If she cannot remember all four lines, repeat them additional times.

Tell the student to stop at the end of each line so that you can tell her the proper punctuation (do not expect her to guess, correctly, that the first two lines end with commas and the last ends with a dash—there's no way she could know this). Watch her as she writes, and correct her at once if she begins to make a mistake.

WEEK 6

DAY ONE: Narration Exercise   *Student Pages 37–39*

Focus: *Identifying the central narrative thread in a passage*

Pull out Student Pages 37–38 and 39. Ask the student to write his name on Student Page 39.
   Allow the student to read the story on Student Pages 37–38, either silently or aloud.
   Help the student begin to identify the central elements in the narrative by asking the following questions. He should try to answer these questions without looking back at the story, but if he cannot remember an answer after thinking for a few minutes, allow him to reread. Remind him to answer in complete sentences.

> **Instructor:** Where did the oarsmen take Jason and Gareth?
> **Student:** *The oarsmen took them to the Great House.*
>
> **Instructor:** Can you name two of the three things that King Neter-Khet did in the first few minutes that Jason was at the Great House?
> **Student:** *He declared wars, signed peace treaties, and began a new pyramid.*
>
> **Instructor:** When the Chief Scribe approached one of the clerks and told him to record the addition of grain, oil, and gold, what else did he add to the list of the Pharoah's possessions?
> **Student:** *He added one black cat.*
>
> **Instructor:** What did Jason say when he heard this?
> **Student:** *He said that his cat was not one of Pharaoh's possessions.*
>
> **Instructor:** Where did Jason and the cat go as soon as Jason protested?
> **Student:** *Jason was put in a tiny room, and the Chief Scribe took the cat away.*
>
> **Instructor:** Did Jason stay in the tiny room?
> **Student:** *No, two guards came and got him.*
>
> **Instructor:** Where did the two guards take him?
> **Student:** *They took him to King Neter-Khet.*
>
> **Instructor:** Who was sitting in front of the throne?
> **Student:** *Gareth the cat was sitting in front of the throne.*

Now ask the student the general question, "Can you give me a brief summary of this passage?" The student should answer by summarizing the plot, rather than listing details. His answer should be no more than three sentences and should resemble one of the following:

> "Gareth and Jason were taken to the Great House of King Neter-Khet. The Chief Scribe took Gareth away, and Jason was shut up in a tiny room. But before long, guards came and got Jason and took him to the throne room."

"The Chief Scribe said that Gareth was one of King Neter-Khet's possessions. Jason tried to protect Gareth, but he was shoved into a tiny room. He stayed in the room for just a little while, and then guards took him to see King Neter-Khet and Gareth."

"The Chief Scribe took Gareth for the king and shut Jason in a cell. Before long, though, guards came to get Jason and took him to see King Neter-Khet. He saw Gareth there, sitting in front of the throne."

If the student has difficulty condensing the selection, ask him the following three questions:

What happened to Gareth?

How did Jason react?

When did Jason see Gareth again?

Then have the student repeat his answer in order; this will form his brief summary. Write down the student's narration on Student Page 39 as he watches.

DAY TWO: Dictation Exercise   *Student Page 40*

Focus: *Possessive adjectives*

Pull out Student Page 40. Ask the student to write his name and the date.

Tell the student that today's dictation sentences are from Rudyard Kipling's story "The Cat That Walked by Himself" from the *Just So Stories*. Read the student the first paragraph of the story:

> Hear and attend and listen; for this befell and behappened and became and was, O my Best Beloved, when the tame animals were wild. The Dog was wild, and the Horse was wild, and the Cow was wild, and the Sheep was wild, and the Pig was wild—as wild as wild could be—and they walked in the Wet Wild Woods by their wild lones. But the wildest of all the wild animals was the Cat. He walked by himself and all places were alike to him.

Also tell the student that, in the story, the Dog goes to live with Man and Woman and becomes tame—but the Cat refuses to be tamed.

Dictate the following sentences to the student two times. Before you read, tell the student that this is what Woman says about the Dog after he is tamed. Tell the student that "Wild Dog" and "First Friend" are capitalized because Rudyard Kipling is using them as proper names. Also tell him that you will pause briefly at the comma and for a longer time at the first period.

His name is not Wild Dog any more, but the First Friend, because he will be our friend for always and always and always. Take him with you when you go hunting.

Now ask the student to repeat the sentences back to you before he writes. If he cannot remember both sentences, you may repeat them additional times.

Watch the student as he writes, and correct him at once if he begins to make a mistake. When he is finished, ask him to underline the phrases "His name" and "our friend." Explain that "his" and "our" are particular kinds of adjectives. They are adjectives that answer the question *whose*. We call these *possessive adjectives*.

DAY THREE: Narration and Dictation   *Student Pages 41–43*

Focus: *Identifying the central theme and writing original sentences from dictation*

Pull out Student Pages 41–42 and 43. Ask the student to write his name and the date on Student Page 43.

Today's exercise will combine narration and dictation. Allow the student to read the story on Student Pages 41–42, either silently or aloud.

Now help the student begin to identify the central theme in the selection by asking the following questions. He should try to answer these questions without looking back at the story, but if he cannot remember an answer after thinking for a few minutes, allow him to reread. Remind him to answer in complete sentences.

> **Instructor:** What did Gareth do when King Neter-Khet ordered him to play?
> **Student:** *He did nothing OR He did not move.*

> **Instructor:** How did Jason try to make Gareth play?
> **Student:** *He pulled a jeweled mouse on a golden chain back and forth in front of the cat.*

> **Instructor:** Did Gareth play with the mouse?
> **Student:** *No, he did not.*

> **Instructor:** What did Gareth do when King Neter-Khet ordered him to purr and be agreeable?
> **Student:** *He did nothing OR He did not move.*

> **Instructor:** What did Gareth do when Jason put him in the king's lap?
> **Student:** *He leaped down OR He wriggled away and accidentally scratched the king.*

> **Instructor:** What explanation did Jason give the king for Gareth's behavior?
> **Student:** *He said that Gareth didn't feel like playing or being agreeable OR He said that's just the way cats are.*

Now say to the student, "Try to tell me, in one sentence, how Gareth behaved in front of the king—and why." The student should respond, "Gareth refused to play or purr because he didn't feel like it," OR "Gareth would not do what the king asked because that's just the way cats are," OR "Gareth wouldn't play or sit in the king's lap because he didn't want to." Prompt the student, if he seems uncertain, by asking the first and last comprehension questions again.

Once the student has come up with this sentence, say, "Now give me two more sentences with specific details in them about how Jason and the king tried to make Gareth obey, and for each specific detail, tell me how Gareth reacted." The purpose of this exercise is to guide the student into stating the central theme of the passage and supporting that theme with specifics.

The answer should resemble one of the following:

"Gareth refused to play or purr because he didn't feel like it. Jason tried to get him to play with a mouse, but Gareth was in no mood for games. Jason tried to put Gareth in the king's lap, but Gareth leaped down."

"Gareth would not do what the king asked because that's just the way cats are. Jason tried to put him in the king's lap, so that the king could stroke him. But Gareth jumped off and scratched the king."

"Gareth wouldn't play or sit in the king's lap because he didn't want to. The Chief Scribe told Jason to make the cat play, but Jason could tell that Gareth wasn't in the mood. He put Gareth on the king's lap, but the cat wriggled away and jumped down."

Write down the student's narration on the lines below, but do not allow him to watch.

_____

_____

_____

_____

Then choose one or two sentences (about 12–15 words) to dictate back to the student. Repeat the sentences twice and ask the student to repeat them back to you before he writes on Student Page 43. If he cannot repeat the sentences, read them again until he is able to keep them in mind.

Give all necessary help in spelling and punctuation.

DAY FOUR: Dictation Exercise

Focus: *Possessive adjectives*

Pull out Student Page 44. Ask the student to write his name and the date.

Tell the student that today's dictation sentences are also from Rudyard Kipling's story "The Cat That Walked by Himself" from the *Just So Stories*. This is what the Cat says to Woman.

Dictate the following sentences to the student two times. Before you read, tell the student that "Cat" is capitalized because Kipling is using it as a proper name. Also tell the student that you will pause briefly at the commas and for a longer time at the first period.

> I am not a friend, and I am not a servant. I am the Cat who walks by
> himself, and I wish to come into your cave.

Now ask the student to repeat the sentences back to you before he writes. If he cannot remember both sentences, you may repeat them additional times.

Watch the student as he writes, and correct him at once if he begins to make a mistake. When he is finished, ask him to find and underline the possessive adjective that answers the question *whose*. (The answer is "your" in the phrase "your cave.")

WEEK 7

DAY ONE: Narration Exercise   *Student Pages 45–47*

Focus: *Identifying the central narrative thread in a passage*

Pull out Student Pages 45–46 and 47. Ask the student to write her name and the date on Student Page 47.

Allow the student to read the story on Student Pages 45–46, either silently or aloud.

Help the student begin to identify the central thread in the narrative by asking the following questions. She should try to answer these questions without looking back at the story, but if she cannot remember an answer after thinking for a few minutes, allow her to reread. Remind her to answer in complete sentences.

Instructor: What did Shi Huangdi mean?
Student: *It meant "First Emperor."*

Instructor: What two things did Shi Huangdi do to prevent revolt?
Student: *He sent his soldiers to guard and report on his enemies, and he burned books that might encourage his people to rebel.*

Instructor: Who lived in the north, outside the borders of China?
Student: *The ferocious tribes called Mongols lived in the north.*

Instructor: What had some of the Warring States done to keep Mongols away?
Student: *They built walls.*

Instructor: Why wouldn't the walls keep the Mongols out?
Student: *The walls had huge gaps in them.*

Instructor: What did Shi Huangdi decide to do?
Student: *He decided to build a Great Wall along China's northern border.*

Instructor: What was the problem with this plan?
Student: There wasn't enough stone to build a Great Wall.

Instructor: The architects found a solution to this problem. They figured out how to build a wall out of dirt in four steps. What were those four steps? [If necessary, you may allow the student to look back at the text as she answers.]
Student: They made a wooden frame. They put the frame on the ground and filled it with dirt. Workers stamped and packed the earth until it was as hard as concrete. Then they lifted the frame up and set it on top of the packed earth.

Now ask the student the general question, "Can you give me a brief summary of this passage?" The student should answer by telling you about the Mongols and the building of the Great Wall. Her answer should be no more than three sentences. It should resemble one of the following:

> "Tribes were coming down from the north and attacking China. Shi Huangdi told his architects to build a Great Wall to stop them. They figured out how to make the wall out of dirt."

> "The First Emperor wanted to build a Great Wall to keep out the Mongols. But there wasn't enough stone. So his builders made a wooden frame, packed it with dirt, and made a dirt wall that was as hard as concrete."

> "The First Emperor was afraid that the Mongols would invade through gaps in the old walls. He ordered his builders to build a new wall—the Great Wall. There wasn't enough stone to make the Great Wall, so his builders made it out of packed dirt."

Write down the student's narration on Student Page 47 as she watches.

DAY TWO: Dictation Exercise   *Student Page 48*

Focus: *Possessive adjectives*

Pull out Student Page 48. Ask the student to write her name and the date.

Tell the student that today's dictation sentences are also from *The Story of the World, Volume 1: Ancient Times.* They describe what China was like before Shi Huangdi conquered the Warring States and united them into one country.

Dictate the following sentences to the student two times. Instead of telling the student that there are two sentences, simply pause at the period.

> China was ruled by strong warriors called warlords. Each warlord had his own, separate kingdom and his own army.

Ask the student to repeat the sentences back to you before she writes. If she cannot remember both sentences, you may repeat them additional times.

Watch the student as she writes, and correct her at once if she begins to make a mistake. When she is finished, ask her to underline the possessive adjectives that answer the question *whose.* (The answer is "his" in the phrases "his own, separate kingdom" and "his own army.")

You may also want to point out "kingdom" has three adjectives that modify it: his, own, and separate. Ask the student how may adjectives modify "army." (The answer is two: "his," and "own.")

DAY THREE: Narration and Dictation   *Student Pages 49–51*

Focus: Identifying the central details in a passage and writing original sentences from dictation

Pull out Student Pages 49–50 and 51. Ask the student to write her name and the date on Student Page 51.

Allow the student to read the story on Student Pages 49–50, either silently or aloud.

Help the student begin to identify the central details in the narrative by asking the following questions. She should try to answer these questions without looking back at the story, but if she cannot remember an answer after thinking for a few minutes, allow her to reread. Remind her to answer in complete sentences.

Instructor: What did the Mongols live in?
Student: *They lived in felt tents.*

Instructor: What did they do to protect themselves from the cold?
Student: *They wore furs and leather and rubbed their skin with grease.*

Instructor: What did they eat instead of raising crops?
Student: *They ate foxes, rabbits, and other small wild creatures.*

Instructor: What did they do if they were in danger of starving?
Student: *They would open the veins of their horses and drink blood.*

Instructor: What did Genghis Khan want the separate Mongol clans to do?
Student: *He wanted them to join together and attack Beijing.*

Instructor: What was in Beijing that Genghis Khan wanted? The passage lists four things.
Student: *There were warm houses, soft beds, plenty of food, and bags of gold.*

Instructor: What did Genghis Khan tell his people about the disappearance of his rival's body?
Student: *He told them that the gods had taken the body away as punishment.*

Instructor: After that, did the Mongols follow Genghis?
Student: *Yes, they did.*

Now ask the student the general question, "Can you give me a brief summary of this passage?" The student should answer by describing the Mongols and what Genghis Khan wanted. Her answer should be no more than three sentences and should resemble one of the following:

"The Mongols lived in felt tents and rubbed grease on their skins to protect them from the cold. They ate small wild creatures and sometimes they drank the blood of their horses. Genghis Khan wanted them to conquer the city of Beijing."

"The Mongols lived in the wild, cold north. They were nomads who didn't grow crops or build houses. But Genghis Khan wanted them to conquer the rich city of Beijing."

"The Mongols lived in felt tents and wore fur and leather because it was so cold in the north. But there were warm houses and soft beds in Beijing. Genghis Khan wanted them to join together and conquer this rich city."

Write down the student's narration on the lines below, but do not allow her to watch.

_____

_____

_____

_____

Then choose one or two sentences (about 12–15 words) to dictate back to the student. Repeat the sentences twice and ask the student to repeat them back to you before she writes on Student Page 51. If she cannot repeat the sentences, read them again until she is able to keep them in mind.

Give all necessary help in spelling and punctuation.

DAY FOUR: Dictation   *Student Page 52*

Focus: *Possessive adjectives and hyphenated words*

Pull out Student Page 52. Ask the student to write her name and the date.

Tell the student that today's dictation sentences are also from *The Story of the World, Volume 2*. After Genghis Khan's death, his grandson Kublai Khan tried to fight his way even further to the south of China, to conquer more of the Chinese empire. These sentences describe one of the problems he encountered.

Dictate the following sentences to the student two times. Before you read, tell the student that there is a hyphenated word in the first sentence. The word is "well-educated." The hyphen links together the two separate words "well" and "educated" into one single word. If necessary, write the word on the bottom of Student Page 52 and show the student how to form the hyphen. Be sure to pause at the commas and to make a longer pause at the period.

> **The Mongols were ferocious warriors, but the Chinese were shrewd and well-educated. Their scientists had developed new weapons to defend against invasion. They knew how to make poisonous fogs which could be blown across a battlefield.**

Ask the student to repeat the sentence back to you before she writes. If she cannot remember the entire selection, you may repeat it additional times. This is a longer dictation selection, intended to stretch the student's ability, and if necessary you may break it into two parts.

Watch the student as she writes, and correct her at once if she begins to make a mistake. You may need to help her spell "ferocious" and "poisonous."

When she is finished, ask her to find and underline the possessive adjective that answers the question *whose*. (The answer is "their" in "their scientists.")

WEEK 8

DAY ONE: Narration Exercise   *Student Pages 53–55*

Focus: *Identifying the central narrative thread in a passage*

Pull out Student Pages 53–54 and 55. Ask the student to write his name and the date on Student Page 55.

Allow the student to read the story on Student Pages 53–54, either silently or aloud.

Help the student begin to identify the central elements in the narrative by asking the following questions. He should try to answer these questions without looking back at the story, but if he cannot remember an answer after thinking for a few minutes, allow him to reread. Remind him to answer in complete sentences.

Instructor: What did Lucy see inside the wardrobe?
Student: *She saw long fur coats.*

Instructor: Why did she get into the wardrobe?
Student: *She liked the smell and the feel of fur OR She wanted to rub her face against the fur.*

Instructor: As she pushed towards the back of the wardrobe, what sound did she hear under her feet?
Student: *She heard crunching under her feet.*

Instructor: What did she think it was?
Student: *She thought it was moth-balls.*

Instructor: What did she feel rubbing against her face and hands instead of soft fur?
Student: *She felt something rough and prickly OR She felt branches.*

Instructor: When she came out of the back of the wardrobe, where was she?
Student: *She was standing in the middle of a wood.*

Instructor: What time was it?
Student: *It was night-time.*

Instructor: What did she see falling through the air?
Student: *She saw snow falling through the air.*

Instructor: How did Lucy feel?
Student: *She felt frightened, inquisitive, and excited.*

Instructor: What could she see behind her?
Student: *She could see the open door of the wardrobe OR She could see the room where the wardrobe was.*

Instructor: What did she do instead of going back?
Student: *She began to walk forward OR She began to walk towards the light.*

Now ask the student the general question, "Can you give me a brief summary of this passage?" The student should answer by summarizing the forward movement of the story, rather than listing details. His answer should be no more than three sentences and should resemble one of the following:

> "Lucy got into the wardrobe to feel the fur coats. As she pushed her way towards the back of the wardrobe, the soft fur turned to hard branches. She came out of the wardrobe into a little wood in the middle of the night."

> "Lucy pushed her way towards the back of the wardrobe. The fur turned into branches, and she came out into a little wood where it was snowing. When she looked behind her, she could see the room through the door of the wardrobe."

> "Lucy got into the wardrobe, but she discovered that the wardrobe was actually a door into a little wood. It was snowing and dark in the wood, and she could see a light. She decided to walk forward towards the light."

The student will probably attempt to put too much information into the summary. If he has difficulty condensing the story, ask the following three questions:

> Why did Lucy get into the wardrobe?

> What did she find at the back of the wardrobe?

What did she do next?

Then have the student repeat his answers in order; this will form his brief summary. Write down the student's narration on Student Page 55 as he watches.

DAY TWO: Dictation Exercise   *Student Page 56*

Focus: *Adverbs that tell how, when, where, and how often*

Pull out Student Page 56. Ask the student to write his name and the date.

Tell the student that today's dictation sentence comes from a little later in *The Lion, the Witch and the Wardrobe*. This time, when Lucy gets into the wardrobe, she shuts the door all the way.

Dictate the following sentence to the student two times. Pause at the comma, but don't tell the student ahead of time that the comma is there; give him a chance to put it in on his own.

> She shut the wardrobe door tightly behind her and looked around, panting for breath.

Ask the student to repeat the sentence back to you before he writes. If he cannot remember the entire sentence, you may repeat it additional times.

Watch the student as he writes, and correct him at once if he begins to make a mistake. When he is finished, tell him that this sentence has two adverbs in it. An adverb is a word that answers the questions "how, when, where, how often?" Tell him to underline the adverb "tightly." Ask the student what question this adverb answers. (It answers the question "how?" How did Lucy shut the door? She shut the door tightly.) Now tell him to underline the adverb "around." Ask the student what question this adverb answers. (It answers the question "where?" Where did Lucy look? She looked around.)

DAY THREE: Narration and Dictation   *Student Pages 57–59*

Focus: *Identifying the central details in a description and writing original sentences from dictation*

Pull out Student Pages 57–58 and 59. Ask the student to write his name and the date on Student Page 59.

Today's exercise will combine narration and dictation. Allow the student to read the story on Student Pages 57–58, either silently or aloud.

Help the student begin to identify the central details in the narrative by asking the following questions. He should try to answer these questions without looking back at the story, but if he cannot remember an answer after thinking for a few minutes, allow him to reread. Remind him to answer in complete sentences.

Instructor: Can you list three of the six things that the girls helped Mrs. Beaver to do in the very first sentence of the passage?
Student: *The girls helped Mrs. Beaver fill the kettle, lay the table, cut the bread, put the plates in the oven, draw a jug of beer, and put on the frying pan.*

Instructor: Why did they put plates in the oven?
Student: *They put plates in the oven to heat.*

Instructor: What was missing from the walls?
Student: *There were no books or pictures.*

Instructor: What did the beavers have instead of beds?
Student: *They had bunks built into the wall.*

Instructor: What two things were hanging from the roof?
Student: *Hams and strings of onions were hanging from the roof.*

Instructor: Name five of the ten things against the walls.
Student: *There were gum boots, oilskins, hatchets, shears, spades, trowels, things for carrying mortar, fishing rods, fishing nets, and sacks against the walls.*

Instructor: What did Mr. Beaver and Peter bring for the meal?
Student: *They brought fresh fish.*

Instructor: The children and the beavers had four things in their dinner. What were they?
Student: *They had fish, potatoes, milk (Mr. Beaver had beer), and butter.*

Instructor: What two things did they have for dessert?
Student: *They had marmalade roll and tea.*

Instructor: What did they sit on?
Student: *They sat on three-legged stools.*

Now ask the student the general question, "Can you give me a brief summary of this passage?" The student should answer with two sets of details: one about the house and one about the meal. His answer should be no more than three sentences and should resemble one of the following:

> "The beavers lived in a little home with bunks, but with no pictures on the walls. Instead they had hams hanging from the ceiling and all sorts of tools leaning against the walls. For dinner, the children and the beavers ate fish and potatoes, with marmalade roll for dessert."

> "The girls helped Mrs. Beaver get ready for dinner while Peter helped Mr. Beaver fish. The beavers' home had boots, hatchets, fishing nets, and sacks leaning against the wall. They all sat on three-legged stools and ate fish and potatoes for dinner."

> "The girls warmed plates, cut bread, and set the table for dinner. The cloth on the table was very rough, and they only had three-legged stools to sit on. The dinner was fish, potatoes, creamy milk, butter, and a marmalade roll for dessert."

If the student has difficulty summarizing the passage, ask him the following three questions:

What did the house look like?

What did the girls do to get ready for the meal?

What did the beavers and the children eat for dinner?

The student's answers will serve as his narration.

Write down the student's narration on the lines below, but do not allow him to watch.

_____

_____

_____

_____

Then choose one or two sentences (about 12–15 words) to dictate back to the student. Repeat the sentences twice and ask the student to repeat them back to you before he writes on Student Page 59. If he cannot repeat the sentences, read them again until he is able to keep them in mind.

Give all necessary help in spelling and punctuation.

DAY FOUR: Dictation Exercise   *Student Page 60*

Focus: *Adverbs that tell how, when, where, how often, to what extent*

Pull out Student Page 60. Ask the student to write his name and the date.

Tell the student that today's dictation sentence comes from a little later in *The Lion, the Witch and the Wardrobe*. The children and the beavers set out on a journey and travel until they are very weary.

Dictate the following sentence to the student two times.

> Everyone was feeling very tired and very hungry when suddenly the trees began to get thinner in front of them and the ground to fall steeply downhill.

Ask the student to repeat the sentence back to you before he writes. If he cannot remember the entire sentence, you may repeat it additional times.

Watch the student as he writes, and correct him at once if he begins to make a mistake. When he is finished, tell him that this sentence has four adverbs in it. Remind him that an adverb is a word that answers the questions "how, when, where, how often?"

Tell him to underline the two adverbs "very." Tell the student that "very" answers another adverb question: "to what extent?" To what extent were the children tired? They were *very* tired. To what extent were the children hungry? They were *very* hungry. These adverbs modify the adjectives "tired" and "hungry."

Now tell the student to underline the adverb "suddenly." Ask the student what question this adverb answers. (It answers the question "how?" How did the trees get thinner? They got thinner *suddenly*. If the student answers "when," you may accept this as a valid answer.)

Finally, tell the student to underline the adverb *steeply*. Ask the student what question this adverb answers. (It answers the question "how?" How did the ground fall downhill? It fell *steeply* downhill. If the student answers "to what extent," you may accept this as a valid answer.)

WEEK 9

DAY ONE: Narration Exercise   *Student Pages 61–63*

Focus: *Identifying the central narrative thread in a passage*

Pull out Student Pages 61–62 and 63. Ask the student to write her name and the date on Student Page 63.

Allow the student to read the story on Student Pages 61–62, either silently or aloud. This selection is a little more difficult than other passages, and some students may need you to read it out loud.

Help the student begin to identify the central elements in the narrative by asking the following questions. She should try to answer these questions without looking back at the story, but if she cannot remember an answer after thinking for a few minutes, allow her to reread. Remind her to answer in complete sentences.

> **Instructor:** Why didn't C. S. Lewis apply to be exempt from the draft?
> **Student:** *He thought it would be dishonorable.*
>
> **Instructor:** What did he do while he was in the officers' training corps?
> **Student:** *He worked on a collection of poems.*
>
> **Instructor:** What country was he sent to fight in?
> **Student:** *He was sent to France.*
>
> **Instructor:** What message was Lewis trying to give his father, in his letters home?
> **Student:** *He was trying to tell his father that he was safe.*

Instructor: What happened to Lewis during the Battle of Arras in France?
Student: *Lewis was wounded.*

Instructor: What did the doctors discover when Lewis was taken to the hospital?
Student: *He had a wound in his chest* **OR** *He was wounded and put out of combat permanently.*

Now ask the student the general question, "Can you give me a brief summary of this passage?" The student should answer by summarizing the progression of the narrative, rather than listing details. Her answer should be no more than three sentences and should resemble one of the following:

"C. S. Lewis decided not to get out of the draft. Instead he was sent to fight in France. He was wounded in a battle and was put out of combat."

"Jack was sent to France to fight for England. He wrote letters to his father telling his father that he was safe. But he was wounded in a battle and no longer had to fight."

"C. S. Lewis trained to be a soldier in the officers' training corps and then went to fight in France. He told his father that he was not in danger. Then he was wounded in the chest during a battle and could no longer fight."

The student will probably attempt to put too much information into the summary. If she has difficulty condensing the story, ask the following three questions:

What did C. S. Lewis do, against his father's wishes?

What did he tell his father in his letters?

What happened to him that made him leave the army?

Then have the student repeat her answers in order; this will form her brief summary. Write down the student's narration on Student Page 63 as she watches.

DAY TWO: Dictation Exercise   *Student Page 64*

Focus: *Adverbs that tell how, when, where, how often, to what extent*

Pull out Student Page 64. Ask the student to write her name and the date.

Tell the student that today's dictation sentence is from *A Child's Story of America* by three authors: Michael J. McHugh, Charles Morris, and Edward J. Shewan.

Dictate the following sentence to the student two times. Before you read, tell the student that "World War I" is a proper name and should be capitalized. You may need to explain that "I" is a Roman numeral (a number used by the Romans in ancient times) and means the same thing as "one" or "1." Be sure to indicate the question with your voice.

> Did you know that World War I was the most terrible war the world had ever seen up to that time?

Now ask the student to repeat the sentence back to you before she writes. Ask her to tell you what punctuation mark comes at the end. If she cannot remember the entire sentence, you may repeat it additional times.

Watch the student as she writes, and correct her at once if she begins to make a mistake. When she is finished, tell her to underline the word "most." This is an adverb. It answers the question "to what extent?" Ask the student to identify the word that "most" modifies. (The answer is "terrible." To what extent was the war terrible? It was *most* terrible.)

Now ask the student to underline the adverb "ever." Tell her that this adverb answers the question "when?"

DAY THREE: Narration and Dictation · · · · · · · · · · · *Student Pages 65–67*

Focus: *Identifying the central theme in a selection*

Pull out Student Pages 65–66 and 67. Ask the student to write her name and the date on Student Page 67.

Allow the student to read the story on Student Pages 65–66, either silently or aloud. This selection is a little more difficult than other passages, and some students may need you to read it out loud.

Help the student begin to identify the central theme in the selection by asking the following questions. She should try to answer these questions without looking back at the story, but if she cannot remember an answer after thinking for a few minutes, allow her to reread. Remind her to answer in complete sentences.

Instructor: Were Germany and Russia on the same side, or on different sides?
Student: *Germany and Russia were on different sides.*

Instructor: How long did the Germans think that World War I would last?
Student: *The Germans thought the war would last four months.*

Instructor: The king of Germany, Kaiser Wilhelm II, told his troops that they would be home before what happened?
Student: *He told them they would be home before the leaves fell.*

Instructor: What did young men rush to do?
Student: *They rushed to join the army.*

Instructor: How long did most Russians think that the war would last?
Student: *They thought it would last two or three months.*

Instructor: What did the Imperial Guard officer want to pack, and why?
Student: *He wanted to pack his uniform so that he could wear it into Berlin.*

Now say to the student, "Try to tell me, in one sentence, what the Germans and Russians thought about the war." The student should respond, "The Germans and Russians thought the war would be over soon," OR "The Germans and Russians thought that the war would only last a few months," OR "The Germans and Russians were eager to fight because both sides expected to win easily." Prompt the student, if she seems uncertain, by asking the first and fifth comprehension questions again.

Once the student has come up with this sentence, say, "Now give me two more sentences with specific details in them about how each side felt." The purpose of this exercise is to guide the student into stating the central theme of the passage and supporting that theme with specifics.

The answer should resemble one of the following:

"The Germans and Russians thought the war would be over soon. The Germans expected the war to last four months. The Russians thought it would only last two or three months."

"The Germans and Russians thought that the war would only last a few months. The German king told his troops that they would be home before the leaves fell. One Russian officer packed his full-dress uniform so that he would be ready for victory."

"The Germans and Russians were eager to fight because both sides expected to win easily. German soldiers wrote 'On to Paris' on the sides of their trains and expected to be in France in weeks. Russians thought they would win in two or three months."

Write down the student's narration on the lines below, but do not allow her to watch.

Then choose one or two sentences (about 12–15 words) to dictate back to the student. Repeat the sentences twice and ask the student to repeat them back to you before she writes on Student Page 67. If she cannot repeat the sentences, read them again until she is able to keep them in mind.

Give all necessary help in spelling and punctuation.

DAY FOUR: Dictation Exercise   *Student Page 68*

Focus: *Adverbs that tell how, when, where, how often, to what extent*

Pull out Student Page 68. Ask the student to write her name and the date.

Tell the student that today's dictation sentence is from the book *Everyday Life: World War I* by Walter A. Hazen.

Dictate the following sentence to the student two times.

All nations now readied their armies for what they thought would be a brief war.

Ask the student to repeat the sentence back to you before she writes. If she cannot remember the sentence, you may repeat it additional times.

Watch the student as she writes, and correct her at once if she begins to make a mistake. When she is finished, tell her to underline the adverb "now." Ask the student what question this adverb answers. (The answer is "when?" When did the nations ready their armies? They readied the armies *now*.)

WEEK 10

Day One: Narration Exercise   *Student Pages 69–71*

Focus: *Identifying the central details in a passage*

Pull out Student Pages 69–70 and 71. Ask the student to write his name and the date on Student Page 71.

Allow the student to read the story on Student Pages 69–70, either silently or aloud.

Help the student begin to identify the central details in the narrative by asking the following questions. He should try to answer these questions without looking back at the story, but if he cannot remember an answer after thinking for a few minutes, allow him to reread. Remind him to answer in complete sentences.

Instructor: There were two kinds of horses in the Horse-Barn. What were they?
Student: *Three-year-old colts and sedate work-horses were in the barn.*

Instructor: The three-year-old colts had soft noses. How soft were they?
Student: *They were as soft as velvet.*

Instructor: Could Almanzo stroke the soft noses of the colts?
Student: *No, he was not allowed to touch them.*

Instructor: What could a boy do to ruin a young horse?
Student: *He could scare it OR He could tease it OR He could strike it OR He could teach it to hate people.*

Instructor: Would Almanzo have done any of those things?
Student: *No, he would not.*

Instructor: What did Almanzo and Royal have to do to the stalls?
Student: *They had to clean out the soiled hay and spread fresh hay.*

Instructor: Which animals did Almanzo own?
Student: *He owned two calves.*

Instructor: What color were they?
Student: *The calves were red.*

Instructor: What did he name them? Why?
Student: *He named one Star, because of the white spot on his forehead. He named the other Bright because he was bright red all over.*

Instructor: What did the calves do when Almanzo scratched around their horns?
Student: *They licked him with their rough tongues.*

Now ask the student the general question, "Can you give me a brief summary of this passage?" The student should answer by listing details about the animals (the horses and calves) and about Almanzo's duties at the barn. His answer should be no more than three sentences and should resemble one of the following:

"Almanzo had to clean out the stalls where the horses, cows, and sheep lived. He loved to see the colts, but he was not allowed to touch them. He had two calves of his own named Star and Bright."

"Almanzo went to the barn every day after school. He had to take care of his two red calves, Star and Bright. He wanted to take care of the colts, but his father wouldn't let him."

"Almanzo loved the colts, but he was not allowed to touch them or clean their stalls. Instead he helped his brother clean out the other stalls. Then he took care of his own two calves, who were named Star and Bright."

If the student has difficulty keeping the narration to three sentences, ask him the following three questions:

How did Almanzo feel about the horses?

What did Almanzo and Royal do to the stalls?

Which animals belonged to Almanzo?

Have the student repeat his answers in order; this will form his brief summary.
Write down the student's narration on Student Page 71 as he watches.

Day Two: Dictation Exercise   *Student Page 72*

Focus: *Adverbs that tell how, when, where, how often, to what extent*

Pull out Student Page 72. Ask the student to write his name and the date.
Tell the student that today's dictation sentence is from *Farmer Boy* and describes the barn.

Dictate the following sentence to the student two times. Before you read, tell the student that the last word of the sentence is actually two words linked together with a hyphen. Do not tell the student that the sentence contains a comma, but pause significantly when you reach it.

The haymows were warm with the warmth of all the stock below, and the hay smelled dusty-sweet.

Now ask the student to repeat the sentence back to you before he writes. If he cannot remember the entire sentence, you may repeat it additional times.

Watch the student as he writes, and correct him at once if he begins to make a mistake or leaves out the comma. When he is finished, ask him to underline the adverb "below." Ask him which question this adverb answers. (The correct answer is "where?" Where is the stock? The stock is *below.*)

Day Three: Narration and Dictation   *Student Pages 73–75*

Focus: *Identifying the central details in a passage and writing original sentences from dictation*

Pull out Student Pages 73–74 and 75. Ask the student to write his name and the date on Student Page 75.

Today's exercise will combine narration and dictation. Allow the student to read the story on Student Pages 73–74, either silently or aloud.

Help the student begin to identify the central details in the narrative by asking the following questions. He should try to answer these questions without looking back at the story, but if he cannot remember an answer after thinking for a few minutes, allow him to reread. Remind him to answer in complete sentences.

Instructor: Can you list four of the seven things that Almanzo saw on the table?
Student: *He saw cheese, headcheese, jams, jellies, preserves, milk, and baked beans with fat pork.*

Instructor: What kind of rug did Mother make for the dining-room?
Student: *She made a rug out of dyed rags.*

Instructor: Can you list two of the four things that sat in the corner cupboards?
Student: *Sea-shells, petrified wood, curious rocks, and books sat in the corner cupboards.*

Instructor: What hung over the center table? What was it made of?
Student: *An air-castle made of wheat straws hung over the center table.*

Instructor: What three words are used to describe Mother?
Student: *She is short, plump, and pretty.*

Instructor: What did Mother's hair look like?
Student: *It was brown and looked like a bird's smooth wings.*

Instructor: What color were her buttons and sleeves?
Student: Her buttons and sleeves were red.

Instructor: What was tied around her waist?
Student: A white apron was tied around her waist.

Instructor: Why did she have to tug her way through the door?
Student: Her hoop-skirts were wider than the door.

Instructor: Whose plate was filled first?
Student: Mr. Corse's OR The schoolmaster's plate was filled first.

Instructor: Whose plate was filled last?
Student: Almanzo's plate was filled last.

Instructor: Almanzo ate twelve different things! Can you list eight of them?
Student: Almanzo ate baked beans, salt pork, potatoes with gravy, ham, bread and butter, mashed turnips, stewed yellow pumpkin, plum preserves, strawberry jam, grape jelly, watermelon-rind pickles, and pumpkin pie.

Now tell the student to describe, in three sentences, either the dinner itself, Mother, or the dining-room. His answer should resemble one of the following:

"When Almanzo came into the house, the ham, cheese, and baked beans smelled so good that he could hardly bear it. He was served last at dinner. But then he ate baked beans, potatoes with gravy, turnips, pumpkin, ham, pickles, and pumpkin pie."

"The dining room in Almanzo's house had brown wallpaper and an air-castle hanging over the table. There were corner cupboards with interesting shells and books in them, and Almanzo's mother had made a rag rug for the floor."

"Almanzo's mother had a hoop-skirt so wide that she had trouble getting through the door. She had smooth brown hair, and her dress had red buttons and red sleeves. She was short and pretty."

Then have the student repeat his answers in order; this will form his brief summary. Write down the student's narration on the lines below, but do not allow him to watch.

_____

_____

_____

_____

Then choose one or two sentences (about 12–15 words) to dictate back to the student. Repeat the sentences twice and ask the student to repeat them back to you before he writes on

Student Page 75. If he cannot repeat the sentences, read them again until he is able to keep them in mind.

Give all necessary help in spelling and punctuation.

DAY FOUR: Dictation Exercise   *Student Page 76*

Focus: *Adverbs that tell how, when, where, how often, to what extent*

Pull out Student Page 76. Ask the student to write his name and the date.

Tell the student that today's dictation sentence is from *Farmer Boy* and describes Almanzo getting ready for bed after his huge dinner.

Dictate the following sentence to the student two times.

> The bedroom was so cold that he could hardly unbutton his clothes and put on his long woolen nightshirt and nightcap.

Now ask the student to repeat the sentence back to you before he writes. If he cannot remember the entire sentence, you may repeat it additional times.

Watch the student as he writes, and correct him at once if he begins to make a mistake. When he is finished, ask him to underline the adverb "so." Tell him that this adverb answers the question "to what extent?" To what extent was the bedroom cold? It was *so* cold.

Now ask the student to underline the adverb "hardly." Ask him which question this adverb answers. (The correct answer is "how?" How could he unbutton his clothes? He could *hardly* unbutton his clothes.)

WEEK 11

DAY ONE: Narration Exercise   *Student Pages 77–79*

Focus: *Identifying the central narrative thread in a passage*

Pull out Student Pages 77–78 and 79. Ask the student to write her name and the date on Student Page 79.

Allow the student to read the story on Student Pages 77–78, either silently or aloud.

Help the student begin to identify the central elements in the narrative by asking the following questions. She should try to answer these questions without looking back at the story, but if she cannot remember an answer after thinking for a few minutes, allow her to reread. Remind her to answer in complete sentences.

> **Instructor:** Who was Hor-em-heb?
> **Student:** *He was the Master Builder.*
>
> **Instructor:** After the doors to the treasure chamber were locked, what was put on them?
> **Student:** *Pharaoh's seal was placed on them.*
>
> **Instructor:** How did Hor-em-heb trick the Pharaoh?
> **Student:** *He built a secret passage into the treasure chamber.*
>
> **Instructor:** The story says that Hor-em-heb was "able to add to the reward which Pharaoh gave to him." What do you think this means?
> **Student:** *He was stealing from the treasure chamber. [You may need to prompt the student for this answer.]*
>
> **Instructor:** After Hor-em-heb died, who began to use the secret passage to steal treasure?
> **Student:** *Hor-em-heb's two sons began to steal the treasure.*
>
> **Instructor:** What did Pharaoh do when he found that his treasure was disappearing?
> **Student:** *He set traps near the treasure.*
>
> **Instructor:** Did the traps work?
> **Student:** *Yes, one of the brothers was caught.*

Now ask the student the general question, "Can you give me a brief summary of this passage?" The student should answer by summarizing the plot, rather than listing details. Her answer should be no more than three sentences and should resemble one of the following:

> "The Pharaoh asked his Master Builder to build him a treasure room. The Master Builder made a secret passage into the treasure room. He and his sons stole the treasure."
>
> "Hor-em-heb, who was the Pharaoh's Master Builder, made a treasure room with a secret passage. He used the passage to steal treasure. He told his sons about the passage before he died, and they used it to steal even more."
>
> "The Master Builder built the Pharaoh a treasure room with a secret passage. He used the passage to steal treasure, and after he died his sons used it too. But the Pharaoh set traps and caught one of the sons."

If the student has trouble condensing the information in the passage, ask the following three questions:

> What did Hor-em-heb do?
>
> What did this allow him and his sons to do?
>
> What did the Pharaoh do about it?

Then have the student repeat her answers in order; this will form her brief summary. Write down the student's narration on Student Page 79 as she watches.

DAY TWO: Dictation Exercise   *Student Page 80*

Focus: *Remembering dictation sentences after three repetitions*

Pull out Student Page 80. Dictate the following sentences to the student three times. Before you read, tell the student that you will read the sentences only three times before asking her to write.

Also tell the student that in these sentences, "pharaoh" should not be capitalized because it does not stand for a particular person. It was capitalized in the story from "The Treasure Thief" because it named a particular pharaoh, Rameses III.

Indicate the period after the first sentence with your voice. You will probably need to remind the student that "pharaoh" is spelled with the *a* before the *o.*

> **The king of Egypt was called the pharaoh. The pharaohs of Egypt built pyramids to protect their treasures and their graves.**

Now ask the student to repeat the sentences back to you before she writes. If she forgets, tell her to go back to the beginning of the sentences and recite them again to jog her memory.

If necessary, you may then prompt the student with single words.

Watch the student as she writes, and correct her at once if she begins to make a mistake.

DAY THREE: Narration and Dictation   *Student Pages 81–82*

Focus: *Identifying the central narrative thread in a passage and writing original sentences from dictation*

Pull out Student Pages 81 and 82. Ask the student to write her name and the date on Student Page 82.

Today's exercise will combine narration and dictation. Allow the student to read the story on Student Page 81, either silently or aloud.

Help the student begin to identify the central elements in the narrative by asking the following questions. She should try to answer these questions without looking back at the story, but if she cannot remember an answer after thinking for a few minutes, allow her to reread. Remind her to answer in complete sentences.

Instructor: In this passage, the treasure chamber isn't built into a pyramid. What building is it part of?
Student: *It is part of the king's palace.*

Instructor: What kind of door did the builder put into the wall?
Student: *He put a stone in the wall that could be taken out.*

Instructor: To whom did the builder tell his secret?
Student: *He told it to his sons.*

Instructor: Why could the king not blame anyone for the thefts? Two reasons were given.
Student: *The seals on the door weren't broken, and the chamber was locked.*

Instructor: What did the king do to protect his treasure?
Student: *He put traps around the treasure.*

Instructor: What happened to the thieves?
Student: *One of them was caught in a trap.*

Now ask the student the general question, "Can you give me a brief summary of this passage?" The student should answer by summarizing the plot, rather than listing details. Her answer should be no more than three sentences and should resemble one of the following:

"The builder built a treasure room onto the king's palace, but he left a loose stone in the wall so that he could steal treasure. He told his sons about the stone before he died. His sons also stole treasure, but one of them got caught in a trap."

"The king told his builder to make a treasure room. The builder left a removable stone in the wall, so that he and his sons could steal the treasure. When the king realized that his treasure was disappearing, he set a trap and caught one of the thieves."

"The builder planned to make himself and his sons comfortable with the king's treasure. So he left a loose stone in the wall, so that they could always get into the treasure room. But the king set traps around the money, and one of the builder's sons was caught."

If she has trouble condensing the information in the passage, ask the following three questions:

What did the builder do to the treasure room?

Who stole the money?

How did the king respond to the disappearing money?

Then have the student repeat her answers in order; this will form her brief summary. Write down the student's narration on the lines below, but do not allow her to watch.

_____

_____

_____

_____

Then choose one or two sentences (about 15–18 words) to dictate back to the student. Repeat the sentences three times and ask the student to repeat them back to you before she writes on Student Page 82.

Give all necessary help in spelling and punctuation.

DAY FOUR: Dictation Exercise   *Student Page 83*

Focus: Remembering dictation sentences after three repetitions

Pull out Student Page 83. Ask the student to write her name and the date.

Dictate the following sentences to the student three times. Before you read, tell the student that you will read the sentences only three times before asking her to write, and will not repeat them afterwards. Tell the student that you will pause briefly for each comma, and for a longer time at the first period.

Now ask the student to repeat the sentences back to you before she writes. If she forgets, tell her to go back to the beginning of the sentences and recite them again to jog her memory.

If necessary, you may then prompt the student with single words.

> Roger Lancelyn Green retold the stories of the Egyptians. When he was younger, he studied at Oxford, where his tutor was C. S. Lewis.

Watch the student as she writes, and correct her at once if she begins to make a mistake. You may need to help her spell "Lancelyn." You may also need to explain that "C." and "S." are capitalized and that each is followed by a period, since those letters are abbreviations for Lewis's full name (Clive Staples).

WEEK 12

DAY ONE: Narration Exercise   *Student Pages 84–86*

Focus: Identifying the central narrative thread in a passage

Pull out Student Pages 84–85 and 86. Ask the student to write his name and the date on Student Page 86.

Allow the student to read the story on Student Pages 84–85, either silently or aloud.

Help the student begin to identify the central elements in the narrative by asking the following questions. He should try to answer these questions without looking back at the story, but if he cannot remember an answer after thinking for a few minutes, allow him to reread. Remind him to answer in complete sentences.

Instructor: How did Ali Baba earn his living?
Student: He sold sticks at the market.

Instructor: How did his brother Kasim earn a living?
Student: He had a rich wife and sold carpets.

Instructor: How did Ali Baba know that the men in the woods were robbers?
Student: They were rough, used bad language, and had plunder on their horses.

Instructor: What happened when the leader of the robbers shouted "Open sesame!"
Student: The rock swung open and a cave appeared.

Instructor: How did they close the door to the cave?
Student: The leader shouted, "Close sesame!"

Instructor: When Ali Baba went into the cave, what did he see?
Student: He saw treasure OR He saw silver, gold, jewels, and carpets.

Instructor: What did Ali Baba take home with him?
Student: He took four bags of gold coins.

Instructor: How did Ali Baba and his wife count the coins?
Student: They borrowed a corn measure from his brother.

Instructor: What did Kasim's wife do to the corn measure?
Student: She put tar on the bottom of the measuring pail.

Instructor: What did she find stuck to the tar when the corn measure was returned?
Student: She found a gold coin.

Now ask the student the general question, "Can you give me a brief summary of this passage?" The student should answer by summarizing the plot, rather than listing details. His answer should be no more than three sentences and should resemble one of the following:

"Ali Baba discovered a cave filled with treasure. He took gold coins home for his wife to count, but his brother's wife found out about the coins."

"Ali Baba was a poor man, but his brother was rich. By accident, Ali Baba found out where robbers were storing their gold. He tried to keep the gold a secret from his brother, but his brother's wife discovered the secret."

"Ali Baba was gathering sticks when he saw robbers storing their plunder in a cave. He took some of the coins home to his wife. They borrowed a corn measure from his brother's wife, but she put tar on the measure and a coin stuck to the tar."

The student will probably attempt to put too much information into the summary. If he has difficulty condensing the story, ask the following three questions:

What did Ali Baba discover?

How did he and his wife measure it?

How did Kasim's wife discover their secret?

Then have the student repeat his answers in order; this will form his brief summary. Write down the student's narration on Student Page 86 as he watches.

DAY TWO: Dictation Exercise   *Student Page 87*

Focus: Proper nouns

Pull out Student Page 87. Ask the student to write his name and the date.

Tell the student that today's dictation sentence is from "The First Voyage of Sinbad," another story in *The Thousand and One Nights*. Sinbad is beginning the story of his adventures.

Dictate the following sentences to the student three times. Before you read, tell the student that you will read the sentences only three times before asking him to write, and will not repeat them afterwards.

Tell the student that the selection has three sentences in it. There is also one comma. You will pause briefly at the comma, and for a longer time at each period.

> We left Baghdad at once. We set sail, and steered our course through the Persian Gulf. The Persian Gulf is formed by the coasts of Arabia on the right and Persia on the left.

Now ask the student to repeat the sentences back to you before he writes. If he forgets, tell him to go back to the beginning of the sentences and recite them again to jog his memory. If necessary, you may then prompt the student with single words.

Remind the student that there are four names, or proper nouns, in the selection: Baghdad, Persian Gulf, Arabia, and Persia. All of these should be capitalized.

Watch the student as he writes, and correct him at once if he begins to make a mistake.

DAY THREE: Narration and Dictation   *Student Pages 88–89*

Focus: Identifying the central narrative thread in a passage and writing original sentences from dictation

Pull out Student Page 88. Ask the student to write his name and the date on Student Page 89.

Today's exercise will combine narration and dictation. Allow the student to read the story on Student Page 88, either silently or aloud.

Help the student begin to identify the central elements in the narrative by asking the following questions. He should try to answer these questions without looking back at the story, but if he cannot remember an answer after thinking for a few minutes, allow him to reread. Remind him to answer in complete sentences.

Instructor: What did Kasim's wife do when she found the golden coin?
Student: *She told her husband about it.*

Instructor: Was Kasim pleased over Ali Baba's good luck?
Student: *No, he was jealous.*

Instructor: What did Ali Baba offer Kasim so that his brother would keep the secret?
Student: *He offered Kasim part of his treasure.*

Instructor: How many treasure chests did Kasim take with him to the cave?
Student: *He took ten chests.*

Instructor: After Kasim filled his treasure chests, he tried to get out. What did he say to the cave door?
Student: *He said, "Open, Barley."*

Instructor: Did the door open?
Student: *No, it did not.*

Now ask the student the general question, "Can you give me a brief summary of this passage?" The student should answer by summarizing the plot, rather than listing details. His answer should be no more than three sentences and should resemble one of the following:

"Kasim's wife was jealous and told her husband about the gold. Kasim discovered Ali Baba's secret. He set off to the cave to take the treasure, but he forgot how to reopen the cave door."

"Kasim learned about Ali Baba's wealth from his wife. Ali Baba told him how to get into the cave, and begged him to keep the secret. Kasim went to the cave alone, but once he was inside, he forgot the words 'Open, Sesame.'"

"Kasim's wife told him all about Ali Baba's wealth. Then Kasim decided to take the treasure for himself. He went to the cave and opened the door, but once he was inside, he forgot how to open it so that he could get back out."

If he has difficulty condensing the story, ask the following three questions:

How did Kasim find out about the treasure?

What did he do?

What went wrong with his plan?

Then have the student repeat his answers in order; this will form his brief summary. Write down the student's narration on the lines below, but do not allow him to watch.

_____

_____

_____

_____

Then choose two or three sentences (15–18 words) to dictate back to the student. Repeat the sentences three times and ask the student to repeat them back to you before he writes on Student Page 89.

Give all necessary help in spelling and punctuation.

DAY FOUR: Dictation Exercise   *Student Page 90*

Focus: Proper nouns and names of books

Pull out Student Page 90. Ask the student to write his name and the date.

Tell the student that today's dictation sentence is from *The Story of the World: The Middle Ages.* This sentence is a little shorter because it has something new in it: the name of a book, *The Thousand and One Nights.*

Tell the student that when he writes the name of a book, he should capitalize the first word of the title and every other important word in the title. In *The Thousand and One Nights,* all of the words except for "and" are capitalized. Also, the names of books are usually put in italics. But when you are writing by hand, you underline the name of a book instead.

Dictate the following sentence to the student three times. Before you read, tell the student that you will read the sentence only three times before asking him to write, and will not repeat it afterwards. Also tell the student that there are two commas in the sentence, and that you will pause briefly at each one.

> One of the most famous Islamic books, <u>The Thousand and One Nights</u>, takes place in the palace of the caliph in Baghdad.

Now ask the student to repeat the sentence back to you before he writes. If he forgets, tell him to go back to the beginning of the sentence and recite it again to jog his memory. If necessary, you may then prompt the student with single words.

Remind the student that the sentence contains two other names besides *The Thousand and One Nights*: "Baghdad" and "Islamic." Both should be capitalized.

Watch the student as he writes, and correct him at once if he begins to make a mistake.

WEEK 13

DAY ONE: Narration Exercise   *Student Pages 91–93*

Focus: *Identifying the central details in a passage*

Pull out Student Pages 91–92 and 93. Ask the student to write her name and the date on Student Page 93.

Allow the student to read the story on Student Pages 91–92, either silently or aloud.

Help the student begin to identify the central details in the narrative by asking the following questions. She should try to answer these questions without looking back at the story, but if she cannot remember an answer after thinking for a few minutes, allow her to reread. Remind her to answer in complete sentences.

Instructor: What is one thing that Oliver found in the first room?
Student: *He found an old bedspring, an empty barrel, and a jar with a large spider.*

Instructor: The second room was filled with treasures. What cave was it like?
Student: *It was like Ali Baba's cave.*

Instructor: What were the two sleds named?
Student: *They were named Snow Demon and Little Kriss Kringle.*

Instructor: What was unusual about the old bicycle?
Student: *The front wheel was very tall and the back wheel was small.*

Instructor: Can you remember three other things that Oliver found in the second room?
Student: *He found a tin bathtub, jars with spiders in them, a doll carriage, a coffee grinder, a crib frame, and books.*

Instructor: What covered all of the objects in the room?
Student: *A layer of white dust covered everything.*

Instructor: What did Oliver spend the rest of the afternoon doing?
Student: *He spent it reading old books OR old magazines.*

Instructor: What three things were missing from the world of the old books?
Student: *There were no cars, no airplanes, and no trains.*

Now ask the student the general question, "Can you give me a brief summary of this passage?" The student should answer by describing the room and what Oliver did there. Her answer should be no more than three sentences and should resemble one of the following:

"Oliver found a room filled with treasures. It had sleds, an old bicycle, old toys, and old books, all covered with dust. He spent all afternoon reading the old books.

"Oliver found a treasure room with sleds, an old bicycle, a tin bathtub, and old books in it. The books were all about a time when there were no cars, planes, or trains."

"Oliver spent all afternoon reading in a secret room. He found the room while he was exploring. It was like a treasure room, filled with things like sleds, an old bike, a bathtub painted blue, old books, and a doll carriage."

Write down the student's narration on Student Page 93 as she watches.

Day Two: Dictation Exercise   *Student Page 94*

Focus: Helping verbs and direct quotations

Pull out Student Page 94. Ask the student to write her name and the date.

Tell the student that today's dictation sentence is also from *The Four-Story Mistake*. This sentence is a little shorter because it has something new in it: a direct quotation.

Tell the student that a direct quotation is the exact words that someone speaks. In this sentence, Cuffy says Oliver's name twice. The student should put quotation marks around these names to show that Cuffy says them.

Show the student the dictation sentences. Point to the quotation marks. Show the student that the quotation marks go right at the beginning of Cuffy's words, and after the punctuation mark that *ends* Cuffy's words. The first word after that, "cried," does not begin with a capital letter because Cuffy's words are *part* of the sentence. This is not the end of the sentence, even though there is an exclamation point after "Oliver! Oliver!"

Now take the book away and dictate the following sentences to the student three times. Before you read, tell the student that you will read the sentence only three times before asking her to write, and will not repeat it afterwards. Be sure to use a different voice for "Oliver! Oliver!" to indicate that these are Cuffy's exact words.

> Hours later his reluctant ear was pierced by the frantically repeated sound of his name. "Oliver! Oliver!" cried Cuffy.

Now ask the student to repeat the sentences back to you before she writes. If she forgets, tell her to go back to the beginning of the sentences and recite them again to jog her memory. If necessary, you may then prompt the student with single words.

Watch the student as she writes, and correct her at once if she begins to make a mistake in either spelling or punctuation. You may need to remind her that there is an exclamation point after each "Oliver!"

When she is finished, tell her to underline the verb "was pierced." Tell her that "pierced" is an action verb and "was" is a helping verb. It would sound silly to say, "His reluctant ear pierced." "Was" has to help out the verb "pierced."

DAY THREE: Narration and Dictation   *Student Pages 95–97*

Focus: Identifying the central details in a passage and writing original sentences from dictation

Pull out Student Pages 95–96 and 97. Ask the student to write her name and the date on Student Page 97.

Today's exercise will combine narration and dictation. Allow the student to read the story on Student Pages 95–96, either silently or aloud.

Help the student begin to identify the central details in the narrative by asking the following questions. She should try to answer these questions without looking back at the story, but if she cannot remember an answer after thinking for a few minutes, allow her to reread. Remind her to answer in complete sentences.

Instructor: What did the children use for sliding down the hill after they tried the sleds?
Student: *They slid down the hill on dishpans.*

Instructor: Which child didn't like the dishpans?
Student: *Oliver didn't like the spinning.*

Instructor: What did they decide to do next?
Student: *They made snow ice cream.*

Instructor: What two ingredients did they get from Cuffy for the ice cream?
Student: *They got milk and sugar.*

Instructor: How did Oliver react to the snow ice cream?
Student: *He ate so much that his stomach felt strange.*

Instructor: After the other three had gone to the house, what did Rush do?
Student: *He went for a walk in the snow.*

Instructor: Who went with him?
Student: *The dog Isaac went with him.*

Instructor: The story draws a contrast between the snowy woods and the house. A contrast is when the differences between two things are pointed out. What two words describe the woods?
Student: *The woods are beautiful and mysterious.*

Instructor: What three things does Rush suddenly long for?
Student: *He longs for noise, warmth, and light.*

Instructor: How are the windows of the kitchen described?
Student: *They are bright.*

Now ask the student the general question, "Can you give me a brief summary of this passage?" The student should answer by describing three things: the sledding, the ice cream, and the walk in the woods. Her answer should be no more than three sentences and should resemble one of the following:

"The children slid down the hill on dishpans that went around and around and made Oliver sick. Then they made snow ice cream, and Oliver ate so much that his stomach felt strange. Then Rush went for a walk in the woods, but he got cold and headed back to the house."

"The children went sledding on sleds and dishpans. Then they made snow ice cream with milk and sugar. Rush took his dog for a walk in the woods, but he decided to go back to where there was light and noise."

"The children sledded on dishpans and made ice cream from snow, milk, and sugar. Then Rush decided to go for a walk in the woods with his dog Isaac. The woods were beautiful and mysterious, but he got cold and wanted to go back to the warm bright kitchen."

Write down the student's narration on the lines below, but do not allow her to watch.

_____

_____

_____

_____

Then choose two or three sentences (15–18 words) to dictate back to the student. Repeat the sentences three times and ask the student to repeat them back to you before she writes on Student Page 97.

Give all necessary help in spelling and punctuation.

DAY FOUR: Dictation Exercise

Focus: *Helping verbs and semicolons*

Pull out Student Page 98. Ask the student to write her name and the date.

Tell the student that today's dictation sentence is from *The Four-Story Mistake*. It describes how the snow looks to the children as it falls.

Dictate the following sentence to the student three times. Before you read, tell the student that you will read the sentence only three times before asking her to write, and will not repeat it afterwards.

Tell the student that there is one comma and one semicolon in the sentence. The semicolon separates two complete sentences and takes the place of a period. Tell the student that you will pause briefly at the comma and for a longer time at the semicolon.

> By lunchtime the valley was lightly coated, like a cake with confectioner's sugar; and by half past three the snow was of a respectable depth.

Now ask the student to repeat the sentence back to you before she writes. Remind her that "confectioner's" is a possessive and has an apostrophe before the *s*. If she forgets part of the sentence, tell her to go back to the beginning of the sentence and recite it again to jog her memory.

If necessary, you may then prompt the student with single words.

Watch the student as she writes, and correct her at once if she begins to make a mistake. You may need to help her spell "confectioner's."

When she is finished, tell her to underline the verbs "was" and "coated" on the first line, and "was" on the second line. Tell her that "coated" is an action verb and "was" is a helping verb. It would sound silly to say, "The valley lightly coated." "Was" has to help out the verb "coated."

Point out that the "was" on the second line is a state of being verb that stands alone. It does not help out an action verb. "Was" can be either a state of being *or* a helping verb.

WEEK 14

DAY ONE: Narration Exercise   *Student Pages 99–101*

Focus: *Identifying the central narrative thread in a passage*

Pull out Student Pages 99–100 and 101. Ask the student to write his name and the date on Student Page 101.

Allow the student to read the story on Student Pages 99–100, either silently or aloud.

Help the student begin to identify the central elements in the narrative by asking the following questions. He should try to answer these questions without looking back at the story, but if he cannot remember an answer after thinking for a few minutes, allow him to reread. Remind him to answer in complete sentences.

Instructor: Why was one kitten named Mask?
Student: *It was a black kitten with a white face.*

Instructor: Why was another kitten named Funny?
Student: *She had one green eye and one blue eye.*

Instructor: What were the rules of the kitten-choosing game? Be sure you tell me what part the hat, the names on four pieces of paper, the four corners of the room, and the kittens play in the game.
Student: The kittens' names were written on pieces of paper put into a hat. Rufus drew the names out of the hat. Each kitten was placed in the middle of the room. The four children went to the four corners of the room and called "Kitty, kitty."

Instructor: What kitten was first to be chosen?
Student: Funny was the first.

Instructor: Which child ended up with Funny?
Student: Sylvie ended up with Funny.

Instructor: When Whiskers was placed in the center of the room, what did he do?
Student: He just sat there.

Instructor: What did the children have to do to get him to play?
Student: They had to get right up next to him.

Instructor: Who ended up with Whiskers?
Student: Rufus got Whiskers.

Now ask the student the general question, "Can you give me a brief summary of this passage?" The student should answer by summarizing the choosing game, rather than listing details. His answer should be no more than three sentences and should resemble one of the following:

> "The four Moffats played a game to choose their kittens. They placed each kitten in the center of the room and called 'Here, kitty, kitty!' Whichever person the kitten went to became the owner of that kitten."

> "The Moffats put the names of the kittens on pieces of paper and drew them out of a hat. Each kitten was placed in the center of the room. The children called, 'Here, kitty, kitty!' and tried to get the kitten to come."

> "The Moffat children placed each kitten in the middle of the room. They went to the four corners of the room and called the kittens. Funny went to Sylvie, and Whiskers went to Rufus, so they were out of the game."

If he has difficulty condensing the game into three sentences, ask the following three questions:

Where did the children stand?

Where were the kittens put?

What did the children try to get the kittens to do?

Then have the student repeat his answers in order; this will form his brief summary.

Write down the student's narration on Student Page 101 as he watches.

DAY TWO: Dictation Exercise   *Student Page 102*

Focus: *Direct objects following action verbs*

Pull out Student Page 102. Ask the student to write his name and the date.

Tell the student that today's dictation sentences are also from *The Moffats.* In these sentences, Jane is watching her mother cook apples for apple pie.

Dictate the following sentences to the student three times. Before you read, tell the student that you will read the sentences only three times before asking him to write, and will not repeat them afterwards.

> She set the blue and white kettle of apples on the stove. She sprinkled sugar and cinnamon on the apples with the same deft fingers.

Now ask the student to repeat the sentences back to you before he writes. If he forgets, tell him to go back to the beginning of the sentences and recite them again to jog his memory. If necessary, you may then prompt the student with single words.

Watch the student as he writes, and correct him at once if he begins to make a mistake. When he is finished, tell him to underline the action verbs "set" and "sprinkled." Ask the student, "Set what?" He should answer "kettle." (If he answers "blue and white kettle of apples," ask him which *one* word represents the thing which is "set.") Tell him that "kettle" is the *direct object* of the verb "set." What did Jane's mother set on the stove? She set the kettle. The kettle "receives" the action of the verb *set.* Tell him to write the initials "d.o." over the word "kettle."

Now ask the student, "Sprinkled what?" He should answer "sugar and cinnamon." Tell him that "sugar" and "cinnamon" are both direct objects of the verb "sprinkled." What did Jane's mother sprinkle? She sprinkled sugar and cinnamon. Sugar and cinnamon both "receive" the action of the verb *sprinkled.* Tell him to write the initials "d.o." over the word "sugar" and also over the word "cinnamon."

DAY THREE: Narration and Dictation   *Student Pages 103–105*

Focus: *Identifying the central narrative thread in a passage and writing original sentences from dictation*

Pull out Student Pages 103–104 and 105. Ask the student to write his name and the date on Student Page 105.

Today's exercise will combine narration and dictation. Allow the student to read the story on Student Pages 103–104, either silently or aloud.

Help the student begin to identify the central elements in the narrative by asking the following questions. He should try to answer these questions without looking back at the story, but if he cannot remember an answer after thinking for a few minutes, allow him to reread. Remind him to answer in complete sentences.

Instructor: What was Boots doing while the game was going on?
Student: *She was clawing at the box and meowing to get out.*

Instructor: What did she do as soon as she was set on the floor?
Student: *She raced madly around and whacked a tassel.*

Instructor: Whom did Jane think Boots would choose?
Student: *She thought Boots would choose Joey.*

Instructor: What did Boots suddenly do?
Student: *She jumped into Jane's lap.*

Instructor: Which kitten went to Joey?
Student: *Mask went to Joey.*

Instructor: What did Joey find to be unusual about Mask? The story lists four things.
Student: *Mask had the longest fur, the prettiest markings, and the longest tail. He was also smallest.*

Instructor: What did Jane do with Boots when the game was over?
Student: *She put Boots back in the box with her mother.*

Now ask the student the general question, "Can you give me a brief summary of this passage?" The student should answer by summarizing the plot, rather than listing details. His answer should be no more than three sentences and should resemble one of the following:

"Jane and Joe both wanted Boots. At first Jane thought that Boots would choose Joe, but then Boots jumped into her lap. Joey got Mask instead."

"Jane wanted to own Boots, even though she thought she didn't deserve to. But Boots jumped in her lap and Mask went to Joey. Joey decided that Mask had the longest fur, the prettiest markings, and the longest tail."

"Boots was the most energetic of all the kittens. Jane wanted her more than anything in the world. She thought that Boots would go to Joey, but then Boots jumped into her lap and became hers."

If he has difficulty condensing the story, ask the following three questions:

What did Jane want?

What did Jane get, and how?

What did Joey get, and how did he feel about it?

Then have the student repeat his answers in order; this will form his brief summary. Write down the student's narration on the lines below, but do not allow him to watch.

_____

_____

_____

_____

Then choose two or three sentences (15–18 words) to dictate back to the student. Repeat the sentences three times and ask the student to repeat them back to you before he writes on Student Page 105.

Give all necessary help in spelling and punctuation.

DAY FOUR: Dictation Exercise   *Student Page 106*

Focus: *Direct objects following action verbs*

Pull out Student Page 106. Ask the student to write his name and the date.

Tell the student that today's dictation sentences are also from *The Moffats*. This happens *before* the choosing game begins.

Dictate the following sentences to the student three times. Before you read, tell the student that you will read the sentences only three times before asking him to write, and will not repeat them afterwards.

Tell him that there are two sentences. One ends with a period and one ends with an exclamation point. When you read, be sure to indicate the exclamation point with your voice.

> Jane clutched the nickel tightly in her fist and walked slowly up the street. Think of all the fine things it might buy!

Now ask the student to repeat the sentences back to you before he writes. If he forgets, tell him to go back to the beginning of the sentences and recite them again to jog his memory. If necessary, you may then prompt the student with single words.

Watch the student as he writes, and correct him at once if he begins to make a mistake. When he is finished, tell him to underline the action verbs "clutched" and "walked." Ask the student, "Clutched what?" He should answer "nickel." Tell him that "nickel" is the *direct object* of the verb "clutched." What did Jane clutch? She clutched the nickel. The nickel "receives" the action of the verb "clutched." Tell him to write the initials "d.o." over the word "nickel."

Now tell the student that "walked" is also an action verb, but in this sentence it doesn't have a direct object. Jane walked what? Jane didn't walk anything. She just walked. Not every action verb has a direct object.

WEEK 15

DAY ONE: Narration Exercise   *Student Pages 107–109*

Focus: *Identifying the central narrative thread in a passage*

Pull out Student Pages 107–108 and 109. Ask the student to write her name and the date on Student Page 109.

Allow the student to read the story on Student Pages 107–108, either silently or aloud.

Help the student begin to identify the central elements in the narrative by asking the following questions. She should try to answer these questions without looking back at the story, but if she cannot remember an answer after thinking for a few minutes, allow her to reread. Remind her to answer in complete sentences.

Instructor: What did Kerby first do to the beaker of water?
Student: *He put two drops of chemical into the water.*

Instructor: What happened?
Student: *Nothing happened.*

Instructor: What did he decide to do with the beaker?
Student: *He decided to empty it.*

Instructor: What did he do with the water on his way to the bathroom?
Student: *He drank it.*

Instructor: Why did Kerby rush into the bathroom to look at himself in the mirror?
Student: *He was afraid that he would turn into a horrible monster.*

Now ask the student the general question, "Can you give me a brief summary of this passage?" The student should answer by summarizing the plot, rather than listing details. Her answer should be no more than three sentences and should resemble one of the following:

"Kerby put two drops of chemical into a beaker of water, but nothing happened. He decided to dump the water out. Instead, he sniffed it, and it smelled so good that he drank it."

"Kerby had a mysterious chemistry set. He mixed one of the chemicals into water. Then, without really meaning to, he drank the water."

"Kerby mixed chemicals and water together. Nothing happened, but the water smelled so good that he drank it. Then he was afraid he would change into a horrible monster."

If the student has difficulty condensing the story, ask the following three questions:

What is Kerby's first experiment?

What does he do with the water?

Why is he afraid?

Then have the student repeat her answers in order; this will form her brief summary. Write down the student's narration on Student Page 109 as she watches.

DAY TWO: Dictation Exercise   *Student Page 110*

Focus: Semicolons and commas

Pull out Student Page 110. Ask the student to write her name and the date.

Tell the student that today's dictation sentence is from Robert Louis Stevenson's story *Dr. Jekyll and Mr. Hyde.* Dr. Jekyll makes a potion that turns him into an evil man named Mr. Hyde. In this sentence, one of Dr. Jekyll's friends goes to see him.

Dictate the following sentence to the student three times. Before you read, tell the student that you will read the sentence four times before asking her to write, and will not repeat it afterwards. (This is a complicated sentence, so you will add an extra repetition.)

Tell the student that this sentence has the name "Dr. Jekyll" in it, and that "Doctor" should be spelled as the abbreviation "Dr."

Tell the student that this long sentence is actually three shorter sentences, attached to each other by semicolons. There are also commas in the sentence. You will pause for a brief time at each comma and for a longer time at each semicolon.

When you read the sentence, let your voice fall on the words that precede each semicolon, so that the student can hear the end of each short sentence.

> The fire burned in the grate; a lamp was set lighted on the chimney shelf, for even in the houses the fog began to lie thickly; and there, close up to the warmth, sat Dr. Jekyll, looking deadly sick.

Now ask the student to repeat the sentence back to you before she writes. If she forgets, tell her to go back to the beginning of the sentence and recite it again to jog her memory. If necessary, you may then prompt the student with single words.

Watch the student as she writes, and correct her at once if she begins to make a mistake. You will probably need to help her spell the name "Jekyll."

DAY THREE: Narration and Dictation   *Student Pages 111–113*

Focus: Identifying the central theme in a selection and writing original sentences from dictation

Pull out Student Pages 111–112 and 113. Ask the student to write her name and the date on Student Page 113.

Allow the student to read the story on Student Pages 111–112, either silently or aloud.

Now help the student begin to identify the central theme in the selection by asking the following questions. She should try to answer these questions without looking back at the story, but if she cannot remember an answer after thinking for a few minutes, allow her to reread. Remind her to answer in complete sentences.

Instructor: There are several different meanings of the word "good." Kerby might be feeling "good" because he feels energetic and happy. Or he might be feeling "good" because he feels like doing the right thing. Which meaning of "good" is the correct one for this story?
Student: *He feels like doing the right thing.*

Instructor: What did he do to the beaker?
Student: *He rinsed it and dried it.*

Instructor: For what did Kerby apologize to Waldo?
Student: *He apologized for dragging Waldo down the hall by the tail.*

Instructor: What did he decide to do to the floors?
Student: *He decided to polish them.*

Instructor: Why did he decide not to do any more experiments in his room?
Student: *He might spill the chemicals and mark his furniture.*

Instructor: What did he then go outside and do?
Student: *He mowed the lawn.*

Instructor: He did two extra things when he mowed the lawn. What were they?
Student: *He trimmed around the trees and fence, and he put the grass clippings on the compost heap.*

Instructor: Do you think that Kerby normally did such a good job cutting the lawn?
Student: *No, he probably didn't.*

Instructor: Why did Kerby's mother nearly fall on her face with surprise?
Student: *Kerby had already fixed lunch.*

Instructor: What did Kerby do all afternoon?
Student: *He worked in the basement.*

Instructor: How did his mother react to this?
Student: *She wondered if he was sick OR She kept asking him if he was all right OR She called his father.*

Now say to the student, "Try to tell me, in one sentence, how Kerby felt after drinking the water in the beaker." The student should respond, "Kerby felt like doing good things," or "Kerby felt helpful and good." The answer should reflect the *ethical* character of Kerby's "feeling good." Prompt the student, if she seems uncertain, by asking the first comprehension question again.

Once the student has come up with this sentence, say, "Now give me two more sentences with specific details in them about the good things Kerby did." The purpose of this exercise is to guide the student into stating the central theme of the passage and supporting that theme with specifics.

The answer should resemble one of the following:

"Kerby felt like doing good things. He apologized to Waldo for dragging him down the hall by the tail. Then he cut the grass, fixed lunch, and cleaned up the basement."

"Kerby felt like doing good things. He put his chemistry set neatly away and decided not to play with it in his room. Then he cut the grass, trimmed around the fence, put the clippings on the compost pile, and fixed lunch."

"Kerby felt helpful and good. He decided to polish the floors for his mother. He cut the grass, cleaned the cellar, and fixed lunch for his mother."

Write down the student's narration on the lines below, but do not allow her to watch.

_____

_____

_____

_____

Then choose two or three sentences (15–18 words) to dictate back to the student. Repeat the sentences three times and ask the student to repeat them back to you before she writes on Student Page 113.

Give all necessary help in spelling and punctuation.

DAY FOUR: Dictation Exercise   *Student Page 114*

Focus: *Direct objects following action verbs*

Pull out Student Page 114. Ask the student to write her name and the date.

Tell the student that today's dictation sentence is also from Robert Louis Stevenson's story *Dr. Jekyll and Mr. Hyde.* In it, Dr. Jekyll describes making and drinking the potion that will change him into the evil Mr. Hyde.

Dictate the following sentence to the student three times. Before you read, tell the student that you will read the sentence only three times before asking her to write, and will not repeat it afterwards.

Tell the student that there are no semicolons in this sentence, just commas.

Late one accursed night, I compounded the elements, watched them boil and smoke together in the glass, and then, with a strong glow of courage, drank the potion.

Now ask the student to repeat the sentence back to you before she writes. Remind her to pause at the commas. If she forgets, tell her to go back to the beginning of the sentence and recite it again to jog her memory.

If necessary, you may then prompt the student with single words.

Watch the student as she writes, and correct her at once if she begins to make a mistake. When she is finished, tell her to underline the action verbs "compounded," "watched," and "drank." (You may need to explain that "compounded" means "mixed together.") Tell the student that each one of these action verbs has a direct object.

> What is the direct object of "compounded?" (The correct answer is "elements." What did he compound? He compounded the elements.) Tell her to write the initials "d.o." over the direct object "elements."

> What is the direct object of "watched?" (The correct answer is "them." What did he watch? He watched them. "Them" is a pronoun, referring back to the elements.) Tell her to write the initials "d.o." over the direct object "them."

> What is the direct object of "drank?" (The correct answer is "potion." What did he drink? He drank the potion.) Tell her to write the initials "d.o." over the direct object "potion."

WEEK 16

DAY ONE: Narration Exercise   *Student Pages 115–117*

Focus: *Summarizing a series of ordered facts*

Pull out Student Pages 115–116 and 117. Ask the student to write his name and the date on Student Page 117.

Allow the student to read the selection on Student Pages 115–116, either silently or aloud.

Help the student summarize the steps outlined in the passage, in order, by asking the following questions. He should try to answer these questions without looking back at the story, but if he cannot remember an answer after thinking for a few minutes, allow him to reread. Remind him to answer in complete sentences.

Instructor: What is the first step in setting up the trick?
Student: *Make a candleholder of clay and put the candle in it.*

Instructor: What is the second step in setting up the trick?
Student: *Put the coin in the dish and cover it with water.*

Instructor: What is the third step in setting up the trick?
Student: *Put food coloring in the water.*

Instructor: What is the audience challenged to do?
Student: *They are challenged to remove the coin without getting their fingers wet.*

Instructor: What is the first step in solving the problem?
Student: *Put the candle and candleholder in the dish.*

Instructor: What is the second step in solving the problem?
Student: *Light the candle.*

Instructor: What is the third step in solving the problem?
Student: *Put the glass over the lit candle.*

Instructor: What happens to the water after the candle uses up the oxygen and goes out?
Student: *Water is pushed up into the glass.*

Instructor: What happens to the dish?
Student: *The dish is dry.*

Instructor: What does the candle use up when it burns?
Student: *The candle uses oxygen.*

Now say to the student, "First, tell me how to set up the trick. Then, tell me how to solve the problem." His answer should be no more than four sentences and should resemble one of the following:

> "Set a candle in a clay candleholder. Put a coin in a dish and cover it with colored water. Then set the candle in the dish and light it. Put a glass over the candle, and the water will be pushed up into the glass."

> "Put a coin in a dish and cover it with water. Put a few drops of food coloring in the water. Set a candle in the dish, light it, and put a glass over it. When the candle uses the oxygen, the water will be pushed up into the glass."

> "Put enough colored water in a dish to cover a coin. Set a lit candle in the dish, far away from the coin. Put a glass over the coin. When the candle uses the oxygen in the glass, water will be sucked away from the coin up into the glass."

Write down the student's narration on Student Page 117 as he watches.

DAY TWO: Dictation Exercise   *Student Page 118*

Focus: *Linking verbs and predicate nominatives*

Pull out Student Page 118. Ask the student to write his name and the date.

Dictate the following sentences to the student three times. Before you read, tell the student that you will read the sentences only three times before asking him to write, and will not repeat them afterwards.

Tell the student that today's dictation is taken from the book *Oxygen* by Michele Thomas. The dictation is three sentences long, and one of the sentences is a question. Ask the student what punctuation mark ends a question. Tell the student to listen for the end of each sentence.

Also tell the student that there are two commas in the sentences. Ask him to listen for the pauses that indicate commas.

When you read the dictation, be sure to indicate the question with your voice. Indicate the end of the second sentence by allowing your voice to fall. Pause at the commas in the third sentence.

> Can you smell the oxygen in the air? Probably not. Oxygen is an odorless, tasteless, and colorless element.

Now ask the student to repeat the sentences back to you before he writes. If he forgets, tell him to go back to the beginning of the sentences and recite them again to jog his memory.

If necessary, you may then prompt the student with single words.

Watch the student as he writes, and correct him at once if he begins to make a mistake. You may need to spell "oxygen" for him.

When he is finished, ask him to underline the word "oxygen" in the third sentence. This is the subject of the sentence. Now ask him to circle the verb "is." This is a state of being verb. (If he knows the state of being verbs, have him chant them now.) In this sentence, however, the state of being verb becomes a linking verb. It links the subject "oxygen" to the noun "element." What is oxygen? Oxygen is an element.

"Element" is a predicate nominative. It is a noun that *renames* the subject. "Oxygen" and "element" are the same thing.

DAY THREE: Narration and Dictation   *Student Pages 119–120*

Focus: Summarizing a series of ordered facts and writing original sentences from dictation

Pull out Student Pages 119 and 120. Ask the student to write his name and the date on Student Page 120.

Allow the student to read the selection on Student Page 119, either silently or aloud.

Help the student summarize the steps outlined in the passage, in order, by asking the following questions. He should try to answer these questions without looking back at the story, but if he cannot remember an answer after thinking for a few minutes, allow him to reread. Remind him to answer in complete sentences.

Instructor: What do you tell the audience you can do?
Student: *You tell them you can read minds.*

Instructor: What does the audience do after you go out of the room?
Student: *The audience chooses an object.*

Instructor: When you come back in, what does your volunteer do?
Student: *Your volunteer points to several objects.*

Instructor: When do you say, "I can read your mind. That is the correct object!"
Student: *You say this when the volunteer points to the object chosen by the audience.*

Instructor: What have you and the volunteer decided ahead of time?
Student: *You have decided on a set of signals.*

Instructor: Give me an example of a signal you might use. (Hint: the signal I want uses the color "red.")
Student: *The volunteer points to something red right before he points to the correct object.*

Instructor: What hand should the volunteer point with if the object itself is red?
Student: *He should point with his left hand.*

Instructor: If the correct object is red and the volunteer is using his left hand, what color object should he point to *before* he points to the correct object?
Student: *He should point to a black object.*

Now say to the student, "Tell me in two or three sentences how you and the volunteer set up the trick." His answer should be no more than three sentences and should resemble one of the following:

> "You decide that the volunteer will point to a red object right before the correct object. If the correct object is red, he will use his left hand and point to a black object right before."

> "You choose your volunteer ahead of time. You decide on signals. Before he points to the right object, he will point to a red object, or he will point to a black object with his left hand."

> "You and the volunteer decide on signals ahead of time. Before he points to the right object, he will point to a red object. If the object itself is red, he will point to a black object with his left hand right before he points to the correct object."

Write down the student's narration on the lines below, but do not allow him to watch.

_____

_____

_____

_____

Then choose two or three sentences (15–18 words) to dictate back to the student. Repeat the sentences three times and ask the student to repeat them back to you before he writes on Student Page 120.

Give all necessary help in spelling and punctuation.

DAY FOUR: Dictation Exercise

Student Page 121

Focus: Linking verbs and predicate adjectives

Pull out Student Page 121. Ask the student to write his name and the date.

Tell the student that today's dictation sentence is from *101 Easy-to-Do Magic Tricks* by Bill Tarr. The sentence is about "presentation"—the art of doing a magic trick in a way that entertains the audience.

Dictate the following sentence to the student three times. Before you read, tell the student that you will read the sentence only three times before asking him to write, and will not repeat it afterwards.

Tell the student to listen carefully for the commas in the sentence, and then pause significantly at each one. Do not tell him ahead of time how many commas there are.

> **Good presentation is clear, direct, easy to follow, and as interesting and absorbing as you can make it.**

Now ask the student to repeat the sentence back to you before he writes. If he forgets, tell him to go back to the beginning of the sentence and recite it again to jog his memory. If necessary, you may then prompt the student with single words.

Watch the student as he writes, and correct him at once if he begins to make a mistake.

When he is finished, ask him to underline the word "presentation" in the sentence. This is the subject of the sentence. Now ask him to circle the verb "is." This is a state of being verb. (If he knows the state of being verbs, have him chant them now.) In this sentence, however, the state of being verb becomes a linking verb. It links the subject "presentation" to several adjectives that describe *what* good presentation is.

Say to the student, "What is good presentation? Underline each word that tells you what good presentation is." The student should underline "clear," "direct," "easy," "interesting," and "absorbing." These are all adjectives that describe "presentation." (If the student asks, tell him that "to follow" is a verb that tells more about "easy," not more about "presentation.")

Now tell the student that because those adjectives come after the linking verb, they are called *predicate adjectives.* Have the student draw an arrow from each predicate adjective back to the subject.

WEEK 17

DAY ONE: Narration Exercise   *Student Pages 122–124*

Focus: *Summarizing a series of ordered facts*

Pull out Student Pages 122–123 and 124. Ask the student to write her name and the date on Student Page 124.

Allow the student to read the selection on Student Pages 122–123, either silently or aloud.

Help the student summarize the steps outlined in the passage, in order, by asking the following questions. She should try to answer these questions without looking back at the story, but if she cannot remember an answer after thinking for a few minutes, allow her to reread. Remind her to answer in complete sentences.

Instructor: The magician tells Ehrich that what a magician actually *does* doesn't really count. What counts?
Student: *What people think you do counts.*

Instructor: When the magician shows the empty bucket with his left hand, what else is he holding in his left hand?
Student: *He is holding coins in his left hand.*

Instructor: Why doesn't the audience see the coins?
Student: *They are looking at the empty bucket.*

Instructor: What does he have in his right hand?
Student: *He has one coin.*

Instructor: Describe how the magician holds the coin in his right hand so that no one can see it. [Note: if the student has trouble answering, you may want to give her a coin to hold between her thumb and first finger so that the coin cannot be seen from the front of her hand.]
Student: *He holds the coin between his thumb and first finger.*

Instructor: When the magician picks a coin out of the air, what is he really doing?
Student: *He is showing the audience the coin already in his hand.*

Instructor: What does he do next with that coin?
Student: *He slips it to the back of his hand again.*

Instructor: Where does he get the coin that goes in the bucket?
Student: *He gets it from his left hand.*

Now say to the student, "Describe how the magician did the coin trick." Her answer should be no more than three sentences and should resemble one of the following:

"The magician hid coins in his left hand and one coin in his right hand. He showed the coin in his right hand and pretended to pick it out of the air. Then he hid that coin again and put a coin into the bucket from his left hand."

"The magician held a bucket and hidden coins with his left hand. He held one coin in his right hand. He pretended to pick the coin in his right hand out of the air and dropped coins from his left hand into the bucket."

"The magician hid a coin in his right hand. He showed the coin and pretended to pick it out of the air, and then hid the coin and pretended to put it in the bucket. Meanwhile, he put coins from his left hand into the bucket."

Write down the student's narration on Student Page 124 as she watches.

Day Two: Dictation Exercise   *Student Page 125*

Focus: *Linking verbs and predicate nominatives*

Pull out Student Page 125. Tell the student that today's dictation sentence is from a book called *The Right Way to Do Wrong* by Harry Houdini himself. Houdini spent many years studying the tricks that criminals use. Here's what Houdini writes in the first chapter of his book: "The object of this book is...to safeguard the public against the practices of the criminal classes by exposing their various tricks and explaining the adroit methods by which they seek to defraud. 'Knowledge is power' is an old saying. I might paraphrase it in this case by saying knowledge is safety. I wish to put the public on its guard, so that honest folks may be able to detect and protect themselves from the dishonest, who labor under the false impression that it is easier to live dishonestly than to thrive by honest means."

Dictate the following sentences to the student three times. Before you read, tell the student that you will read the sentences only three times before asking her to write, and will not repeat them afterwards.

> "Knowledge is power" is an old saying. I might paraphrase it by saying knowledge is safety.

Now ask the student to repeat the sentences back to you before she writes. If she forgets, tell her to go back to the beginning of the sentences and recite them again to jog her memory. If necessary, you may then prompt the student with single words.

Before she begins to write, tell her that the phrase "Knowledge is power" has quotation marks around it. The quotation marks show that Houdini is not using his own words—he is using the words of a traditional saying. (If the student asks, you may also tell her that there is no comma after "power," as there would be in dialogue, because this is not something that Houdini himself is saying out loud.) The phrase "knowledge is safety" doesn't have quotation marks because Houdini is now using his own words.

Watch the student as she writes, and correct her at once if she begins to make a mistake.

When she is finished, point out that there are two predicate nominatives in these sentences. Both of them rename "knowledge." Ask the student to find and circle them. (The correct answers are "power" and "safety.") Both predicate nominatives are linked to "knowledge" by the linking verb "is."

DAY THREE: Narration and Dictation   *Student Pages 126–128*

Focus: *Summarizing a series of ordered facts and writing original sentences from dictation*

Pull out Student Pages 126–127 and 128. Ask the student to write her name and the date on Student Page 128.

Allow the student to read the selection on Student Pages 126–127, either silently or aloud.

Help the student summarize the steps outlined in the passage, in order, by asking the following questions. She should try to answer these questions without looking back at the story, but if she cannot remember an answer after thinking for a few minutes, allow her to reread. Remind her to answer in complete sentences.

Instructor: During the magic trick itself, what was Houdini wearing when he got into the box?
Student: *He was wearing handcuffs and chains.*

Instructor: What did carpenters do to the box?
Student: *They nailed the top shut.*

Instructor: What was placed in front of the box?
Student: *A drapery cabinet stood in front of the box.*

Instructor: When Houdini appeared, what did the box look like?
Student: *It was still nailed closed.*

Instructor: How did Houdini and his assistant actually prepare the box?
Student: *They replaced the nails on one side with short nails.*

Instructor: What did Houdini do as soon as he got out of the box?
Student: *He tapped the long nails back in.*

Instructor: Why didn't the audience hear him?
Student: *The band was playing loudly.*

Instructor: What tool did Houdini use at other times to get out of the box?
Student: *He used a steel jack hidden in his clothes.*

Instructor: Why didn't the audience hear him?
Student: *The band was playing loudly.*

Instructor: Can you remember three of the strange things Houdini escaped from on his American tour?

Student: *He escaped from an envelope, a glass box, a coffin, a sausage skin, and a giant football.*

Now say to the student, "Tell the two ways that Houdini escaped from his boxes." Her answer should be no more than three sentences and should resemble one of the following:

"Houdini and his assistant replaced the long nails in the box with short nails. When no one could see, Houdini pushed the small nails out and nailed the long ones back in. Sometimes Houdini smuggled a steel jack into the box and used that instead."

"Houdini's assistant prepared the box ahead of time by using short nails that were easy to push out. After Houdini pushed the box apart he nailed it back together while the band played. Houdini also used a small steel jack hidden in his clothes to push the box apart."

"Houdini could push the box apart because some of the nails had been taken out and replaced with small ones. Sometimes he also pried the box apart with a hidden steel jack. Afterwards he nailed the box back together while the band played loudly."

Write down the student's narration on the lines below, but do not allow her to watch.

_____

_____

_____

_____

Then choose two or three sentences (15–18 words) to dictate back to the student. Repeat the sentences three times and ask the student to repeat them back to you before she writes on Student Page 128.

Give all necessary help in spelling and punctuation.

DAY FOUR: Dictation Exercise   *Student Page 129*

Focus: *Linking verbs, predicate nominatives, and predicate adjectives*

Pull out Student Page 129. Ask the student to write her name and the date.

Tell the student that today's dictation sentences are also from Harry Houdini's book about criminals, *The Right Way to Do Wrong*. In this paragraph, Houdini describes pickpockets: "Among the most interesting classes of thieves is the pickpocket, whose clever subterfuges and skill of hand have been so often exploited in novel and story-book...It is the usual opinion that a pickpocket is a forbidding and suspicious looking fellow, but a glance at the rogues' gallery in any police headquarters will show you that they look much like ordinary individuals, and are of more than average intelligence."

Dictate the following sentences to the student three times. Before you read, tell the student that you will read the sentences only three times before asking her to write, and will not repeat them afterwards.

You will probably need to tell the student that "prepossessing" means "attractive, creating a good impression."

> The pickpocket is usually very well dressed and of prepossessing appearance. They are entertaining talkers and easy in their manner.

Now ask the student to repeat the sentence back to you before she writes. If she forgets, tell her to go back to the beginning of the sentences and recite them again to jog her memory. If necessary, you may then prompt the student with single words.

Watch the student as she writes, and correct her at once if she begins to make a mistake. You may need to help her spell "prepossessing." When she is finished, point out that there is a predicate adjective in the second sentence. It describes "they." Ask the student to find and circle it. (The correct answer is "easy.") There is also a predicate nominative, which renames "they" (it is "talkers"). Both of these are linked to the subject "they" by the linking verb "are."

WEEK 18

DAY ONE: Narration Exercise   *Student Pages 130–132*

Focus: Identifying the central theme in a selection

Pull out Student Pages 130–131 and 132. Ask the student to write his name and the date on Student Page 132.

Allow the student to read the story on Student Pages 130–131 either silently or aloud.

Help the student begin to identify the central theme in the selection by asking the following questions. He should try to answer these questions without looking back at the story, but if he cannot remember an answer after thinking for a few minutes, allow him to reread. Remind him to answer in complete sentences.

Instructor: How many cooks at a time could work in Paul Bunyan's new kitchen?
Student: Two hundred cooks at a time could work in the kitchen.

Instructor: How long were the tables in the dining room?
Student: The tables were six miles long.

Instructor: How many gallons of soup could the kettle hold?
Student: It could hold eleven hundred gallons.

Instructor: How did Hot Biscuit Slim get vegetables into the soup?
Student: He rowed into the kettle with boatloads of vegetables and shoveled them in.

Instructor: How did the cookhouse boys grease the ten-acre griddle?
Student: They strapped bacon onto their feet and skated back and forth.

Instructor: How many men did one hot cake feed?
Student: It fed five men.

Instructor: What did Slim say that hurt Cream Puff Fatty's pride?
Student: He said that the men wouldn't be able to eat dessert.

Instructor: What did Cream Puff Fatty decide to cook for dessert?
Student: He made cream puffs with whipped cream a foot high.

Instructor: Name three things that Hot Biscuit Slim served for Sunday dinner.
Student: He served soup, vegetables, salads, chicken pie, hot biscuits with jelly, spinach, cucumbers, and young red radishes.

Instructor: Did the men eat the cream puffs anyway?
Student: Yes, they did.

Now say to the student, "Try to complete this sentence with one interesting, vivid word. 'Everything in Paul Bunyan's camp was....'" The student will probably say "big." Help him find another, more vivid word. If necessary, you can offer him the following list to look at:

colossal

enormous

gigantic

huge

immense

mammoth

oversize

tremendous

vast

Once the student has come up with this sentence, say, "Give me two more sentences with two or more details about the size of Paul Bunyan's camp." The purpose of this exercise is to guide the student into stating the central theme of the passage and supporting that theme with specifics.

The answer should resemble one of the following:

"Paul Bunyan's camp was enormous. The dining tables were six miles long, and the soup kettle was so huge that the cook had to row into the middle of it with his boat filled with vegetables. The cookboys greased the griddle by skating on it, and the hot cakes were so big that it took five men to eat one."

"Paul Bunyan's camp was gigantic. Two hundred cooks worked on the meals. The meals were so huge that the men ate soup, vegetables, salads, chicken pie, hot biscuits with jelly, and cream puffs a foot tall."

"Paul Bunyan's camp was oversize. The kettle held eleven hundred gallons, the griddle was ten acres across, and the dining tables were six miles long. The men were served so much food that it took two hundred cooks to prepare it, and boys on roller skates served it."

Write down the student's narration on Student Page 132.

DAY TWO: Dictation Exercise   *Student Page 133*

Focus: *Linking verbs, predicate nominatives and predicate adjectives*

Pull out Student Page 133. Ask the student to write his name and the date.

Dictate the following sentence to the student three times. Before you read, tell the student that you will read the sentence only three times before asking him to write, and will not repeat it afterwards.

Pause at the comma, but do not tell the student that the comma is there.

> By the time Paul Bunyan was sixteen years old, he was the best logger in his father's camp in the Maine woods.

Now ask the student to repeat the sentence back to you before he writes. If he forgets, tell him to go back to the beginning of the sentence and recite it again to jog his memory. If necessary, you may then prompt the student with single words.

Watch the student as he writes, and correct him at once if he begins to make a mistake. You may need to remind him that "father's" has an apostrophe to show possession.

When he is finished, tell him to circle both occurrences of the linking verb "was." In the first phrase, "was" links Paul Bunyan to what phrase? "Sixteen years old." The phrase acts as a predicate adjective; it describes Paul Bunyan.

Now tell the student to underline the pronoun "he." In the second part of the sentence, "he" is the subject. Ask the student to underline the noun that renames "he" and to label it "p.n." for "predicate nominative." (The answer is "logger.") Have the student draw an arrow from the word "logger" back to the pronoun "he."

DAY THREE: Narration and Dictation   *Student Pages 134–135*

Focus: Identifying the central details in a passage and writing original sentences from dictation

Pull out Student Pages 134 and 135. Ask the student to write his name and the date on Student Page 135.

Today's exercise will combine narration and dictation. Allow the student to read the selection on Student Page 134, either silently or aloud.

Help the student begin to identify the central details in the narrative by asking the following questions. He should try to answer these questions without looking back at the story, but if he cannot remember an answer after thinking for a few minutes, allow him to reread. Remind him to answer in complete sentences.

Instructor: The passage says that families and single young men who came to British Canada took on different tasks. What is one thing families did?
Student: *They cleared the forests OR planted new farms OR built up cities and towns.*

Instructor: What are two things that young men did?
Student: *They dug canals around the rapids and waterfalls, hauled timber, salted down codfish, and worked in shipyards.*

Instructor: From what nation did most of the immigrants come?
Student: *Most of them came from Britain. [If the student answers Scotland, Ireland, or England, tell them that this is correct, but that those countries were part of a larger nation: Britain, or Great Britain.]*

Instructor: What does it mean if a country is "a good poor man's country"?
Student: *Anyone willing to work hard can do well.*

Instructor: What time of year did lumberjacks cut wood?
Student: *They cut wood in the winter.*

Instructor: In the spring, what did they do with the logs?
Student: *They floated the logs down the rapids to the sawmills and timber ships.*

Instructor: People told all sorts of tall tales about the lumberjack Joseph Montferrand. Can you remember three of the things that Montferrand could supposedly do?
Student: *He was so strong no boxer could beat him; he could leave bootmarks on a ceiling and land on his feet; he could drink a lake dry; he could dig a channel by dragging his axe; he combed his hair with a pine tree.*

Now ask the student the general question, "Can you give me a brief summary of this passage? Be sure to tell me where the immigrants came from and what at least two groups of them did." His answer should be around three sentences long (he may add a sentence about Joseph Monteferrand for a four-sentence option) and should resemble one of the following:

"Families and young men came from Britain to look for work. Many of the families cleared forests, planted farms, and built towns. Young men became lumberjacks, fishermen or shipbuilders."

"Immigrants came from England, Scotland, and Ireland to British Canada. Families built new farms and cities, while young men cut wood, dug canals, and fished. Lumberjacks cut timber all winter long and then rode the logs down the rivers in the spring."

"British immigrants came to Canada to find new lives and new work. Families cleared forests and built cities and towns. Many young men became lumberjacks, a job which only the strongest men could do. One famous lumberjack was so strong that people said he could drink a lake dry and comb his hair with a pine tree."

Write down the student's narration on the lines below, but do not allow him to watch.

_____

_____

_____

_____

Then choose two or three sentences (15–18 words) to dictate back to the student. Repeat the sentences three times and ask the student to repeat them back to you before he writes on Student Page 135.

Give all necessary help in spelling and punctuation.

DAY FOUR: Dictation Exercise   *Student Page 136*

Focus: *Linking verbs and predicate nominatives*

Pull out Student Page 136. Ask the student to write his name and the date.

Dictate the following sentence to the student three times. Before you read, tell the student that you will read the sentence only three times before asking him to write, and will not repeat it afterwards.

Pause significantly at the comma, but do not tell the student ahead of time that the comma is there.

All through the nineteenth century, lumbering was the greatest industry in many parts of eastern Canada.

Now ask the student to repeat the sentence back to you before he writes. If he forgets, tell him to go back to the beginning of the sentence and recite it again to jog his memory. If necessary, you may then prompt the student with single words.

Watch the student as he writes, and correct him at once if he begins to make a mistake. When he finishes, point out that there is a predicate nominative in the second half of the sentence. It is a noun that describes "lumbering." Ask him to find and circle it. (The correct answer is "industry.") It is linked to the subject, "lumbering," by the linking verb "was."

WEEK 19

DAY ONE: Narration Exercise   *Student Pages 137–139*

Focus: *Identifying the central narrative thread in a passage*

Pull out Student Pages 137–138 and 139. Ask the student to write her name and the date on Student Page 139.

Allow the student to read the story on Student Pages 137–138, either silently or aloud.

Help the student begin to identify the central elements in the narrative by asking the following questions. She should try to answer these questions without looking back at the story, but if she cannot remember an answer after thinking for a few minutes, allow her to reread. Remind her to answer in complete sentences.

Instructor: What kind of rule did the Americans believe to be wrong?
Student: *They believed that absolute rule was wrong.*

Instructor: What had Americans been doing for the last one hundred and fifty years?
Student: *They had been making their own laws.*

Instructor: What did the members of the Continental Congress decide to declare about the colonies?
Student: *They decided to declare the American colonies independent.*

Instructor: Who was chosen to write the official declaration?
Student: *Thomas Jefferson was chosen.*

Instructor: How long did Jefferson work on writing the declaration?
Student: *He worked for two weeks.*

Instructor: The first part of the Declaration of Independence explains American beliefs about what form of government?
Student: *It explains American beliefs about democracy.*

Instructor: Can you remember the three rights that men are born with, according to the Declaration?

Student: *They are born with the right to life, the right to liberty, and the right to try to be happy.*

Instructor: What is a government supposed to do about these rights?

Student: *It is supposed to preserve these rights for all.*

Instructor: The second part of the Declaration contains a list. What does the list describe?

Student: *It describes the tyranny of the king.*

Instructor: How long did the members of the Congress debate the Declaration?

Student: *They debated for almost three days.*

Instructor: When did they approve it?

Student: *They approved it on July 4, 1776.*

Now ask the student the general question, "Can you give me a brief summary of this passage?" The student should answer by summarizing the plot, rather than listing details. She may have four full sentences to answer; her answer should resemble one of the following:

"Kings had absolute rule, but Americans wanted to make laws for themselves. The Continental Congress decided to declare the American colonies to be independent. Thomas Jefferson was chosen to write the Declaration of Independence. The first part explained that men had certain rights; the second part listed all the ways that the king had refused to honor those rights."

"Americans had been making their own laws for 150 years. The Continental Congress decided to declare America independent of the English king. Thomas Jefferson wrote out the official Declaration of Independence. The Continental Congress approved the Declaration on July 4, 1776."

"The Continental Congress declared the American colonies independent and chose Thomas Jefferson to write the official Declaration. The Declaration said that all men had the right to life, the right to liberty, and the right to try to be happy. It also listed many examples of the king's tyranny."

The student will probably attempt to put too much information into the summary. If she has difficulty condensing the story, ask the following three questions:

What did Americans believe?

What did the Continental Congress decide to do?

What official document explained this?

What were the two parts of this document, and what did each say?

Then have the student repeat her answers in order; this will form her brief summary. Write down the student's narration on Student Page 139 as she watches.

DAY TWO: Dictation Exercise   *Student Page 140*

Focus: *Command sentences and understood "you"*

Pull out Student Page 140. Ask the student to write her name and the date.

Tell the student that today's dictation sentence is from a letter written by Thomas Jefferson, who also wrote out the Declaration of Independence for the Continental Congress. Tell her that Thomas Jefferson often wrote letters to the members of his family, giving them advice and telling them about his own work. He wrote many of these letters to his young nephew Peter Carr. Jefferson wanted Peter to be as well educated, healthy, and happy as possible. He gave Peter many commands: he told Peter to read many books and to make a special study of ancient history, to go for walks every day, to avoid ever doing a dishonorable thing, to learn French, and to practice shooting a gun.

These sentences are taken from a letter that Jefferson wrote to Peter Carr in 1785, when Peter was fifteen years old.

Dictate the following sentences to the student three times. Before you read, tell the student that you will read the sentences only three times before asking her to write, and will not repeat them afterwards.

Pause significantly at the comma, and for an even longer time at the period; also indicate the end of the first sentence by allowing your voice to fall. However, do not tell the student ahead of time about the comma or period.

> Write to me once every month or two, and let me know the progress you make. Tell me in what manner you employ every hour in the day.

Now ask the student to repeat the sentences back to you before she writes. If she forgets, tell her to go back to the beginning of the sentences and recite them again to jog her memory. If necessary, you may then prompt the student with single words.

Watch the student as she writes, and correct her at once if she begins to make a mistake. When she is finished, tell her to underline the words "write," "let," and "tell." Explain that each one is the verb of a command sentence. Jefferson is ordering his nephew to write, to let, and to tell.

Tell the student that, in a command sentence, the subject is understood. Jefferson's nephew is not actually *in* the sentences, but he is the one who is supposed to write, let, and tell.

If Thomas Jefferson were standing right next to young Peter Carr, he might turn around and point at Peter and say, "You write to me! You let me know! You tell me!" In a command sentence, the subject is "understood you." The "you" is not written, but we understand without being told that it is there.

DAY THREE: Narration and Dictation

Student Pages 141–143

Focus: Identifying the central narrative thread in a passage and writing original sentences from dictation

Pull out Student Pages 141–142 and 143. Ask the student to write her name and the date on Student Page 143.

Today's exercise will combine narration and dictation. Allow the student to read the story on Student Pages 141–142, either silently or aloud.

Help the student begin to identify the central elements in the narrative by asking the following questions. She should try to answer these questions without looking back at the story, but if she cannot remember an answer after thinking for a few minutes, allow her to reread. Remind her to answer in complete sentences.

> **Instructor:** What was the first bad thing John did (or was suspected of doing) that made him unpopular?
> **Student:** *He may have murdered his nephew Arthur of Brittany.*
>
> **Instructor:** What happened to John's lands in France?
> **Student:** *He lost them.*
>
> **Instructor:** What nickname did he get for this?
> **Student:** *He became known as "Softsword."*
>
> **Instructor:** How did John raise money to attack the French and get his lands back?
> **Student:** *He raised taxes.*
>
> **Instructor:** Even with all this money, was his army able to defeat the French?
> **Student:** *No, his army was defeated.*
>
> **Instructor:** What did the English people and their leaders force John to sign?
> **Student:** *They forced him to sign the Magna Carta.*
>
> **Instructor:** According to the passage, what two things did John promise in the Magna Carta?
> **Student:** *He promised to treat everyone more fairly, and he agreed that people could complain to a committee of twenty-five barons if he did not keep his promises.*
>
> **Instructor:** Did he keep his promises?
> **Student:** *No, he did not.*
>
> **Instructor:** What did the barons do to get rid of John?
> **Student:** *They chose Louis of France to be the new king of England.*
>
> **Instructor:** Who actually became king after John died?
> **Student:** *John's son Henry became king.*
>
> **Instructor:** Was Henry supposed to follow the Magna Carta?
> **Student:** *Yes, he was.*

Now ask the student the general question, "Can you give me a brief summary of this passage?" The student should answer by summarizing the plot, rather than listing details. Her answer should be no more than four sentences and should resemble one of the following:

"King John of England got rid of his nephew and taxed his people heavily. His people and their leaders forced him to sign the Magna Carta. This said that he would treat people more fairly, and that his people could complain to the barons. John did not keep his promises, but when his son became king, the Magna Carta was reissued."

"King John became unpopular because he raised taxes and lost land to the French. The English people rebelled. They forced John to agree that he would treat them more fairly. The treaty they forced him to sign was called the Magna Carta, but John did not keep the promises he made in it."

"King John became so unpopular that his people forced him to sign the Magna Carta. This treaty said that he would treat everyone more fairly, and that his people could complain to a committee of barons. When John didn't keep his promises, the barons made a French prince king of England instead. Finally John's son became king after John's death."

If she has difficulty condensing the story, ask the following four questions:

Why was King John unpopular?

What did his people force him to do?

What two things did the Magna Carta say?

Did John keep his promises?

Then have the student repeat her answers in order; this will form her brief summary. Write down the student's narration on the lines below, but do not allow her to watch.

_____

_____

_____

_____

Then choose two or three sentences (15–18 words) to dictate back to the student. Repeat the sentences three times and ask the student to repeat them back to you before she writes on Student Page 143.

Give all necessary help in spelling and punctuation.

DAY FOUR: Dictation Exercise

Focus: *Command sentences*

Pull out Student Page 144. Ask the student to write her name and the date.

Tell the student that today's dictation sentences are adapted from the Magna Carta. The Magna Carta promised the people of England that no man could be thrown in jail or punished unless it could be proved that he had broken the law. The king of England could no longer arrest men just because he wanted to show his power. This is a paraphrase of the clause that guarantees this freedom (Clause 29). Today we call this right *habeas corpus.*

Dictate the following sentence to the student three times. Before you read, tell the student that you will read the sentence only three times before asking her to write, and will not repeat it afterwards.

Pause significantly at each comma, but do not tell the student that the commas are there.

No free man shall be imprisoned, or be deprived of his land or liberty, or be exiled or outlawed, except by the law of the land.

Now ask the student to repeat the sentence back to you before she writes. If she forgets, tell her to go back to the beginning of the sentence and recite it again to jog her memory. If necessary, you may then prompt the student with single words.

Watch the student as she writes, and correct her at once if she begins to make a mistake.

When she is finished, ask her whether this is a command sentence or a simple statement. (The correct answer is "statement"—although the statement has the sound of a command, it is simply announcing a fact.) Point out that the subject of the sentence is "man," rather than "you."

WEEK 20

DAY ONE: Narration Exercise

Focus: *Identifying the central details in a passage*

Pull out Student Pages 145–146 and 147. Ask the student to write his name and the date on Student Page 147.

Allow the student to read the story on Student Pages 145–146, either silently or aloud.

You will now ask the student to summarize the passage. A detail-oriented summary is more appropriate to this descriptive passage than a summary telling what happens. Since this is the first time the student has summarized without having the help of comprehension questions, use a "directed narration starter." Say to the student, "Describe the garden in three sentences." His answer should resemble one of the following:

> "In the garden, all the flowers can talk. The Tiger-lily is the leader of the flowers. The tree at the center of the garden keeps them safe by saying 'Bough-wow.'"

> "The flowers in the garden can all talk. Alice finds out that this is because the ground is so hard that they stay awake. In most gardens, the ground is so soft that the flowers fall asleep."

> "The Tiger-lily and the Rose both talk to Alice. The daisies talk too, but they all talk at once and make too much noise. The tree at the center of the garden keeps the flowers safe by 'barking.'"

> "The garden has tiger-lilies, roses, and pink daisies in it. All of them can talk because the ground is so hard that it keeps them awake. In the middle of the garden, there is a tree that keeps the flowers safe."

If the student has trouble choosing important details, ask these three questions:

What flowers are in the garden?

What reason does the Tiger-lily give for the flowers' ability to talk?

What is at the center of the garden?

The answers to these questions will make up the student's summary.
Write the narration down on Student Page 147 as the student watches.

DAY TWO: Dictation Exercise   *Student Page 148*

Focus: *Direct quotations*

Pull out Student Page 148. Ask the student to write his name and the date.

Tell the student that today's dictation sentence is from the same chapter of *Through the Looking-Glass*. In the garden, Alice meets the Red Queen from her chess set, now grown to life size. The Red Queen is quite bossy.

Before reading the selection, remind the student of the proper form for direct quotations. The Red Queen's actual words should be surrounded by quotation marks. The ending punctuation for each of the Red Queen's sentences should go *inside* the closing quotation marks. The phrase "said the Red Queen" is part of the previous sentence, so "said" should not be capitalized. "And" is capitalized because it begins a new sentence. Also remind the student that "Red Queen" is used as a proper name, so both words should be capitalized.

Now tell the student that you will read the selection three times. Be sure to indicate questions and statements with your voice; also, use a different voice for the Red Queen's actual words and your normal voice for the phrase "said the Red Queen."

Tell the student that you will only read the sentences three times and will not repeat them afterwards.

> "Where do you come from?" said the Red Queen. "And where are you going? Look up, speak nicely, and don't twiddle your fingers all the time."

Now ask the student to repeat the sentences back to you before he writes. If he forgets, tell him to go back to the beginning of the sentences and recite them again to jog his memory. If necessary, you may then prompt the student with single words.

Watch the student as he writes, and correct him at once if he begins to make a mistake.

Day Three: Narration and Dictation   *Student Pages 149–151*

Focus: *Identifying the central narrative thread in a passage and writing original sentences from dictation*

Pull out Student Pages 149–150 and 151. Ask the student to write his name and the date on Student Page 151.

Today's exercise will combine narration and dictation. Allow the student to read the story on Student Pages 149–150, either silently or aloud.

You will now ask the student to summarize the passage. This selection lends itself to a narrative, story-like retelling. To guide the student towards this type of summary, ask him, "In three sentences, what happened at the dinner party?" His answer should resemble one of the following:

> "The Red Queen introduced Alice to the leg of mutton, so then the waiters carried it off. Then she introduced Alice to the plum pudding, but Alice cut a slice out of it anyway. When she did, the pudding spoke to her."

> "At the dinner, the Red Queen kept introducing Alice to the food. Then the waiters carried it off, because it isn't polite to eat food that you've been introduced to. Finally Alice cut the pudding—but the pudding talked back to her."

> "Alice was hungry, but she couldn't eat her meat because she had been introduced to it. The Red Queen also introduced her to the pudding, but she decided to eat it anyway. When she cut a slice, it said, 'How would like me to cut a slice out of you?'"

If the student has difficulty with this summary, ask the following three questions to help focus his thoughts:

> Why couldn't Alice eat her leg of mutton?

> What did she do to the pudding?

> What did the pudding do in response?

Then have the student repeat his answers in order; this will form his brief summary.
Write down the student's narration on the lines below, but do not allow him to watch.

_____

_____

_____

_____

Then choose two or three sentences (16–20 words) to dictate back to the student. Repeat
the sentences three times and ask the student to repeat them back to you before he writes on
Student Page 151.

Give all necessary help in spelling and punctuation.

DAY FOUR: Dictation Exercise

Student Page 152

Focus: *Comma use*

Pull out Student Page 152. Ask the student to write his name and the date.

Tell the student that today's dictation sentences are from the chapter of *Through the
Looking-Glass* where Alice meets the two strange brothers, Tweedledum and Tweedledee. Spell
those names for the student. Then warn him that this selection is one very long sentence with
seven commas in it. Make sure to indicate the commas by pausing significantly when you
reach each one.

Dictate the following sentence to the student three times. Before you read, tell the student
that you will read the sentence only three times before asking him to write. However, tell the
student that you will repeat additional times if necessary, since this is a difficult selection.

> So she wandered on, talking to herself as she went, till, on turning a
> sharp corner, she came upon two fat little men, so suddenly that she
> could not help starting back, but in another moment she recovered
> herself, feeling sure that they must be Tweedledum and Tweedledee.

Now ask the student to repeat the sentence back to you before he writes. If he forgets, tell
him to go back to the beginning of the sentence and recite it again to jog his memory. You
may repeat the sentence as many additional times as necessary.

Watch the student as he writes, and correct him at once if he begins to make a mistake.

WEEK 21

Day One: Poetry Exercise   *Student Page 153*

Focus: *Definitions of poetic terms*

Pull out Student Page 153.

   Allow the student to read the poem on Student Page 153, either silently or aloud.

   Tell the student that, instead of asking questions about the poem, you are going to discuss it with her.

   Remind the student that a "rhyme scheme" is a pattern of rhyming words. Ask the student to fill in the rhyme scheme as in Week 5. If necessary, remind her to give each ending rhyme a letter and write these letters in the blanks at the end of the lines.

   The pattern is:

   A

   A

   B

   A

   B

   B

   C

   B

   C

   C

   D

   C

   D

   D

   D

   D

(***Optional:*** if the student is interested, you may point out to her that the rhyme scheme
   of the poem can be divided into quatrains—sets of four lines. Each of the first three
   quatrains has the same pattern, while the last quatrain has the same rhyme for all four
   lines.

   AABA

BBCB

CCDC

DDDD)

Now ask the student to read the two lines written below the poem out loud, stressing each bolded syllable. Remind her that this is iambic meter, because it falls into this pattern: unstress **stress.**

Ask the student to write "iambic" on the blank that follows "meter (unstress **stress**)." Help her to spell the word properly if necessary.

DAY TWO: Dictation Exercise   *Student Page 154*

Focus: Poetic form, exclamations

Pull out Student Page 154. Ask the student to write her name and the date.

Tell the student that today's dictation sentence is from Robert Frost's poem "Blueberries." Explain that when Robert Frost wrote a poem, he often drew very clear pictures of a natural scene as part of his work. Tell her that you will read her the first lines of "Blueberries." As you read, she should pay attention to how many different words Robert Frost used to describe the blueberries.

> You ought to have seen what I saw on my way
> To the village, through Mortenson's pasture to-day:
> Blueberries as big as the end of your thumb,
> Real sky-blue, and heavy, and ready to drum
> In the cavernous pail of the first one to come!
> And all ripe together, not some of them green
> And some of them ripe! You ought to have seen!

Think about how many different kinds of descriptions of blueberries are in these seven lines: size (as big as the end of your thumb), color (sky-blue), weight (heavy), sound (ready to drum into a pail).

Now dictate the following lines to the student three times. Before you read, tell the student that you will read the lines only three times before asking her to write, and will not repeat them afterwards. Tell her that you will pause briefly at each comma, but that you will pause for a longer time at the end of the first line. Remind her that she should begin the second line right beneath the first line, and that the first word in each line is capitalized.

Be sure to indicate the exclamation point with an excited voice. You will also need to tell her that "sky-blue" is hyphenated.

Real sky-blue, and heavy, and ready to drum
In the cavernous pail of the first one to come!

Now ask the student to repeat the lines back to you before she writes. If she forgets, tell her to go back to the beginning of the lines and recite them again to jog her memory. If necessary, you may then prompt the student with single words.

Watch the student as she writes, and correct her at once if she begins to make a mistake.

DAY THREE: Poetry Exercise   *Student Pages 155–157*

Focus: *Definitions of poetic terms*

Pull out Student Page 155. Do not allow the student to see Student Page 156.

Allow the student to read the poem on Student Page 155, either silently or aloud.

Tell the student that, instead of asking questions about the poem, you are going to discuss it with her.

Begin by asking the student whether the poem tells you who the Listeners are. You may allow her to try several explanations, but eventually you should tell her that the poem is deliberately mysterious. We don't know who the Listeners are! The poet, Walter de la Mare, doesn't *want* us to know. All we are supposed find out is that the Traveller had a promise to keep, and he kept it.

Now tell the student to assign a letter to each ending rhyme—but only the ending rhymes of *every other line*, where blanks are provided in the workbook. The first two blanks in the workbook are filled out already. (You may need to explain that "stone" and "gone" rhymed for the author, Walter de la Mare, because he had a British accent.)

Now, have the student check her answers against Student Page 156.

Once the student has checked her answers, ask her to read the bolded words at the ends of the remaining lines on Student Page 156: **Traveller, grasses, turret, time, Traveller, eyes, listeners, moonlight, stair, shaken, strangeness, turf, even, answered, listeners, house, stirrup, backward.** Ask her whether any of these words rhyme. She should answer that they do *not* rhyme. Tell the student that in this poem, rhymes happen only on every other line. This rhyme scheme gives the poet, Walter de la Mare, more freedom to choose words that will tell his story; he doesn't have to worry about finding a rhyme for the end of every line.

Finally, ask the student to read the poetic lines on Page 157, stressing each bolded syllable. When she is finished, point out that the patterns of **stress** unstress are different for every one of these lines. This poem isn't trochaic, or iambic. It isn't any other meter either. It has "uneven meter"—there is no single pattern of **stress** unstress.

DAY FOUR: Dictation Exercise   *Student Page 158*

Focus: *Poetic form, questions*

Pull out Student Page 158. Ask the student to write her name and the date.

Tell the student that today's dictation exercise is from the poem "Will Ever?" by Walter de la Mare. Begin by reading the first two stanzas of the poem to the student:

> Will he ever be weary of wandering,
> The flaming sun?
> Ever weary of waning in lovelight,
> The white still moon?
> Will ever a shepherd come
> With a crook of simple gold,
> And lead all the little stars
> Like lambs to the fold?
>
> Will ever the Wanderer sail
> From over the sea,
> Up the river of water,
> To the stones to me?
> Will he take us all into his ship,
> Dreaming, and waft us far,
> To where in the clouds of the West
> The Islands are?

Now read the first four lines of the poem to the student, using your voice to emphasize the questions at the ends of the second and fourth lines:

> Will he ever be weary of wandering,
> The flaming sun?
> Ever weary of waning in lovelight,
> The white still moon?

Tell the student that you will dictate these lines to her three times. First, however, show the lines briefly to the student. Point out the commas at the ends of lines 1 and 3, and also point out that lines 2 and 4 are indented. Remind the student that each line begins with a capital letter.

Now remove the selection from the student's sight. Read these four lines three times, pausing significantly at the end of each line. Ask the student to repeat them back to you. If she cannot remember all four lines, repeat them additional times.

Watch the student as she writes, and correct her at once if she begins to make a mistake.

WEEK 22

DAY ONE: Narration Exercise   *Student Pages 159–161*

Focus: *Identifying the central theme in a selection*

Pull out Student Pages 159–160 and 161. Ask the student to write his name and the date on Student Page 161.

Allow the student to read the story on Student Pages 159–160, either silently or aloud.

You will now ask the student to summarize the passage. This selection has a strong central theme which the student should identify. To guide him towards this type of summary, ask him, "In four sentences, tell me about Melvin's problem." His answer should resemble one of the following:

> "Melvin's father owned an ice cream factory, so all of Melvin's schoolmates came to his house to eat it. Melvin knew that his friends came over for the ice cream, so he told his father to give the ice cream away. Most of his friends stopped coming—until he started fixing bicycles. Then they all started bringing their broken chains for him to fix."

> "Melvin had a problem. His friends didn't like him for himself. At first, they came over to eat the ice cream from his father's factory. Then, they came over so he could fix their broken bicycles."

> "Melvin lived in a fancy house, and his father owned an ice cream factory. But Melvin knew that his friends only came over to eat ice cream, so he told his father to give it to orphans. Most of his friends stopped coming. But then Melvin started fixing bicycles, and his friends started coming again with their broken bicycle parts."

If the student has difficulty with this summary, say, "Try to tell me, in one sentence, what Melvin wanted his friends to do." The student should respond, "Melvin wanted his friends to like him for himself," OR "Melvin wanted his friends to come over because they liked him."

Once the student has come up with this sentence, say, "Now give me three more sentences with specific details in them about why Melvin's friends *actually* liked him, and how he reacted to them." The purpose of this exercise is to guide the student into stating the central theme of the passage and supporting that theme with specifics.

Write down the student's narration on Student Page 161 as he watches.

DAY TWO: Dictation Exercise   *Student Page 162*

Focus: *Prepositions*

Pull out Student Page 162. Ask the student to write his name and the date.

Tell the student that today's dictation sentences are from another book by Jan Wahl, the author of *The Furious Flycycle*. Wahl wrote many other children's books. *Humphrey's Bear* is the story of a boy who dreams of his teddy bear coming to life and going on adventures with him. As the story begins, Humphrey's father has just said, "Isn't Humphrey getting a little too old to sleep with a teddy bear?"

Dictate the following sentences to the student three times. Before you read, tell the student that you will read the sentences only three times before asking him to write, and will not repeat them afterwards.

Pause at each comma, and indicate the end of the first sentence by allowing your voice to fall and pausing for a longer time. Do not warn the student ahead of time about the commas and periods.

> Humphrey didn't hear what his mom said. He just jumped under the
> blanket, snuggled with the brown bear, and slept.

Now ask the student to repeat the sentences back to you before he writes. If he forgets, tell him to go back to the beginning of the sentences and recite them again to jog his memory. If necessary, you may then prompt the student with single words.

Watch the student as he writes, and correct him at once if he begins to make a mistake.

When he is finished, tell him to circle the words "under" and "with" in the second sentence. Tell him that these words are *prepositions*—words that show the relationship between two different words. Who was under what? *He* was *under* the *blanket*. "Under" shows the relationship between "he" and the "blanket."

Who snuggled with what? *He* snuggled *with* the *bear*. "With" shows the relationship between "he" and the "bear."

Day Three: Narration and Dictation   *Student Pages 163–165*

Focus: *Identifying the central narrative thread in a passage and writing original sentences from dictation*

Pull out Student Pages 163–164 and 165. Ask the student to write his name and the date on Student Page 165.

Today's exercise will combine narration and dictation. Allow the student to read the story on Student Pages 163–164, either silently or aloud.

You will now ask the student to summarize the passage. This selection lends itself to a narrative, story-like retelling. To guide the student towards this type of summary, say to him, "In three or four sentences, what two important things happened in this passage?" His answer should resemble one of the following:

> "Melvin got very good at repairing things. He even fixed his father's ice cream freezer. His father was so grateful that he bought Melvin a beautiful silver bicycle. Then the great inventor Professor Mickimecki moved into town."

"Melvin repaired his father's ice cream freezer when it broke down. His father bought him a Silver Zephyr bicycle, and Melvin rode it everywhere. Then a great inventor moved into town."

"Melvin's father bought him a bicycle because Melvin fixed the freezer at the ice cream factory. Melvin rode the bicycle everywhere. Then a great inventor came to town. Melvin was very excited that the great inventor now lived in his town."

If the student has difficulty with this summary, ask the following four questions to help focus his thoughts:

What did Melvin do for his father?

What did his father do for him in return?

Who moved to town?

Why was this exciting for Melvin?

Then have the student repeat his answers in order; this will form his brief summary. Write down the student's narration on the lines below, but do not allow him to watch.

_____

_____

_____

_____

Then choose two or three sentences (16–20 words) to dictate back to the student. Repeat the sentences three times and ask the student to repeat them back to you before he writes on Student Page 165.

Give all necessary help in spelling and punctuation.

DAY FOUR: Dictation Exercise   *Student Page 166*

Focus: *Prepositions, direct quotations*

Pull out Student Page 166. Ask the student to write his name and the date.

Tell the student that today's dictation sentences are from *Humphrey's Bear* by Jan Wahl. Humphrey has fallen asleep now, and is dreaming about his teddy bear.

Dictate the following sentences to the student three times. Before you read, tell the student that these sentences have a direct quotation in them. Remind him that a direct quotation has quotation marks on either side of it. Also tell him that this direct quote ends with an exclamation point.

Pause at each comma, and indicate the end of the first sentence by allowing your voice to fall and pausing for a longer time. Be sure to use a different voice for the direct quotation "Get up!" and indicate the exclamation point by using an excited tone.

> As soon as Humphrey was asleep, the bear grew big, as it always did, and took him by the hand. "Get up!" called the bear, standing in the moonlight.

Now ask the student to repeat the sentences back to you before he writes. If he forgets, tell him to go back to the beginning of the sentences and recite them again to jog his memory. Since these sentences have a number of different elements in them (commas, periods, direct quotation, exclamation point), you may then repeat them additional times if necessary.

Watch the student as he writes, and correct him at once if he begins to make a mistake. You may need to remind him that "called" in the second sentence is not capitalized, because it does not begin a new sentence—it follows a direct quotation.

When he is finished, tell him to circle the word "in" in the second sentence. Remind him that this word is a *preposition*—a word that shows the relationship between two different words. The bear was standing in what? The *bear* was standing *in* the *moonlight*.

WEEK 23

Day One: Narration Exercise   *Student Pages 167–169*

Focus: *Identifying the central narrative thread in a passage*

Pull out Student Pages 167–168 and 169. Ask the student to write her name and the date on Student Page 169.

Allow the student to read the story on Student Pages 167–168, either silently or aloud.

You will now ask the student to summarize the passage. This selection lends itself to a narrative, story-like retelling. To guide the student towards this type of summary, ask her, "In three or four sentences, tell me about the three books Laura decided to write, and the order she wrote them in." Her answer should resemble one of the following:

> "Laura Ingalls Wilder wrote *Little House in the Big Woods*, and everyone loved it. For her next book, she decided to write about Almanzo's childhood in New York. She had a hard time getting her husband Almanzo to tell her about it! Then she decided to write her third book about living on the prairie in Kansas."

> "*Little House in the Big Woods* was Laura's first book. Next, she wrote *Farmer Boy* about Almanzo's childhood. Then she decided that her third book should be about the year

her family lived on the prairie. She even drove to Kansas to find the place where the log cabin had been, and found oil wells instead."

"Laura's first book, *Little House in the Big Woods*, was a success. So she wrote a second book, called *Farmer Boy*, about her husband when he was a little boy. Her husband didn't tell her stories about his childhood, but his brother and sister did. Laura's third book was about life on the Kansas prairie.

If the student has difficulty with this summary, ask the following four questions to help focus her thoughts:

Did people like Laura's first book?

What did she decide to write about for her second book?

What was the subject of her third book?

What did she do as research for the third book?

The answers to these questions will make up the student's summary.
Write the narration down on Student Page 169 as the student watches.

DAY TWO: Dictation Exercise

Student Page 170

Focus: Prepositions, objects of prepositions, prepositional phrases

Pull out Student Page 170. Tell the student that today's dictation sentence is from Laura Ingalls Wilder's biography by Beatrice Gormley. The "she" in the sentence is Laura, getting down to work on the story of her life.

Dictate the following sentence to the student three times. Before you read, tell the student that you will read the sentence only three times before asking her to write, and will not repeat it afterwards.

Pause significantly at each comma, but do not warn the student about the commas.

> In spare moments, while soup simmered on the stove or between hanging out the wash and starting dinner, she would pick up her pencil and step back into the world of her childhood.

Now ask the student to repeat the sentence back to you before she writes. If she forgets, tell her to go back to the beginning of the sentence and recite it again to jog her memory. If necessary, you may then prompt the student with single words.

Watch the student as she writes, and correct her at once if she begins to make a mistake.

When she is finished, tell her to circle the words "on" and "into." Tell her that these words are *prepositions*—words that show the relationship between two different words. Soup simmered on what? *Soup* simmered *on* the *stove*. "On" shows the relationship between "soup" and "stove."

She would step back into what? *She* would step back *into* the *world* of her childhood.

Tell the student to put a box around the words "stove" and "world." Explain to her that these words are known as "objects of the preposition." The object of the preposition is the word that follows the preposition and answers the question "what?" On what? On the *stove*. Into what? Into the *world*. Ask the student to write the abbreviation "p." over each circled preposition, and "o.p." over each boxed object of the preposition.

Now tell the student to underline the words "on the stove" and "into the world." Explain to her that each set of three words is a *prepositional phrase*. A prepositional phrase is made up of a preposition, its object, and any words (like "the") that modify the object.

> [**Note:** If the student asks, you may tell her that "in spare moments" is a prepositional
> phrase that tells *when*. Although "between" can be a preposition, in this sentence
> it is acting as an adverb that answers the question "when?" "Out" in this sentence
> functions as part of the compound verb "hanging out," while "up" functions as part of
> the compound verb "pick up." "Of her childhood" is a prepositional phrase indicating
> ownership. The prepositional phrases "on the stove" and "into the world" are the
> simplest examples of prepositional phrases in this sentence.]

DAY THREE: Narration and Dictation   *Student Pages 171–173*

***Focus:** Identifying the central narrative thread in a passage and writing original sentences from dictation*

Pull out Student Pages 171–172 and 173. Ask the student to write her name and the date on Student Page 173.

Today's exercise will combine narration and dictation. Allow the student to read the story on Student Pages 171–172, either silently or aloud.

You will now ask the student to summarize the passage. This selection lends itself to a narrative, story-like retelling. To guide the student towards this type of summary, say to the student, "In three or four sentences, tell me first about the teacher who discouraged Ted, and then about the teacher who encouraged him." Her answer should resemble one of the following:

> "In Ted's first art class, he had to draw daisies in a milk bottle. He tried to turn his
> paper upside down to draw the daisies, but his art teacher told him that he had to
> follow the rules and draw right side up. But Ted's English teacher, Mr. Smith, told Ted
> that he could be a writer. He told Ted to try different kinds of writing and to keep on
> sending his writing to the school paper."

> "Ted's art teacher told him that he had to follow the rules. But his English teacher told
> Ted that he could be a writer. He encouraged Ted to write for the school newspaper, to
> experiment with words, and to try different kinds of writing."

> "Ted was discouraged in his art class because he was forced to follow the rules. But he
> liked his English teacher, Red Smith. Red recited funny poems with him and helped

him to write poetry. He also told Ted that all writers get rejected, and that Ted should keep trying."

If the student has difficulty with this summary, ask the following three questions to help focus her thoughts:

Why was Ted discouraged by his art class?

What did Mr. Smith tell Ted that he could be?

What were two things that Mr. Smith encouraged Ted to do?

Then have the student repeat her answers in order; this will form her brief summary. Write down the student's narration on the lines below, but do not allow her to watch.

_____

_____

_____

_____

Then choose two or three sentences (16–20 words) to dictate back to the student. Repeat the sentences three times and ask the student to repeat them back to you before she writes on Student Page 173.

Give all necessary help in spelling and punctuation.

DAY FOUR: Dictation Exercise   *Student Page 174*

Focus: Prepositions, objects of prepositions, prepositional phrases

Pull out Student Page 174. Ask the student to write her name and the date.

Tell the student that today's dictation sentences are from the biography *Dr. Seuss, Young Author and Artist.* They describe how hard it was for Dr. Seuss to write his stories.

Dictate the following sentences to the student three times. Before you read, tell the student that you will read the sentences only three times before asking her to write, and will not repeat them afterwards.

Pause significantly at the periods, but do not tell the student how many periods are in the dictation exercise.

He wrote a few words. He stared into space. He erased the words he had written and tried again.

Now ask the student to repeat the sentences back to you before she writes. If she forgets, tell her to go back to the beginning of the sentences and recite them again to jog her memory. If necessary, you may then prompt the student with single words.

Watch the student as she writes, and correct her at once if she begins to make a mistake.

When she is finished, tell her to circle the word "into" in the second sentence. Tell her that this word is a *preposition*—a word that shows the relationship between two different words. He stared into what? *He* stared *into space.* "Into" shows the relationship between his staring, and space. He stared *into* space.

Tell the student to put a box around the word "space." Ask her if she remembers what this word is called. If she cannot remember, explain to her that this word is the "object of the preposition." The object of the preposition is the word that follows the preposition and answers the question "what?" Stared into what? Into *space.* Ask the student to write the abbreviation "p." over the circled preposition, and "o.p." over the boxed object of the preposition.

Now tell the student to underline the words "into space." Remind her that this is a *prepositional phrase*. A prepositional phrase is made up of a preposition, its object, and any words that modify the object (this prepositional phrase doesn't happen to have any modifying words).

WEEK 24

DAY ONE: Narration Exercise   *Student Pages 175–177*

Focus: *Identifying the central theme in a selection*

Pull out Student Pages 175–176 and 177. Ask the student to write his name and the date on Student Page 177.

Allow the student to read the story on Student Pages 175–176, either silently or aloud.

You will now ask the student to summarize the passage. This selection has a strong central theme which the student should identify. To guide him towards this type of summary, say to the student, "Tell me, in one sentence, what obnoxious habit both Timmy and Wendy had." The student should respond with some variation of, "Timmy and Wendy were both tattletales." (If he says, "They were tattletales," encourage him to use the names of the children instead of the pronoun.)

Once the student has come up with this sentence, say, "Now give me two or three more sentences with specific details in them about *how* both Timmy and Wendy tell tales." The purpose of this exercise is to guide the student into stating the central theme of the passage and supporting that theme with specifics.

The answer should resemble one of the following:

"Timmy and Wendy were both tattletales. Wendy told her teacher whenever anyone whispered, cheated, or wrote notes. Timmy told their mother that Wendy didn't eat her toast or wipe up Spot's water when she spilled it."

"Timmy and Wendy were both tattletales. Wendy told on the other children in her class when they whispered or sucked their paintbrushes. She also told her mother that Timmy hadn't brushed his teeth and that he bought candy with his Sunday School money. Then Timmy told their mother that Wendy ate half the candy and that she spilled water and didn't wipe it up."

"Timmy and Wendy were both tattletales. Wendy was a tattletale at school and at home. She told her teacher that Jimmy sucked on his paintbrush, and she told her mother that Timmy didn't brush his teeth or eat his liver. Then Timmy said that Wendy put her toast in the silverware drawer and ate half of his candy, and Wendy said that Timmy called her 'dog eyes.'"

If the student has difficulty with these details, ask these three questions:

What did Wendy tattle about at school?

What did Wendy tattle about at home?

What did Timmy tell their mother about Wendy?

The answers to these questions will make up the rest of the student's summary.
Write the narration down on Student Page 177 as the student watches.

Day Two: Dictation Exercise   *Student Page 178*

Focus: *Adverbs that tell to what extent*

Pull out Student Page 178. Ask the student to write his name and the date.

Tell the student that today's dictation sentence is from the story "The Tattletale Cure" in *Mrs. Piggle-Wiggle's Magic.* Mrs. Hamilton becomes so desperate that she calls Mrs. Piggle-Wiggle and asks her how to stop Timmy and Wendy from tattling. Mrs. Piggle-Wiggle has just the thing—special tattletale pills.

Now dictate the following sentences to the student three times. Before you read, tell the student that you will read the sentences only three times before asking him to write, and will not repeat them afterwards.

Indicate the end of the first sentence by allowing your voice to drop, but do not tell the student ahead of time that the selection contains two sentences.

I do think we should start the tattletale cure right away. The pills look and taste just like licorice drops but the effect is quite remarkable.

Now ask the student to repeat the sentences back to you before he writes. If he forgets, tell him to go back to the beginning of the sentences and recite them again to jog his memory. If necessary, you may then prompt the student with single words.

Watch the student as he writes, and correct him at once if he begins to make a mistake.

When he is finished, tell him to circle the word "quite" in the second sentence. Tell him that this is an adverb. Remind him that an adverb is a word that modifies a verb, an adjective, or another adverb. It answers the questions "how, when, where, how often, to what extent?"

Ask the student what word "quite" modifies. If he is not sure, say, "The effect is quite what?" The answer is "remarkable."

Now ask the student to draw a line from the work "remarkable" back to the noun it describes. What is quite remarkable? The effect is quite remarkable. The line should point back to "effect."

Since "effect" is a noun, "remarkable" is an adjective. The adverb "quite" modifies an adjective.

Finally, ask the student which question this adverb answers: how, when, where, how often, to what extent? The answer is "to what extent." To what extent is the effect remarkable? It is *quite* remarkable.

DAY THREE: Narration and Dictation *Student Pages 179–181*

Focus: *Identifying the central narrative thread in a passage and writing original sentences from dictation*

Pull out Student Pages 179–180 and 181. Ask the student to write his name and the date on Student Page 181.

Today's exercise will combine narration and dictation. Allow the student to read the story on Student Pages 179–180, either silently or aloud.

You will now ask the student to summarize the passage. This selection lends itself to a narrative, story-like retelling. To guide the student towards this type of summary, ask him, "In three or four sentences, how did the magic pills begin to cure Wendy and Timmy?" His answer should resemble one of the following:

> "First, Wendy began to tell on Timmy, but a big puff of black smoke with little black tails on the bottom came out of her mouth instead. Then Timmy started to tattle, but a big puff of smoke with a tattletail on it came out of his mouth too. The next time they started to tell on each other, the same thing happened. So they stopped arguing and went out to shovel snow."

> "Whenever Wendy and Timmy started to tell on each other, big black puffs of smoke came out of their mouths. Each puff had a tail hanging on the bottom of it for each tattletale. Wendy and Timmy didn't want the puffs to come out of their mouths at school."

"Wendy started to tell four tales about Timmy, and black smoke with four tails hanging from it came out of her mouth. Then Timmy started to tell a tale about Wendy, and black smoke with one tail came out of his mouth. Wendy decided that she would not want that to happen at school."

If the student has difficulty with this summary, ask the following three questions to help focus his thoughts:

What happened when Wendy started to tell on Timmy?

What happened when Timmy started to tell on Wendy?

How did the children feel about this?

Then have the student repeat his answers in order; this will form his brief summary. Write down the student's narration on the lines below, but do not allow him to watch.

_____

_____

_____

_____

Then choose two or three sentences (16–20 words) to dictate back to the student. Repeat the sentences three times and ask the student to repeat them back to you before he writes on Student Page 181.

Give all necessary help in spelling and punctuation.

DAY FOUR: Dictation Exercise   *Student Page 182*

Focus: *Adverbs that tell to what extent*

Pull out Student Page 182. Ask the student to write his name and the date.

Tell the student that today's dictation sentences are also from "The Tattletale Cure."

Dictate the following sentences to the student three times. Before you read, tell the student that you will read the sentences only three times before asking him to write, and will not repeat them afterwards.

During dinner the children were surprisingly quiet and surprisingly pleasant. In fact, there wasn't a cross word spoken the entire evening.

Now ask the student to repeat the sentences back to you before he writes. If he forgets, tell him to go back to the beginning of the sentences and recite them again to jog his memory. If necessary, you may then prompt the student with single words.

Watch the student as he writes, and correct him at once if he begins to make a mistake.

When he is finished, tell him to circle both occurrences of the word "surprisingly" in the first sentence. Tell him that these are adverbs that answer the question "to what extent?" Both adverbs modify adjectives. Ask the student to underline the adjectives that each adverb modifies. (The first modifies "quiet" and the second modifies "pleasant.").

Now ask the student to draw a line from "quiet" back to the noun that "quiet" modifies. Ask him to do the same with the adjective "pleasant." Both lines should point back to "children."

WEEK 25

DAY ONE: Narration Exercise   *Student Pages 183–185*

Focus: *Identifying the central details in a passage*

Pull out Student Pages 183–184 and 185. Ask the student to write her name and the date on Student Page 185.

Allow the student to read the story on Student Pages 183–184, either silently or aloud.

You will now ask the student to summarize the passage. A detail-oriented summary is more appropriate to this descriptive passage than a summary telling what happens. Say to the student, "In three sentences, explain where at least three different names for money came from." The student can add details, but should not go over three sentences. Her answer should resemble one of the following:

> "The word 'money' comes from Moneta, one of the names of the Roman goddess Juno. The word 'coin' comes from the Latin word for 'wedge,' because the first coins were shaped like pieces of pie. The word 'cash' comes from the Chinese, but they borrowed it from the Portuguese."

> "The words 'money' and 'coin' both come from Latin, but the word 'dollar' comes from German. We call a dollar a 'buck' because North American Indians used to trade with buckskins. Germans call coins 'pinke-pinke' because the money jingles in your pocket."

> "The name for 'dollar' came from the German word 'thaler.' Spanish explorers brought this word to the Americas. 'Money' comes from a nickname of the goddess Juno, because the Romans made their money right next to Juno's temple."

If the student has trouble choosing important details, ask these three questions:

What two money words come from Latin, and why?

Where does the word "dollar" come from?

Can you tell me two nicknames, or slang terms, for money?

The answers to these questions will make up the student's summary.

Write the narration down on Student Page 185 as the student watches. (Note: put quotation marks around the money words that the student is describing, as shown above.)

DAY TWO: Dictation Exercise   *Student Page 186*

Focus: *Poetic form, titles of respect (abbreviations)*

Pull out Student Page 186. Ask the student to write her name and the date.

Tell the student that today's dictation sentence is from another poem by Walter de la Mare, called "Miss T." Read the student the poem:

> It's a very odd thing—
> As odd as can be—
> That whatever Miss T. eats
> Turns into Miss T.;
> Porridge and apples,
> Mince, muffins and mutton,
> Jam, junket, jumbles—
> Not a rap, not a button
> It matters; the moment
> They're out of her plate,
> Though shared by Miss Butcher
> And sour Mr. Bate;
> Tiny and cheerful,
> And neat as can be,
> Whatever Miss T. eats
> Turns into Miss T.

Now tell the student that you will dictate the final six lines of the poem three times. The student should listen carefully to discover where each line ends and the next begins. Pause significantly at the end of each line.

> Though shared by Miss Butcher
> And sour Mr. Bate;
> Tiny and cheerful,
> And neat as can be,
> Whatever Miss T. eats
> Turns into Miss T.

Now ask the student to repeat the lines back to you before she writes. If she forgets, tell her to go back to the beginning of the lines and recite them again to jog her memory. If necessary, you may then repeat the lines additional times, until the student can remember all six.

Tell the student to stop writing at the end of each line and look up at you, so that you can tell her the proper punctuation for at each line's end.

Watch the student write and correct her at once if she begins to make a mistake. You may need to remind her that each poetic line begins right beneath the one above it. You may also need to prompt her to use capital letters for "Butcher" and "Bate," since these are proper names.

When she is finished, ask her to underline the titles of respect in the poem: "Miss" and "Mr." Beneath her dictation exercise, write out the word "Mister." Remind her that "Mr." is an abbreviation for "Mister," but that "Miss" is not abbreviated.

DAY THREE: Narration and Dictation   *Student Pages 187–188*

Focus: *Identifying the central details in a passage and writing original sentences from dictation*

Pull out Student Pages 187 and 188. Ask the student to write her name and the date on Student Page 188.

Today's exercise will combine narration and dictation. Allow the student to read the story on Student Page 187, either silently or aloud.

You will now ask the student to summarize the passage. A detail-oriented summary is more appropriate to this descriptive passage than a summary telling what happens. Say to the student, "Tell me about three different kinds of coins described in this passage. Try to tell me when or where each coin was made. Try to use no more than four sentences." Her answer should resemble one of the following:

> "John Hull made coins with a date on one side and a tree on the other for the Massachusetts Bay colony. In the 1700s [or in the eighteenth century], many different colonies made copper coins. In 1878, James Jarvis made a coin called the Fugio cent. It was the first official United States coin."

> "It was easy for thieves to shave pieces off the edges of early coins like the New England pine tree coins. Most of the different colonies made copper coins—more than three hundred kinds. Finally James Jarvis made the first official United States coin. It said 'Time flies' on one side and 'Mind your business' on the other."

> "One of the first coins was the New England pine tree coin. Other colonies made their own coins. This got confusing, so Congress chose James Jarvis to make an official coin. It was called the Fugio cent."

If the student has trouble choosing important details, ask these three questions:

What kind of coin did John Hull make in Massachusetts?

What sort of coin did most of the colonies make for themselves?

What was the first official United States coin like?

The answers to these questions will make up the student's summary.
Write down the student's narration on the lines below, but do not allow her to watch.

———————————————————————————————————————

———————————————————————————————————————

———————————————————————————————————————

———————————————————————————————————————

Then choose two or three sentences (16–20 words) to dictate back to the student. Repeat the sentences three times and ask the student to repeat them back to you before she writes on Student Page 188.

Give all necessary help in spelling and punctuation.

DAY FOUR: Dictation Exercise   *Student Page 189*

Focus: *Titles of respect (abbreviations)*

Pull out Student Page 189. Ask the student to write her name and the date.

Tell the student that today's dictation sentences are a silly poem which was made up four hundred years ago. Here is the poem:

> I do not love thee, Dr. Fell,
> The reason why I cannot tell;
> But this I know, and know full well,
> I do not love thee, Dr. Fell.

Tell her that there is a story behind this poem. Dr. John Fell was the Bishop of Oxford over three hundred years ago. It was part of his job to expel students (force them to leave university) if they didn't study or follow the rules.

One student who had a hard time studying and following the rules was a young man named Tom Brown. Dr. Fell was ready to expel Tom Brown, but he gave Tom one chance to stay in school. He told Tom that he could remain at Oxford if he could translate, on the spot, a Latin poem written by the Latin poet Martial.

Martial's poem is written to one of his ancient enemies, a man named Sabidius. The poem goes like this: "Non amo te, Sabidi, nec possum dicere - quare; Hoc tantum possum dicere, non amo te." (It's OK to simply pronounce all of the Latin words as though they are English words.)

In English, the poem means something like, "I don't like you, Sabidius, and I can't say why. But I can say this: I don't like you."

Tom Brown was a quick thinker. He immediately answered,

> I do not love thee, Dr. Fell,
> The reason why I cannot tell;
> But this I know, and know full well,
> I do not love thee, Dr. Fell.

Dr. Fell was amused, and he let Tom Brown stay in school.

After explaining the poem, read it three more times to the student, pausing significantly at the commas within the lines. You may need to repeat it additional times. When the student can repeat it back to you, tell her to begin to write. She should look up at the end of every line so that you can tell her the correct punctuation.

Watch the student write and correct her at once if she begins to make a mistake. You may need to remind her that each poetic line begins right beneath the one above it.

When she is finished, ask her to underline the title of respect in the poem: "Dr." Beneath her dictation exercise, write out the word "Doctor." Remind her that "Dr." is an abbreviation for "Doctor."

WEEK 26

Day One: Narration Exercise   *Student Pages 190–192*

Focus: *Identifying the central narrative thread in a passage*

Pull out Student Pages 190–191 and 192. Ask the student to write his name and the date on Student Page 192.

Allow the student to read the story on Student Pages 190–191, either silently or aloud.

You will now ask the student to summarize the passage. This selection lends itself to a narrative, story-like retelling. To guide the student towards this type of summary, say to him, "In three or four sentences, tell me what happened when Babe met Fly and her puppies." His answer should resemble one of the following:

> "Fly and her puppies looked over into the loose box and saw Babe. The puppies said that Babe was stupid, but Fly was kind to the little pig. She asked him his name and said that she would take care of him from now on."

"Farmer Hogget put his new piglet in a loose box. The puppies and Fly looked down at the piglet and Fly asked the piglet his name. He said that his name was Babe, and he missed his mother. Fly said that she would look after him."

"When Fly and her puppies saw Babe in the barn, the puppies started to make fun of him. But Fly felt sorry for the piglet. She sent her puppies to play in the yard, and then jumped down to take care of Babe. She told him that she would look after him."

If the student has difficulty with this summary, ask the following four questions to help focus his thoughts:

Where was the piglet when Fly and her puppies first saw him?

How did the puppies react to the piglet?

How did Fly feel when she saw that Babe was unhappy?

What did she promise?

The answers to these questions will make up the student's summary.
Write the narration down on Student Page 192 as the student watches.

DAY TWO: Dictation Exercise
Student Page 193

Focus: *Abbreviations for months and days of the week*

Pull out Student Page 193. Ask the student to write his name and the date.

Tell the student that today's dictation sentences give more information about Dick King-Smith, the author of *Babe: The Gallant Pig* and many other books about animals.

Dictate the following sentences to the student three times. Before you read, tell the student that he should abbreviate the month of March. You will read "March," but he should write the abbreviation instead. Also tell him that there is a hyphen between "King" and "Smith."

When you read, indicate the commas in the second and third sentence by pausing. Indicate the end of each sentence by pausing for a longer time, and by allowing your voice to fall slightly. Do not tell the student ahead of time that there will be three separate sentences.

Now tell the student that you will read the sentences four times before asking him to write, and will not repeat them afterwards. (Since there are three sentences, an extra repetition is appropriate.)

> Dick King-Smith was born Mar. 27, 1922. For twenty years, he worked as a farmer in England. When he began to write for children, he often told stories about farm animals.

Now ask the student to repeat the sentences back to you before he writes. If he forgets, tell him to go back to the beginning of the sentences and recite them again to jog his memory. If necessary, you may then prompt the student with single words.

Watch the student as he writes, and correct him at once if he begins to make a mistake.

DAY THREE: Narration and Dictation   *Student Pages 194–196*

Focus: *Identifying the central details in a passage and writing original sentences from dictation*

Pull out Student Pages 194–195 and 196. Ask the student to write his name and the date on Student Page 196.

Today's exercise will combine narration and dictation. Allow the student to read the story on Student Pages 194–195, either silently or aloud.

You will now ask the student to summarize the passage. A detail-oriented summary is more appropriate to this descriptive passage than a summary telling what happens. Say to the student, "Describe what the sheep was like, from Babe's point of view, in three sentences." His answer should resemble one of the following:

> "The sheep was stamping her foot and complaining about wolves. She told Babe she was a ewe, and Babe thought she was stupid. He also thought that her name was Ma."

> "The sheep thought that Babe was a wolf until she saw him. She told him that her name was Ma, and that she had foot rot and a cough. Then she burped and started to chew her cud."

> "At first, the sheep thought that Babe was a wolf. She told him that she was a ewe, and that her name was Ma. She had a cough and foot rot, and she was chewing her cud."

If the student has trouble choosing important details, ask these three questions:

What did the sheep think of Babe, at first?

What two names did Babe learn for the sheep?

What was wrong with the sheep?

Then have the student repeat his answers in order; this will form his brief summary. Write down the student's narration on the lines below, but do not allow him to watch.

_____

_____

_____

_____

Then choose two or three sentences (16–20 words) to dictate back to the student. Repeat the sentences three times and ask the student to repeat them back to you before he writes on Student Page 196.

Give all necessary help in spelling and punctuation.

DAY FOUR: Dictation Exercise   *Student Page 197*

Focus: *Abbreviations for months and days of the week*

Pull out Student Page 197. Ask the student to write his name and the date.

Dictate the following sentences to the student three times. Before you read, tell the student that he should use the abbreviations for "Saturday" and "October," even though you will read the entire words as you dictate. Tell the student that "Cinderella May" is two separate words making up the dog's full name, so both should be capitalized. Also tell him that the sentences contain the words "68 inches"; he should write 68 inches with the *numeral* "68" and the *word* "inches."

When you read the sentences, pause significantly at each comma. Make a longer pause at the period and indicate the end of the first sentence by allowing your voice to fall. Do not tell the student how many commas or sentences are in the selection.

Now tell the student that you will read the sentences only four times before asking him to write, and will not repeat them afterwards. (Since the student will need to keep several different things in mind as he listens, an extra repetition is appropriate.)

> On Sat., Oct. 7, 2006, a dog named Cinderella May jumped higher than any other dog in the world. Cinderella May cleared a wooden rail set at 68 inches, which is over five feet high.

Now ask the student to repeat the sentences back to you before he writes. If he forgets, tell him to go back to the beginning of the sentences and recite them again to jog his memory. If necessary, you may then prompt the student with single words.

Watch the student as he writes, and correct him at once if he begins to make a mistake.

WEEK 27

DAY ONE: Narration Exercise   *Student Pages 198–199*

Focus: *Identifying the central theme in a selection*

Pull out Student Pages 198 and 199. Ask the student to write her name and the date on Student Page 199.

Allow the student to read the passage on Student Page 198, either silently or aloud.

You will now ask the student to summarize the passage. This selection has a strong central theme which the student should identify. To guide her towards this type of summary, say to her, "Tell me in one sentence what border collies are good at." The student should respond, "Border collies are good at driving animals," OR "Border collies are good at gathering animals together and herding them towards a farmer," OR "Border collies are good at obeying commands and working on farms."

Once the student has come up with this sentence, say, "Now give me two or three more sentences with specific details in them about what border collies do." The purpose of this exercise is to guide the student into stating the central theme of the passage and supporting that theme with specifics.

The answer should resemble one of the following:

"Border collies are good at driving animals. They gather sheep together by glaring at them, and they have an instinct that helps them drive animals towards farmers. They can work out of sight of the farmer, and they can understand twenty different commands."

"Border collies are good at gathering animals together and herding them towards a farmer. They crouch down and glare at sheep to make them obey. They can also be taught to drive a herd of animals away from a farmer."

"Border collies are good at obeying commands and working on farms. They naturally drive animals towards a farmer, and they can also learn to drive animals away. They can understand nearly twenty different commands. They can even learn to solve problems by themselves when the farmer is not there."

If the student has difficulty with this summary, ask the following three questions to help focus his thoughts.

What do border collies naturally do?

What can border collies learn to do, with some practice?

How many commands can a border collie understand?

The answers to these questions will make up the student's summary.

Write the narration down on Student Page 199 as the student watches.

DAY TWO: Dictation Exercse

Focus: *Commas in a series*

Pull out Student Page 200. Ask the student to write her name and the date.

Tell the student that today's dictation sentences are from the book *Border Collies* by Michael DeVine. Before you give the dictation sentences, you will read a paragraph from the book to give the student some background.

Here is what the book says about border collies and the way they herd sheep: "Modern border collies are typified by a working style that involves a quiet, head-down style that is remarkably similar to a wolf creeping up on its prey. Instead of barking and nipping excessively, border collies use 'eye.' A border collie with strong 'eye' will stare at bunched stock until they decide there are better places to be. Some people are even a little put off by the breed's tendency to stare at them."

The book then describes several famous border collies who won prizes for herding sheep and cattle, and who all won the highest prize for border collies: the International Supreme Championship.

Now dictate the following sentences to the student three times. Before you read, tell the student that you will read the sentences only three times before asking her to write, and will not repeat them afterwards.

Pause significantly at each comma. Indicate the end of the first sentence by allowing your voice to fall and pausing for a slightly longer time.

> These dogs ranged greatly in size, color, and hair coat. But they shared extreme intelligence, instinctive stock sense, and a quiet working style.

Now ask the student to repeat the sentences back to you before she writes. If she forgets, tell her to go back to the beginning of the sentences and recite them again to jog her memory. If necessary, you may then prompt the student with single words.

Watch the student as she writes, and correct her at once if she begins to make a mistake. Be sure to remind her to insert the commas.

When the student is finished writing, ask her to underline "size," "color," and "hair coat" in the first sentence. Tell her that this is a list, or series, of items. The items are the three ways in which the dogs were different. When there are more than two items in a series, the items should be separated by commas.

Now ask her to underline the words "intelligence," "stock sense," and "working style" in the second sentence. (You may need to explain that "stock sense" is an instinct that allows the dog to guess what an animal is about to do.) Tell her that this is also a list, or series. In this list, the items are the ways in which the dogs were alike. Because there are three items, they are separated by commas.

DAY THREE: Narration and Dictation   *Student Pages 201–202*

Focus: *Summarizing a series of ordered facts and writing original sentences from dictation*

Pull out Student Pages 201 and 202. Ask the student to write her name and the date on Student Page 202.

Today's exercise will combine narration and dictation. Allow the student to read the passage on Student Page 201, either silently or aloud.

You will now ask the student to summarize the passage. This passage lists a series of ordered steps. The student doesn't need to remember all six phases of the sheepdog trial in order! Instead, ask her to look at the six phases listed on Student Page 202. While looking at these phases, the student should summarize the trial in four or five sentences, keeping the phases in their correct order. Tell her that she does not need to use the name of the phases; instead she should describe what the dog is doing, in order, and add a few details about what the sheep and the handler are doing as well.

She should attempt to do this without looking back at the passage, but if necessary you may allow her to glance at Student Page 201. This is a difficult exercise, so give whatever help is necessary.

Her answer should resemble one of the following:

"The dog leaves the post and contacts the sheep so he can bring them back to the handler. He is supposed to drive them in a straight line, but the sheep like to wander off. Then the dog herds the sheep through gates. Next, he cuts two sheep with special collars off from the flock. Then he herds all the sheep into a pen."

"The dog leaves the post, contacts the sheep, and brings them back to the handler. Then he herds the sheep through special gates, without upsetting them. He cuts off two special sheep from the rest, and then herds all the sheep into a pen. The handler can try to keep the sheep from wandering off, but he can't let go of the gate."

"First, the dog leaves the post. He circles around to the right or left of the sheep to make contact with them. He herds them back to the handler in a straight line. Then the dog herds them through gates, cuts two sheep off from the rest, and then drives them into the pen. The sheep do not like to go in straight lines, and they keep trying to wander off and turn the wrong way."

Write down the student's narration on the lines below, but do not allow her to watch.

_____

_____

_____

_____

Then choose two or three sentences (16–20 words) to dictate back to the student. Repeat the sentences three times and ask the student to repeat them back to you before she writes on Student Page 202.

Give all necessary help in spelling and punctuation.

DAY FOUR: Dictation Exercise   *Student Page 203*

Focus: *Commas in a series*

Pull out Student Page 203. Ask the student to write her name and the date.

Tell the student that today's dictation sentences are based on information found in *The Shetland Sheepdog,* by Charlotte Wilcox.

Dictate the following sentences to the student three times. Before you read, tell the student that you will read the sentences only three times before asking her to write, and will not repeat them afterwards.

Be sure to pause significantly at each comma. Indicate the end of the first sentence by allowing your voice to fall and pausing for a longer time. Indicate the exclamation point at the end of the second sentence by using an excited voice. After you read the sentences the first time, ask the student if she noticed your excited voice. Ask her what punctuation mark shows excitement.

Then complete the dictation by reading the sentences twice more in the same way.

> Sheepdogs are loyal, intelligent, and good with children. Some sheepdogs actually herd children together into groups to keep them safe as they play!

Now ask the student to repeat the sentences back to you before she writes. If she forgets, tell her to go back to the beginning of the sentences and recite them again to jog her memory. If necessary, you may then prompt the student with single words.

Watch the student as she writes, and correct her at once if she begins to make a mistake. Be sure to remind her to insert the commas and exclamation point.

When the student is finished writing, ask her to underline "loyal," "intelligent," and "good with children" in the first sentence. Tell her that this is a list, or series, of items. The items are the three qualities of sheepdogs. When there are more than two items in a series, the items should be separated by commas.

WEEK 28

DAY ONE: Narration Exercise   *Student Pages 204–206*

Focus: *Identifying the central narrative thread in a passage*

Pull out Student Pages 204–205 and 206. Ask the student to write his name and the date on Student Page 206.

Allow the student to read the story on Student Pages 204–205, either silently or aloud.

You will now ask the student to summarize the passage. This selection lends itself to a narrative, story-like retelling. To guide the student towards this type of summary, ask him, "In three sentences, what happened when Marilla and Anne met each other?" His answer should resemble one of the following:

> "Marilla was surprised to see that Matthew had brought home a girl. The little girl realized that she wasn't wanted, and burst into tears. Marilla told her not to cry, and asked her what her name was."

> "When Matthew and Anne came into the house, Marilla asked where the boy was. Anne began to cry because no one wanted her, and Marilla asked what her name was. Anne asked Marilla to call her Cordelia, but Marilla said that Anne was a good plain name."

> "Matthew told Marilla that he had to bring Anne home even though she was a girl. Anne realized that she wasn't supposed to be there, and began to cry. But Marilla told her that she could stay while they found out what the mistake was."

If the student has difficulty with this summary, ask the following three questions to help focus his thoughts:

What was Marilla's reaction when she saw Anne?

What did Anne do when she realized that there had been a mistake?

When Anne began to cry, how did Marilla respond?

The answers to these questions will make up the student's summary.
Write the narration down on Student Page 206 as the student watches.

DAY TWO: Dictation Exercise   *Student Page 207*

Focus: *Ending exclamation points*

Pull out Student Page 207. Ask the student to write his name and the date.

Tell the student that today's dictation sentence is from Chapter One of *Anne of Green Gables,* "Mrs. Rachel Lynde Is Surprised." Mrs. Rachel Lynde, the Cuthberts' nosy neighbor, has just found out that Marilla and Matthew have sent to the orphanage for a boy.

Dictate the following sentences to the student three times. Before you read, tell the student that you will read the sentences only three times before asking him to write, and will not repeat them afterwards.

Before you read, tell the student that there are two exclamation points in the selection; indicate them with your voice while you read. You may also want to point out that the last two sentences are fragments; this is an appropriate use of a fragment in writing.

> Mrs. Rachel felt that she had received a severe mental jolt. She thought in exclamation points. A boy! Marilla and Matthew Cuthbert of all people adopting a boy!

Now ask the student to repeat the sentences back to you before he writes. If he forgets, tell him to go back to the beginning of the sentences and recite them again to jog his memory. If necessary, you may then prompt the student with single words.

Watch the student as he writes, and correct him at once if he begins to make a mistake. You may need to help him spell "Marilla," "Matthew," and "Cuthbert." If necessary, remind him that "Mrs." is an abbreviation for a married woman.

DAY THREE: Narration and Original Sentence Exercise　　　*Student Pages 208–210*

Focus: *Identifying the central details in a passage and writing original sentences*

Pull out Student Pages 208–209 and 210. Ask the student to write his name and the date on Student Page 210.

Today's exercise will require the student to write an original sentence. Allow the student to read the story on Student Pages 208–209, either silently or aloud. Before he reads, tell him that you will be asking him to describe Prince Edward Island in his summary (although he certainly does not need to remember every detail!).

You will now ask the student to summarize the passage. To guide him towards a detail-oriented summary, say, "Describe Prince Edward Island in two or three sentences. Be sure to use specific names for trees, plants, and animals." His answer should resemble one of the following:

> "Prince Edward Island has pines, willows, maples, and many other trees. The island also has strawberries, raspberries, grain, and peas. There are many pigeons in the forests."

> "The forests on Prince Edward Island are many different colors of green because there are so many different trees—like pines, elms, and beeches. The island is pleasant and warm, and there are gooseberries, strawberries, peas, and raspberries growing there."

"Jacques Cartier sailed to the north end of Prince Edward Island and described it. He said that there were many different trees, such as pines and maples, and wild berries, like strawberries and raspberries."

If the student has trouble choosing important details, ask these three questions:

Name three trees that were in the forests.

Name three foods that grew in the meadows and forests.

Can you remember one more thing about the island?

(If the student draws a blank, ask him what the weather was like, whether there were any birds, or which explorer landed on it.)

Write down the student's narration on the lines below, but do not allow him to watch.

_____

_____

_____

_____

Now ask him whether he can repeat the first sentence of the narration to himself. If not, read him the first sentence of the narration only. Tell him to listen carefully, since you will only read it once. Encourage him to repeat it to himself until he can remember it, and then to say it out loud to himself as he writes it down on Student Page 210.

Give all necessary help in spelling and punctuation.

DAY FOUR: Dictation Exercise   *Student Page 211*

Focus: *Ending question marks*

Pull out Student Page 211. Ask the student to write his name and the date.

Tell the student that today's dictation sentences are also from *Anne of Green Gables.*

Explain that although Prince Edward Island is cold in the winter, Jacques Cartier landed on the island in midsummer. Anne also arrived at the Cuthbert farm in summer. This selection from Chapter Four, "Morning at Green Gables," describes when she first looked out of her window.

Dictate the following sentences to the student three times. Before you read, tell the student that you will read the sentences only three times before asking her to write, and will not repeat them afterwards.

Be sure to indicate the period by pausing. Tell the student before you read that there are two question marks in the selection, and use a questioning voice for the two questions at the end.

> Anne dropped on her knees and gazed out into the June morning, her eyes glistening with delight. Oh, wasn't it beautiful? Wasn't it a lovely place?

Now ask the student to repeat the sentences back to you before he writes. If he forgets, tell him to go back to the beginning of the sentences and recite them again to jog his memory. If necessary, you may then prompt the student with single words.

Watch the student as he writes on Student Page 211, and correct him at once if he begins to make a mistake. You may need to remind him that "wasn't" is a contraction and has an apostrophe between the last two letters.

WEEK 29

DAY ONE: Narration Exercise   *Student Pages 212–214*

Focus: *Identifying the central details in a passage*

Pull out Student Pages 212–213 and 214. Ask the student to write her name and the date on Student Page 214.

Allow the student to read the story on Student Pages 212–213, either silently or aloud.

You will now ask the student to summarize the passage. A detail-oriented summary is more appropriate to this descriptive passage than a summary telling what happens. Use a "directed narration starter": say to the student, "Describe the Britons in three sentences." Her answer should resemble one of the following:

> "The Britons were tall men with red hair and plaid clothes. They lived in houses that were piles of stones. The men hunted wild boars, the women raised corn, and they had fortresses in the woods built out of tree trunks."

> "Julius Caesar tried to conquer the Britons. He found out that they lived in houses of stone, with strong places made out of tree trunks. He couldn't conquer these, but he made the Britons give him pearls and call the Romans their masters."

> "The Britons had long red streaming hair and fought the Romans with darts. They hunted boars, wolves, and stags, grew corn for bread, and spun wool into clothes. Caesar forced them to pay tribute."

If the student has trouble choosing important details, ask these three questions:

What were the men of the Britons like?

What did the men and women do for food?

What did Caesar force the Britons to do?

The answers to these questions will make up the student's summary.
Write the narration down on Student Page 214 as the student watches.

DAY TWO: Dictation Exercise *Student Page 215*

Focus: *Commas in direct address*

Pull out Student Page 215. Ask the student to write her name and the date.

Tell the student that today's dictation sentences are from *Julius Caesar* by William Shakespeare. In Shakespeare's famous play about Caesar, the Roman soldier Mark Antony gives a funeral oration, or speech, after Caesar's death. The dictation sentences are the first two lines of that oration. Tell the student that the sentences are poetry: each sentence begins a new line.

Now dictate the following sentence to the student three times. Before you read, tell the student that you will read the sentences only three times before asking her to write, and will not repeat them afterwards.

Be sure to pause at each comma; pause for a longer time at the end of the first line, and indicate the end of the sentence by allowing your voice to drop.

> Friends, Romans, countrymen, lend me your ears.
> I come to bury Caesar, not to praise him.

Now ask the student to repeat the sentences back to you before she writes. If she forgets, tell her to go back to the beginning of the sentences and recite them again to jog her memory. If necessary, you may then prompt the student with single words.

You may need to remind her that the second line of poetry begins immediately beneath the first; you will probably also need to help her spell "Caesar." If necessary, remind her that "Caesar" and "Romans" are both proper names and should be capitalized.

Watch the student as she writes, and correct her at once if she begins to make a mistake. When she is finished writing, ask her to read the words "Friends, Romans, countrymen" out loud. Tell her that all three of these are words of direct address: they are words that *name* the people to whom the speaker is talking.

Ask the student to circle the commas after "Friends," "Romans," and "countrymen." Tell her that words of direct address should be followed by commas.

DAY THREE: Narration and Original Sentence Exercise   *Student Pages 216–218*

Focus: *Identifying the central theme in a selection and writing original sentences*

Pull out Student Pages 216–217 and 218. Ask the student to write her name and the date on Student Page 218.

Today's exercise will require the student to write an original sentence. Allow the student to read the story on Student Pages 216–217, either silently or aloud.

You will now ask the student to summarize the passage. This selection has a central theme which the student should identify. To guide the student towards this type of summary, say to her, "Tell me in one sentence what happened to the Britons." The student should respond, "The Britons were driven into Wales," OR "The Britons were driven into the north and west of Britain," OR, "The Angles took Britain away from the Britons."

Once the student has come up with this sentence, say, "Now give me three more sentences with specific details in them about how this happened to the Britons. Be sure to mention the Romans and the Angles." The purpose of this exercise is to guide the student into stating the central theme of the passage and supporting that theme with specifics.

The answer should resemble one of the following:

"The Britons were driven into Wales. First, the Romans lived in Britain for four hundred years. Then the Angles came across the North Sea and took Britain. Now Britain is called England."

"The Britons were driven into the north and west of Britain. The Romans had taken Britain and built roads and towns for themselves. But then tall, blue-eyed men called Angles came over the ocean and fought against the Romans. They took Britain for themselves."

"The Angles took Britain away from the Britons. First, the Romans lived in England. Then the Angles invaded and fought against the Romans and the Britons. King Arthur fought against the Angles, but he could not drive them away."

If the student has difficulty with this summary, ask the following three questions to help focus her thoughts:

How long did the Romans live in Britain?

Who arrived in Britain next?

What did these invaders do to the British?

Then have the student repeat her answers in order; this will form her brief summary. Write down the student's narration on the lines below, but do not allow her to watch.

_____

_____

_____

_____

Now ask her whether she can repeat the first sentence of the narration to herself. If not, read her the first sentence of the narration only. Tell her to listen carefully, since you will only read it once. Encourage her to repeat it to herself until she can remember it, and then to say it out loud to herself as he writes it down on Student Page 218.

Give all necessary help in spelling and punctuation.

DAY FOUR: Dictation Exercise   *Student Page 219*

Focus: Commas in direct address

Pull out Student Page 219. Ask the student to write her name and the date.

Tell the student that today's dictation sentences are from the story of King Arthur. These are the words that Arthur spoke as he lay dying to his friend, a knight named Bedivere.

Dictate the following sentences to the student three times. Before you read, tell the student that you will read the sentences only three times before asking her to write, and will not repeat them afterwards.

Remind the student that Arthur's words should have quotation marks around them. Pause at each comma; indicate the end of the first sentence by pausing for a slightly longer time and allowing your voice to fall. Be sure to use a slightly different voice for Arthur's exact words.

Arthur said, "Take the sword, good knight, and throw it into the water. Then come back and tell me what you see."

Now ask the student to repeat the sentences back to you before she writes. If she forgets, tell her to go back to the beginning of the sentences and recite them again to jog her memory. If necessary, you may then prompt the student with single words.

Watch the student as she writes, and correct her at once if she begins to make a mistake.

When she is finished writing, ask her to read the words "good knight" out loud. Tell her that these words *name* the friend to whom Arthur is speaking. They are words of direct address.

Ask the student to circle the commas before and after "good knight." Tell her that words of direct address should be surrounded by commas when they come in the middle of a sentence.

WEEK 30

DAY ONE: Narration Exercise   *Student Pages 220–222*

Focus: *Identifying the central narrative thread in a passage*

Pull out Student Pages 220–221 and 222. Ask the student to write his name and the date on Student Page 222.

Allow the student to read the story on Student Pages 220–221, either silently or aloud.

You will now ask the student to summarize the passage. This selection lends itself to a narrative, story-like retelling. To guide the student towards this type of summary, say to him, "Tell me in three or four sentences how Alec fell off the ship and was rescued by the Black." His answer should resemble one of the following:

> "The Black knocked Alec off the ship just before it sank. There were no lifeboats, but he grabbed onto the rope attached to the Black's halter. The Black pulled him through the water all night."

> "Alec went to let the Black out, and the horse knocked him off the ship and into the water. When he came up, he saw the ship sinking. The Black swam by him, and Alec grabbed the horse's rope. He tied it to his waist so that the Black could tow him through the water."

> "The Black leaped off the ship and knocked Alec into the water. Alec grabbed the rope attached to the Black's halter and tied it to his waist. The horse pulled him through the water until they got close to land."

If the student has difficulty with this summary, ask the following three questions to help focus his thoughts:

> What made Alec fall off the ship?

> What did he grab to save him?

> What did the Black do for the next few hours?

The answers to these questions will make up the student's summary.
Write the narration down on Student Page 222 as the student watches.

DAY TWO: Dictation Exercise   *Student Page 223*

Focus: *Contractions*

Pull out Student Page 223. Ask the student to write his name and the date.

Tell the student that today's dictation sentences are also from *The Black Stallion*. The Black tows Alec to an island, where the boy and horse are marooned together. In these sentences, Alec tries to figure out how to survive.

Dictate the following sentences to the student three times. Before you read, tell the student that you will read the sentences only three times before asking him to write, and will not repeat them afterwards.

Be sure to indicate the exclamation point with an excited voice. Pause briefly at both commas.

You may need to remind the student that "Black" is capitalized because it is the horse's proper name.

> He wasn't licked yet! He'd find some way to make a shelter, and if that
> wasn't possible, then he'd sleep outside like the Black.

Now ask the student to repeat the sentences back to you before he writes. If he forgets, tell him to go back to the beginning of the sentences and recite them again to jog his memory. If necessary, you may then prompt the student with single words.

Watch the student as he writes, and correct him at once if he begins to make a mistake.

When he is finished, ask him to find and underline the four contractions in the sentences. He should underline both occurrences of "wasn't" and "he'd." Ask him to write the contracted words out in full beneath his dictation. He should write "was not" and "he would." Point out that in the contraction "he'd," four letters drop out!

DAY THREE: Narration and Original Sentence Dictation   *Student Pages 224–226*

Focus: *Identifying the central narrative thread in a passage and writing original sentences*

Pull out Student Pages 224–225 and 226. Ask the student to write his name and the date on Student Page 226.

Today's exercise will require the student to write an original sentence. Allow the student to read the story on Student Pages 224–225, either silently or aloud.

You will now ask the student to summarize the passage. This selection lends itself to a narrative, story-like retelling. To guide the student towards this type of summary, say to him, "In three or four sentences, tell me how Alec finally got onto the Black and rode him. Be sure to also tell me what the ride was like, and how it ended." His answer should resemble one of the following:

> "At first, the Black bucked Alec off. But then Alec got onto his back and the Black broke into a run. The Black galloped through a ravine and jumped over a gully. Finally the Black slowed down and Alec slipped off."

> "Alec tried to climb onto the Black by standing on a sand dune. At first he fell off, but then he managed to stay on. The Black raced down the beach and into a ravine. When the Black slowed down, Alec was able to slip off his back."

"Alec finally managed to get onto the Black by standing on a sand dune. As soon as he got on, the Black raced off. After a wild ride, the Black slowed down and Alec was able to slip off."

If the student has difficulty with this summary, ask the following three questions to help focus his thoughts:

How did Alec get onto the Black?

Where did the Black run?

When he finally slowed down, what did Alec do?

Then have the student repeat his answers in order; this will form his brief summary. Write down the student's narration on the lines below, but do not allow him to watch.

_____

_____

_____

_____

Now ask him whether he can repeat the first sentence of the narration to himself. If not, read him the first sentence of the narration only. Tell him to listen carefully, since you will only read it once. Encourage him to repeat it to himself until he can remember it, and then to say it out loud to himself as he writes it down on Student Page 226.

Give all necessary help in spelling and punctuation.

DAY FOUR: Dictation Exercise   *Student Page 227*

Focus: *Contractions*

Pull out Student Page 227. Ask the student to write his name and the date.

Tell the student that today's dictation sentences are also from *The Black Stallion*.

Dictate the following sentences to the student three times. Before you read, tell the student that you will read the sentences only three times before asking him to write, and will not repeat them afterwards.

Pause briefly at the comma in the last sentence. Be sure to indicate the end of each sentence by allowing your voice to fall and pausing for a longer time.

The next day he mounted the Black again. The horse half-reared but didn't fight him. Alec spoke softly in his ear, and the Black stood still.

Now ask the student to repeat the sentences back to you before he writes. If he forgets, tell him to go back to the beginning of the sentences and recite them again to jog his memory. If necessary, you may then prompt the student with single words.

Watch the student as he writes, and correct him at once if he begins to make a mistake.

When he is finished, ask him to find and underline the contraction. He should underline the word "didn't." Ask him to write the contracted words out in full beneath his dictation. He should write "did not."

WEEK 31

Day One: Narration Exercise   *Student Pages 228–230*

Focus: *Identifying the central narrative thread in a passage*

Pull out Student Pages 228–229 and 230. Ask the student to write her name and the date on Student Page 230.

Allow the student to read the story on Student Pages 228–229, either silently or aloud.

You will now ask the student to summarize the passage. This selection lends itself to a narrative, story-like retelling. To guide the student towards this type of summary, ask her, "In three or four sentences, tell me about the sword in the anvil." Her answer should resemble one of the following:

> "The knights in Britain fought over who would be their leader. Then Merlin came to London and gathered all the knights together on Christmas Day. They all saw a sword in an anvil, sitting on a stone. The knights tried to pull out the sword, because the man who pulled it out would be the king of Britain, but no one could move it."

> "There was no king in Britain, so Merlin came to London and gathered the knights together. They saw a sword in an anvil with gold letters saying, 'Whoever pulls out this sword will be king of Britain.' But none of the knights could pull the sword out."

> "The men of Britain were quarrelling and the Saxons were conquering them. Britain needed a king, so Merlin made a sword in an anvil appear. The anvil was sitting on a stone that said, 'Whoso pulleth out this sword is the king of all Britain.'"

If the student has difficulty with this summary, ask the following three questions to help focus her thoughts:

> What problem did the knights of Britain have?

> What appeared when Merlin came to London?

> How did the knights react?

Write the narration down on Student Page 230 as the student watches.

DAY TWO: Dictation Exercise

Focus: *Contractions*

Pull out Student Page 231. Ask the student to write her name and the date.

Tell the student that contractions make a story sound modern. Read her this excerpt from a retelling of the King Arthur story by Andrew Lang, who lived over a hundred years ago (1844–1912). He writes, "When Arthur reached the house, the door was locked, and though Arthur tried his best to get in, he could not. Then he rode away in great anger and said to himself, 'Kay will not be without a sword this day. I will take that sword in the churchyard and give it to him.'"

Tell the student to repeat after you, "Though Arthur tried his best to get in, he could not." As soon as the student can repeat this sentence, ask him to contract the words "could not." He should answer "couldn't." Then have him repeat the sentence one more time, using the contraction: "Though Arthur tried his best to get in, he couldn't."

Now have the student repeat, "Kay will not be without a sword this day." As soon as he can repeat this sentence, ask him to contract the words "will not." He should answer "won't." Point out that "won't" is an irregular contraction because the *ill* actually changes to an *o*. Then have him repeat the sentence one more time, using the contraction: "Kay won't be without a sword this day."

Finally, have the student repeat, "I will take that sword in the churchyard." As soon as he can repeat this sentence, ask him to contract the words "I will." He should answer "I'll." Then have him repeat the sentence one more time, using the contraction: "I'll take that sword in the churchyard."

Tell the student you will read him the excerpt twice more. The first time you will use contractions, but the second time you will not. Tell him to listen carefully for the difference.

Read: "When Arthur reached the house, the door was locked, and though Arthur tried his best to get in, he couldn't. Then he rode away in great anger and said to himself, 'Kay won't be without a sword this day. I'll take that sword in the churchyard and give it to him.'"

Next, read: "When Arthur reached the house, the door was locked, and though Arthur tried his best to get in, he could not. Then he rode away in great anger and said to himself, 'Kay will not be without a sword this day. I will take that sword in the churchyard and give it to him.'"

Now dictate the following sentences to the student three times. Before you read, tell the student that you will read the sentences only three times before asking her to write, and will not repeat them afterwards.

> Kay won't be without a sword this day. I'll take that sword in the churchyard and give it to him.

Ask the student to repeat the sentences back to you before she writes. If she forgets, tell her to go back to the beginning of the sentences and recite them again to jog her memory. If necessary, you may then prompt the student with single words.

Watch the student as she writes, and correct her at once if she begins to make a mistake.

DAY THREE: Narration and Original Sentence Exercise   *Student Pages 232–234*

Focus: *Identifying the central narrative thread in a passage and writing original sentences*

Pull out Student Pages 232–233 and 234. Ask the student to write her name and the date on Student Page 234.

Today's exercise will require the student to write an original sentence. Allow the student to read the story on Student Pages 232–233, either silently or aloud.

You will now ask the student to summarize the passage. This selection lends itself to a narrative, story-like retelling. To guide the student towards this type of summary, say, "In three or four sentences, tell me how Arthur pulled the sword from the anvil—both times." Her answer should resemble one of the following:

> "Arthur went to get a sword for his brother Kay. He saw the sword in the stone and pulled it out. Sir Ector told him to put it back in. Arthur put it back in and drew it back out again. Sir Ector knelt down and said that Arthur was king of the Britons."

> "Arthur and Kay were at the tournament, but Kay forgot his sword. Arthur rode back and pulled out the sword in the stone and brought it to Kay. When Sir Ector saw the sword, he told Arthur to put it back and then pull it out a second time."

> "Arthur pulled the sword out of the anvil so that Kay could use it in the tournament. When Sir Ector saw the sword, he asked Arthur how he got it. Arthur said that he pulled it from the anvil. Then he put it back into the anvil and pulled it out a second time."

If the student has difficulty with this summary, ask the following three questions to help focus her thoughts:

Why did Arthur go get the sword in the anvil?

When Sir Ector saw the sword, what did he tell Arthur to do?

What did Arthur do then?

Then have the student repeat her answers in order; this will form her brief summary. Write down the student's narration on the lines below, but do not allow her to watch.

_____

_____

_____

_____

Now ask her whether she can repeat the first sentence (or first and second sentences, depending on length) of the narration to herself. If not, read her the first one or two sentences of the narration only. Tell her to listen carefully, since you will only read once. Encourage her to repeat the sentence or sentences to herself until she can remember, and then to say the words out loud to herself as she writes on Student Page 234.

Give all necessary help in spelling and punctuation.

Day Four: Dictation Exercise   *Student Page 235*

Focus: *Memory*

Pull out Student Page 235. Ask the student to write her name and the date.

Tell the student that today's dictation sentences are from T. H. White's book *The Once and Future King*, a retelling of the Arthur legends.

First, tell the student that you will read the entire description of Sir Ector's castle as she listens.

Read: "Sir Ector's castle stood in the enormous clearing in a still more enormous forest. It had a big green courtyard and a moat with pike in it. The moat was crossed by a strongly-fortified stone bridge which ended half-way across it: the other half was covered by a wooden draw-bridge which was wound up every night. As soon as you had crossed the draw-bridge you were at the top of the village street—it had only one street—and this extended for about half a mile, with little white thatched houses of mud on either side of it. The street divided the clearing into two huge fields, that on the left being cultivated in hundreds of long narrow strips, while that on the right ran down to a little river and was used as pasture. Half of the right-hand field was fenced off for hay."

Now tell the student that you will dictate the first three sentences of the paragraph to her. Tell her that this is a memory-stretcher; you don't expect her to remember the whole thing, but you would like her to write as much as she can remember before asking you to repeat.

Read the following sentences three times. Before you read, tell the student that the last sentence is divided not by a period, but by a colon. If she is not familiar with colons, write one on the bottom of Student Page 235 and tell her that colons can sometimes be used in the place of periods. When you read, pause at the colon, but pause for a longer time at each period.

> Sir Ector's castle stood in the enormous clearing in a still more enormous forest. It had a big green courtyard and a moat with pike in it. The moat was crossed by a strongly-fortified stone bridge which ended half-way across it: the other half was covered by a wooden draw-bridge which was wound up every night.

Watch the student as she writes, and correct her at once if she begins to make a mistake. You will need to tell her that there is a hyphen in "strongly-fortified" and another in "half-way."

WEEK 32

Day One: Narration Exercise   *Student Pages 236–238*

Focus: *Identifying the central narrative thread in a passage*

Pull out Student Pages 236–237 and 238. Ask the student to write his name and the date on Student Page 238.

Allow the student to read the story on Student Pages 236–237, either silently or aloud.

You will now ask the student to summarize the passage. This selection lends itself to a narrative, story-like retelling. To guide the student towards this type of summary, say to him, "Tell me in three sentences why the tailor wrote 'Seven in one stroke' on his belt." His answer should resemble one of the following:

> "The tailor bought some jam from a peasant woman. The flies descended on the jam, so the tailor hit them with a cloth. He killed seven flies, so he wrote 'Seven at one stroke!' on his belt."

> "A woman came along selling jam, and the tailor bought some. He was finishing a jacket, so he left the jam on the table. Then he killed seven of the flies that swarmed around the jam with one blow."

> "The little tailor bought some jam and spread it on bread. He left the bread and jam on the table, and flies swarmed all around it. The little tailor killed seven of them with a cloth, and wrote 'Seven at one stroke!' on his belt."

If the student has difficulty with this summary, ask the following three questions to help focus his thoughts:

What did the tailor buy from the woman?

What happened to the jam while it was sitting on the table?

What did the tailor kill?

The answers to these questions will make up the student's summary.

Write the narration down on Student Page 238 as the student watches.

DAY TWO: Dictation Exercise

Focus: *Direct quotations at beginning, middle, and end of sentences*

> ***Note:*** Today's exercise covers direct quotations at the beginning, middle, and end of
> sentences. The student should have learned the rules for writing direct quotations from
> his grammar program. If he has not (or needs a reminder), show him the following
> rules and read through them with him. Ask the student to find the place where each
> rule is demonstrated in the dialogue.
>
> "If the direct quote is at the beginning of a sentence, it should have a comma after it,"
> the teacher said. "The comma should go inside the closing quotation mark. The first
> word after the quotation should not be capitalized."
>
> "What if the quote is a question?" the student asked.
>
> "Good point!" the teacher said. "Question marks and exclamation points go inside the
> closing quotation mark as well. But you still shouldn't capitalize the first word after the
> quotation."
>
> The student said, "What if the quotation is at the end of the sentence?"
>
> The teacher said, "Then the comma should come right before the direct quotation, and
> the quotation should begin with a capital letter."
>
> "What if the words 'he said' come in the middle of the quotation?" the student asked.
>
> "In that case," the teacher said, "commas come after the first part of the quotation and
> also after the word 'said.'"

Pull out Student Page 239. Ask the student to write his name and the date.

Tell the student that today's dictation sentences are from the fairy tale "Briar Rose,"
another story collected by the Brothers Grimm. He may know it by the name "Sleeping
Beauty."

Before you dictate, read the first paragraph of the story to the student: "A king and queen
once upon a time reigned in a country a great way off, where there were in those days fairies.
Now this king and queen had plenty of money, and plenty of fine clothes to wear, and plenty
of good things to eat and drink, and a coach to ride out in every day: but though they had
been married many years they had no children, and this grieved them very much indeed. But
one day as the queen was walking by the side of the river, at the bottom of the garden, she saw
a poor little fish, that had thrown itself out of the water, and lay gasping and nearly dead on
the bank. Then the queen took pity on the little fish, and threw it back again into the river."

Now dictate the following sentences to the student three times. Before you read, tell the
student that you will read the sentences only three times before asking him to write, and will
not repeat them afterwards. Also tell him that there is a direct quote in the selection. Remind
him that a direct quote should have quotation marks around it, and that it should be separated

from the sentence before it by a comma. Be sure to use a different voice for the fish's exact words.

> **Before the little fish swam away, it lifted its head out of the water and said, "I know what your wish is, and it shall be fulfilled, in return for your kindness to me. You will soon have a daughter."**

Now ask the student to repeat the sentences back to you before he writes. If he forgets, tell him to go back to the beginning of the sentences and recite them again to jog his memory. If necessary, you may then prompt the student with single words.

Watch the student as he writes, and correct him at once if he begins to make a mistake. If he writes "it's" instead of "its," remind him that "its" is the possessive form of "it," while "it's" is a contraction for "it is" ("it lifted it is head out of the water" wouldn't make any sense!).

DAY THREE: Narration and Original Sentence Exercise   *Student Pages 240–242*

Focus: *Identifying the central narrative thread in a passage and writing original sentences*

Pull out Student Pages 240–241 and 242. Ask the student to write his name and the date on Student Page 242.

Today's exercise will require the student to write an original sentence. Allow the student to read the story on Student Pages 240–241, either silently or aloud.

You will now ask the student to summarize the passage. This selection lends itself to a narrative, story-like retelling. To guide the student towards this type of summary, say to him, "Tell me the three things that the tailor did to impress the giant." (Do not give him a sentence limit.) His answer should resemble one of the following:

> "First, the tailor squeezed the liquid out of a cheese, and the giant thought he was squeezing a rock. Then, the tailor threw a bird into the air, and the giant thought he was throwing a stone. Then the tailor told the giant he would carry the branches of a tree, but instead he rode on it while the giant carried it."

> "The giant squeezed a rock until water ran out, and the tailor did the same thing with a piece of cheese. Next the giant threw a rock into the air. The tailor threw a bird, which flew up out of sight. Then the giant told the tailor to carry a tree. Instead, the tailor let the giant carry it while he rode in the branches."

> "When the giant told the tailor to squeeze water out of a rock, the tailor squeezed water out of a cheese. The giant threw a rock high into the air and told the tailor to do the same. The tailor threw a bird into the air, and the bird did not come back. Then the giant told the tailor to help carry a tree. The tailor said that he would carry the branches, but he let the giant do all the work while he rode on the tree."

If the student has difficulty with this summary, ask the following three questions to help focus his thoughts:

Why did the tailor squeeze the cheese?

Why did the tailor throw the bird into the air?

Why did the tailor ride in the branches of the tree?

Then have the student repeat his answers in order; this will form his brief summary. Write down the student's narration on the lines below, but do not allow him to watch.

_____

_____

_____

_____

Now ask him whether he can repeat the first sentence (or first and second sentences, depending on length) of the narration to himself. If not, read him the first one or two sentences of the narration only. Tell him to listen carefully, since you will only read once. Encourage him to repeat the sentence or sentences to himself until he can remember, and then to say the words out loud to himself as he writes on Student Page 242.

Give all necessary help in spelling and punctuation.

DAY FOUR: Dictation Exercise   *Student Page 243*

Focus: *Direct quotations at beginning, middle, and end of sentences*

Pull out Student Page 243. Ask the student to write his name and the date.

Tell the student that today's dictation sentences are also from the fairy tale "Briar Rose." Read the following paragraphs of the story to the student:

> The queen had a little girl, so very beautiful that the king said he would hold a great feast and make merry, and show the child to all the land. So he asked his kinsmen, and nobles, and friends, and neighbours. But the queen said, "I will have the fairies also, that they might be kind and good to our little daughter." Now there were thirteen fairies in the kingdom; but as the king and queen had only twelve golden dishes for them to eat out of, they were forced to leave one of the fairies without asking her. So twelve fairies came, and after the feast was over they gathered round in a ring and gave all their best gifts to the little princess. One gave her goodness, another beauty, another riches, and so on till she had all that was good in the world.
>
> Just as eleven of them had done blessing her, a great noise was heard in the courtyard, and word was brought that the thirteenth fairy was come.

Now, as she had not been asked to the feast she was very angry, and scolded the king and queen very much, and set to work to take her revenge. So she cried out, "The king's daughter shall, in her fifteenth year, be wounded by a spindle, and fall down dead." Then the twelfth of the friendly fairies, who had not yet given her gift, came forward, and said that the evil wish must be fulfilled, but that she could soften its mischief; so her gift was, that the king's daughter, when the spindle wounded her, should not really die, but should only fall asleep for a hundred years.

However, the king hoped still to save his dear child altogether from the threatened evil; so he ordered that all the spindles in the kingdom should be bought up and burnt. But all the gifts of the first eleven fairies were in the meantime fulfilled; for the princess was so beautiful, and well behaved, and good, and wise, that everyone who knew her loved her.

It happened that, on the very day she was fifteen years old, the king and queen were not at home, and she was left alone in the palace. So she roved about by herself, and looked at all the rooms and chambers, till at last she came to an old tower, to which there was a narrow staircase ending with a little door. In the door there was a golden key, and when she turned it the door sprang open, and there sat an old lady spinning away very busily.

Tell the student that the next two sentences of the story are today's dictation exercise. Dictate the following sentences to the student three times. Before you read, tell the student that you will read the sentences four times before asking him to write, since he will need to remember several different types of punctuation as he writes.

Be sure to use different voices for the princess and the old lady. Indicate the question at the end of the first sentence with your voice. Pause briefly at each comma.

"Why, good mother," said the princess, "what are you doing there?"
"Spinning," said the old lady, and nodded her head, humming a tune.

Now ask the student to repeat the sentences back to you before he writes. If he forgets, tell him to go back to the beginning of the sentences and recite them again to jog his memory. If necessary, you may then prompt the student with single words.

Remind the student that there should be commas between each speech and the words "said" in each sentence. Also remind him that in the first sentence, the word "what" should not be capitalized because it is part of the same sentence as "Why, good mother."

Watch the student as he writes on Student Page 243, and correct him at once if he begins to make a mistake. You will probably need to tell him to begin a new paragraph with the second speech.

When the student is finished writing, tell him that when an author writes a story, he usually begins a new paragraph whenever a new speaker begins to talk.

WEEK 33

DAY ONE: Narration Exercise   *Student Pages 244–246*

Focus: *Identifying the central details in a passage*

Pull out Student Pages 244–245 and 246. Ask the student to write her name and the date on Student Page 246.

Allow the student to read the story on Student Pages 244–245, either silently or aloud.

You will now ask the student to summarize the passage. A detail-oriented summary is more appropriate to this descriptive passage than a summary telling what happens. Say to the student, "In three or four sentences, describe four things that Bambi saw in the meadow." Her answer should resemble one of the following:

"The meadow was filled with white daisies, red and purple clover, and golden dandelions. Bambi saw butterflies that looked like flying flowers. When he looked down at the ground, he saw ants running in swarms and a grasshopper jumping."

"Bambi saw the meadow covered with green grass and beautiful flowers. Butterflies were fluttering above the grass. A swarm of ants ran under his hooves. A grasshopper jumped up in front of Bambi, and Bambi thought he was a piece of grass."

"The green meadow was filled with white daisies and golden dandelions. Butterflies flew above the grass like flying flowers. Bambi saw ants beneath his hoofs and a grasshopper leaping in front of him."

If the student has trouble choosing important details, give her these three pointers:

Describe the meadow and the flowers.

Tell me about the butterflies.

Describe the two kinds of insects that Bambi saw.

The answers to these questions will make up the student's summary.
Write the narration down on Student Page 246 as the student watches.

DAY TWO: Dictation Exercise   *Student Page 247*

Focus: *Direct quotations at beginning, middle, and end of sentences*

Pull out Student Page 247. Ask the student to write her name and the date.

Tell the student that today's dictation sentences are also from the book *Bambi*. Before you dictate, read the following dialogue to the student. Tell her that Bambi and his mother have this conversation while walking in the woods.

Once he asked, "Whom does this trail belong to, Mother?"

His mother answered, "To us."

Bambi asked again, "To you and me?"

"Yes."

"To us two?"

"Yes."

"Only to us two?"

"No," said his mother, "to us deer."

"What are deer?" Bambi asked, and laughed.

His mother looked at him from head to foot and laughed too. "You are a deer and I am a deer. We're both deer," she said. "Do you understand?"

Now dictate the following sentences to the student three times. Before you read, tell the student that you will read the sentences only three times before asking her to write, and will not repeat them afterwards.

Be sure to use a different voice for the mother's voice. Indicate the periods by pausing and allowing your voice to fall; remember to indicate the question mark by using a questioning voice for the last phrase.

His mother looked at him from head to foot and laughed too. "You are a deer and I am a deer. We're both deer," she said. "Do you understand?"

Now ask the student to repeat the sentences back to you before she writes. If she forgets, tell her to go back to the beginning of the sentences and recite them again to jog her memory. If necessary, you may then prompt the student with single words.

Watch the student as she writes on Student Page 247. Correct her at once if she begins to make a mistake.

DAY THREE: Narration and Original Sentence Exercise   *Student Pages 248–250*

Focus: *Identifying the central details in a passage and writing original sentences*

Pull out Student Pages 248–249 and 250. Ask the student to write her name and the date on Student Page 250.

Today's exercise will require the student to write an original sentence. Allow the student to read the story on Student Pages 248–249, either silently or aloud.

You will now ask the student to summarize the passage. A detail-oriented summary is more appropriate to this descriptive passage than a summary telling what happens. Say to the student, "In three or four sentences, describe Bambi's meeting with the Hare." Her answer should resemble one of the following:

"Bambi saw his mother standing still, and he went over to see what she was doing. She was talking to the Hare. He had tall spoonlike ears with black stripes, stiff whiskers, and big round eyes. Bambi did not feel any respect for the Hare."

"Bambi saw the Hare's two long ears in the grass. The Hare had a mild face, good-natured features, and big round eyes. His mouth and nose twitched, and Bambi had to laugh at him."

"The Hare had spoonlike, grayish-brown ears with black stripes. The Hare was polite and mild, and Bambi did not feel any respect for him. The Hare sat up suddenly with his nose twitching and then hopped quickly away."

If the student has difficulty with this summary, ask the following three questions to help focus her thoughts:

What did Bambi see when he went over to his mother?

Can you describe the Hare's ears and face?

How did Bambi feel towards the Hare?

Then have the student repeat her answers in order; this will form her brief summary. Write down the student's narration on the lines below, but do not allow her to watch.

_____

_____

_____

_____

Now ask her whether she can repeat the first sentence (or first and second sentences, depending on length) of the narration to herself. If not, read her the first one or two sentences of the narration only. Tell her to listen carefully, since you will only read once. Encourage her to repeat the sentence or sentences to herself until she can remember, and then to say the words out loud to herself as she writes on Student Page 250.

Give all necessary help in spelling and punctuation.

DAY FOUR: Dictation Exercise   *Student Page 251*

Focus: *Direct quotations at beginning, middle, and end of sentences*

Pull out Student Page 251. Ask the student to write her name and the date.

Tell the student that today's dictation sentences are also from the book *Bambi*. Before you dictate, read the following paragraph to the student. It describes how Bambi develops the ability to smell what is going on in the woods.

> He knew how to snuff the air now, too. Soon he would do it as well as his mother. He could breathe in the air and at the same time analyze it with his senses. "That's clover and meadow grass," he would think when the wind blew off the fields. "And Friend Hare is out there, too. I can smell him plainly."

Now dictate the following sentences to the student three times. Before you read, tell the student that you will read the sentences only three times before asking her to write, and will not repeat them afterwards.

Use a different voice for Bambi's thoughts. Be sure to indicate the periods by allowing your voice to fall. Pause briefly at the comma in the second sentence. Before the student writes, tell her that "Friend Hare" is capitalized because Bambi is using it as a proper name.

> "That's clover and meadow grass," he would think when the wind blew off the fields. "And Friend Hare is out there, too. I can smell him plainly."

Now ask the student to repeat the sentences back to you before she writes. If she forgets, tell her to go back to the beginning of the sentences and recite them again to jog her memory. If necessary, you may then prompt the student with single words.

Watch the student as she writes on Student Page 251. Correct her at once if she begins to make a mistake. You may need to remind her to use an apostrophe in "that's" because it is a contraction of "that is."

WEEK 34

Day One: Narration Exercise   *Student Pages 252–254*

Focus: *Identifying the central narrative thread in a passage*

Pull out Student Pages 252–253 and 254. Ask the student to write his name and the date on Student Page 254.

Allow the student to read the story on Student Pages 252–253, either silently or aloud.

You will now ask the student to summarize the passage. This selection lends itself to a narrative, story-like retelling. To guide the student towards this type of summary, ask him, "Tell me what happened to Prince Wicked and the three animals. Be sure to include how the animals and the prince felt towards the poor man after they were rescued." He should take five or six sentences for his answer, which should resemble one of the following:

> "Prince Wicked was swept into the river. He climbed onto a log. A rat, a snake, and a parrot were also forced to climb onto the log. A poor man rescued them and took care of the animals first. The animals were grateful to him, but the prince secretly hated him."

> "Prince Wicked was so wicked that his servants left him to drown. He climbed onto a log and floated down the river. A rat and a snake were also swept into the river and climbed onto the log. Then a parrot was forced to land on it. They were all rescued by a poor man. The animals thanked the poor man, but the prince hated him because the poor man took care of the animals first."

> "Prince Wicked fell into the river and floated down it on a log. A rat, a snake, and a parrot also climbed onto the log for safety. A poor man rescued all of them and took care of the animals first, because they were weaker. The snake promised him gold, the rat promised him money, and the parrot promised him rice. But the prince hated him."

If the student has difficulty condensing this story into a summary, ask the following four questions to help focus his thoughts:

> What happened to Prince Wicked at the beginning of the story?

> What three animals joined him?

> When they were rescued, how were the animals treated differently?

> How did the animals and the prince feel towards the poor man?

The answers to these questions will make up the student's summary.
Write the narration down on Student Page 254 as the student watches.

Day Two: Dictation Exercise   *Student Page 255*

Focus: *Comparative and superlative adjectives*

Pull out Student Page 255. Ask the student to write his name and the date.

Tell the student that today's dictation sentence is from another of the Jataka tales retold by Ellen Babbitt. The tale is called "The Wise Goat and the Wolf."

Before you dictate, read the beginning paragraph to the student: "Once upon a time, many, many wild goats lived in a cave in the side of a hill. A wolf lived with his mate not far from this cave. Like all wolves they liked the taste of goat. So they caught the goats, one after another, and ate them all but one who was wiser than all the others. Try as they might the wolves could not catch her."

Now dictate the following sentences to the student three times. Before you read, tell the student that you will read the sentences only three times before asking him to write, and will not repeat them afterwards.

> **Like all wolves they liked the taste of goat. So they caught the goats, one after another, and ate them all but one who was wiser than all the others.**

Now ask the student to repeat the sentences back to you before he writes. If he forgets, tell him to go back to the beginning of the sentences and recite them again to jog his memory. If necessary, you may then prompt the student with single words.

Watch the student as he writes, and correct him at once if he begins to make a mistake.

When the student is finished, ask him to underline the word "wiser" in the second sentence. Tell him that this is a *comparative adjective*. Most adjectives have three forms: the regular form, the comparative form, and the superlative form. The regular form of this adjective is "wise." All of the goats might be wise. The comparative form is "wiser." One goat is "wiser" than the rest. Can the student guess the superlative form? It is "wisest." Maybe this goat is the "wisest" of all the goats in the world!

DAY THREE: Narration and Original Sentence Exercise   *Student Pages 256–258*

Focus: *Identifying the central narrative thread in a passage and writing original sentences*

Pull out Student Pages 256–257 and 258. Ask the student to write his name and the date on Student Page 258.

Today's exercise will require the student to write an original sentence. Allow the student to read the story on Student Pages 256–257, either silently or aloud.

You will now ask the student to summarize the passage. This selection lends itself to a narrative, story-like retelling. To guide the student towards this type of summary, say to him, "Tell me about the poor man and the animals. Then tell me about the poor man and Prince Wicked." His answer should be five or six sentences long and should resemble one of the following:

> "The poor man went to see each one of the animals to see if they would keep their promises. All of them did. Then the poor man went to see the prince. The prince was now the king. He ordered the poor man beaten and put to death. But the people killed the king instead and made the poor man king in his place."

> "The snake showed the poor man where the gold was. The rat showed him where money was buried. The parrot said that he and his family and friends would gather rice. But the prince, who was now king, was afraid that he would have to give the poor man riches. He ordered the poor man put to death. Instead, the people made the poor man king in his place."

"The snake, the rat, and the parrot all kept their promises. So the poor man went to the city to see Prince Wicked, who was now the king. The king didn't want to keep his promise, so he told his servants to arrest and beat the poor man. The poor man told his story to some wise men in the city. The wise men and the rest of the people killed the wicked king and made the poor man king instead."

If the student has difficulty with this summary, ask the following four questions to help focus his thoughts:

What did the three animals do when the poor man went to see them?

What had happened to the prince in the meantime?

When the king saw the poor man, what did he tell his servants to do?

How did the people of the city react to this?

Then have the student repeat his answers in order; this will form his brief summary. Write down the student's narration on the lines below, but do not allow him to watch.

_____

_____

_____

_____

Now ask him whether he can repeat the first sentence (or first and second sentences, depending on length) of the narration to himself. If not, read him the first one or two sentences of the narration only. Tell him to listen carefully, since you will only read once. Encourage him to repeat the sentence or sentences to himself until he can remember, and then to say the words out loud to himself as he writes on Student Page 258.

Give all necessary help in spelling and punctuation.

DAY FOUR: Dictation Exercise   *Student Page 259*

Focus: *Comparative and superlative adjectives*

Pull out Student Page 259. Ask the student to write his name and the date.

Tell the student that today's dictation sentence is from another of the Jataka tales retold by Ellen Babbitt. It is called "The Quarrel of the Quails." Before you dictate, read the first paragraphs of the story to the student:

Once upon a time many quails lived together in a forest. The wisest of them all was their leader.

A man lived near the forest and earned his living by catching quails and selling them. Day after day he listened to the note of the leader calling the quails. By and by this man, the fowler, was able to call the quails together. Hearing the note the quails thought it was their leader who called.

When they were crowded together, the fowler threw the net over them and off he went into the town, where he soon sold all the quails that he had caught.

Tell the student that the leader of the quails thought of a plan to escape from the fowler, but he'll have to find the story and read it to find out what the plan was.

Now dictate the following sentences to the student three times. Before you read, tell the student that you will read the sentences only three times before asking him to write, and will not repeat them afterwards.

Once upon a time many quails lived together in a forest. The wisest of them all was their leader.

Now ask the student to repeat the sentences back to you before he writes. If he forgets, tell him to go back to the beginning of the sentences and recite them again to jog his memory. If necessary, you may then prompt the student with single words.

Watch the student as he writes on Student Page 259. Correct him at once if he begins to make a mistake.

When the student is finished, ask him to underline the word "wisest" in the second sentence. Ask him if he remembers what form of the adjective "wise" this is. The correct answer is the "superlative" form. Remind him that most adjectives have three forms: the regular form, the comparative form, and the superlative form. The regular form of this adjective is "wise." All of the quails might be wise. The comparative form is "wiser." Some of the quails might be "wiser" than the others. The superlative form is "wisest." The leader of the quails is the "wisest" of them all.

WEEK 35

DAY ONE: Narration Exercise   *Student Pages 260–262*

Focus: *Identifying the central narrative thread in a passage, along with relevant details*

Pull out Student Pages 260–261 and 262. Ask the student to write her name and the date on Student Page 262.

Allow the student to read the story on Student Pages 260–261, either silently or aloud.

You will now ask the student to summarize the passage. This passage has a strong narrative thread, but it also contains important details. To help the student in summarizing, say, "Give me two sentences telling what the Monkey People are like, and then two sentences telling what they do to Mowgli." Her answer should resemble one of the following:

"The Monkey People lived in the treetops and threw sticks and nuts at other animals. They had no leader or laws or customs of their own. They decided to kidnap Mowgli because he could help them make houses to live in. So they grabbed Mowgli during his nap and dragged him away through the treetops."

"The Monkey People lived in the trees, and none of the other animals would notice them. They howled and shrieked and started fights over nothing. They kidnapped Mowgli while he was sleeping and carried him away through the treetops. Mowgli enjoyed rushing through the branches, even though it frightened him."

"The Monkey People lived in the trees and had their own roads and crossroads in the treetops. They always intended to have leaders and laws, but they could never remember this the next day. When they saw Mowgli making play huts, they decided that he could live with them and be their leader. They snatched him away from Baloo and Bagheera and carried him off through the treetops."

If the student has difficulty condensing the selection, ask these four questions:

Where did the monkeys live?

Why didn't they have leaders and laws?

Why did they decide to kidnap Mowgli?

How did they get him away from Baloo and Bagheera?

The answers to these questions will make up the student's summary.
Write the narration down on Student Page 262 as the student watches.

DAY TWO: Dictation Exercise

Focus: *Interjections*

Pull out Student Page 263. Ask the student to write her name and the date.

Tell the student that today's dictation sentences are from Rudyard Kipling's story "Rikki-tikki-tavi," found in *The Jungle Book*. Rikki-tikki is a mongoose who lives with a British family in India. His instinct is to kill snakes, so when he finds two cobras living in the garden, he tries to get rid of them. The following sentence tells what happens when Rikki-tikki destroys all of the cobra's eggs except for one.

Dictate the following sentences to the student three times. Before you read, tell the student that you will read the sentences only three times before asking her to write, and will not repeat them afterwards.

Also tell the student that "Ah!" is spelled *ah* and should be followed by an exclamation point. Be sure to use a different voice for the snake's words. Pause briefly at the comma in the first sentence. Pause for a longer time at the period, and indicate the end of the sentence by allowing your voice to fall.

> The big snake turned half round, and saw the egg on the veranda. "Ah!
> Give it to me," she said.

Now ask the student to repeat the sentences back to you before she writes. If she forgets, tell her to go back to the beginning of the sentences and recite them again to jog her memory. If necessary, you may then prompt the student with single words.

Watch the student as she writes, and correct her at once if she begins to make a mistake.

When the student is finished writing, ask her to underline the word "Ah!" Tell her that this is an *interjection*. An interjection shows emotion and doesn't have any grammatical relationship to the rest of the sentence. It can be in a sentence all by itself, like "Ah!"

DAY THREE: Narration and Original Sentence Exercise

Focus: *Identifying the central details in a passage and writing original sentences*

Pull out Student Pages 264–265 and 266. Ask the student to write her name and the date on Student Page 266.

Today's exercise will require the student to write an original sentence. Allow the student to read the story on Student Pages 264–265, either silently or aloud.

You will now ask the student to summarize the passage. A detail-oriented summary is more appropriate to this descriptive passage than a summary telling what happens. Say to the student, "Give me two sentences describing the Lost City, and two sentences describing what the monkeys did there." Her answer should resemble one of the following:

"The Lost City had trees and creepers growing through it. The palace had no roof, and rows and rows of houses with no roofs lined the streets. The monkeys pretended that they were men and used the council chamber. They explored the city, but they could never remember what they saw."

"The gates of the Lost City were ruined and the battlements had fallen down. The domes of the temples were shattered and the houses had no roofs. The monkeys lived in the city and pretended to be men, but they didn't know what the buildings were for. They played in the garden, explored the tunnels, and drank from the tanks."

"The monkeys called the Lost City their city, but they didn't know what the buildings were for. The city was ruined; the palace on the hill had no roof, and trees and vines grew everywhere. Rows and rows of roofless houses made up the rest of the city. The monkeys collected bits of brick and plaster, fought with each other, and pretended to be men."

If the student has difficulty with this summary, ask the following three questions to help focus her thoughts:

Describe the palace in the Lost City.

Describe something else seen in the streets of the Lost City.

Now tell me what the monkeys pretended to be, and how.

Then have the student repeat her answers in order; this will form her brief summary. Write down the student's narration on the lines below, but do not allow her to watch.

_____

_____

_____

_____

Now ask her whether she can repeat the first sentence (or first and second sentences, depending on length) of the narration to herself. If not, read her the first one or two sentences of the narration only. Tell her to listen carefully, since you will only read once. Encourage her to repeat the sentence or sentences to herself until she can remember, and then to say the words out loud to herself as she writes on Student Page 266.

Give all necessary help in spelling and punctuation.

Day Four: Dictation Exercise   *Student Page 267*

Focus: *Interjections*

Pull out Student Page 267. Ask the student to write her name and the date.

Tell the student that today's dictation sentences are also from Rudyard Kipling's story "Rikki-tikki-tavi," found in *The Jungle Book*. In this selection, Rikki-tikki is startled by the mother and father of the family, who have come into the room where he is sleeping.

Begin by reading the following two paragraphs to the student:

> "Oh, it's you," said he. "What are you bothering for? All the cobras are dead; and if they weren't, I'm here."
>
> Rikki-tikki had a right to be proud of himself; but he did not grow too proud, and he kept that garden as a mongoose should keep it, with tooth and jump and spring and bite, till never a cobra dared show its head inside the walls.

Now dictate the following sentences to the student three times. Before you read, tell the student that you will read the sentences only three times before asking her to write, and will not repeat them afterwards.

Be sure to indicate the commas by pausing slightly. Indicate the question by allowing your voice to rise. Before you read, tell the student that there is a semicolon in the selection. The semicolon will be a longer pause than a comma, but a shorter pause than a period, and it will separate two complete sentences. Tell the student to listen carefully for the semicolon.

> "Oh, it's you," said he. "What are you bothering for? All the cobras are dead; and if they weren't, I'm here."

Now ask the student to repeat the sentences back to you before she writes. If she forgets, tell her to go back to the beginning of the sentences and recite them again to jog her memory. If necessary, you may then prompt the student with single words.

Watch the student as she writes, and correct her at once if she begins to make a mistake. You may need to remind her that "it's" is the contraction of "it is" and has an apostrophe.

When the student is finished writing, ask her to underline the word "Oh." Tell her that this is another *interjection*. An interjection can be in a sentence all by itself—like "Ah!"—but it can also be connected to another sentence with a comma.

WEEK 36: EVALUATION

Before moving to Level Four, the student should be able to read a passage independently and sum it up in two to six sentences (depending on length). He should be able to write down at least the first sentence of his own narration. He should also be able to take down dictation exercises of two to three sentences after three repetitions.

Use the following assignments to evaluate the student's mastery of these skills; you may do these over several days or all at once, depending on the student's maturity.

If the student still struggles with narration or dictation skills, spend a few more weeks on these skills before moving on.

NARRATION AND ORIGINAL SENTENCE EVALUATION   *Evaluation Pages 1–3*

Pull out Evaluation Pages 1–3. Ask the student to write his name and the date on Evaluation Page 3.

Give Evaluation Pages 1–2 to the student to read independently.

When he is finished reading, ask him to summarize the passage in three sentences. His answer should resemble one of the following:

"Little Georgie ran away from the Old Hound, so fast that it felt like flying. But when he came over a hill, he saw Deadman's Brook in front of him. He leaped all the way over the brook, and the Old Hound gave up and went slowly home."

"The Old Hound was chasing Little Georgie, and Little Georgie could not find anywhere to hide. He wondered why the Old Hound didn't give up, until he came to Deadman's Brook. He had to jump over it, even though he was frightened."

"Little George was running away from the Old Hound when he saw a stream in front of him. It was so wide that he didn't think he could jump across it. But he leaped as hard as he could, sailed across, and landed safely on the other side."

Write down the student's narration on the lines below, but do not allow him to watch.

_____

_____

_____

_____

Now ask him to repeat the first sentence of the narration to himself. If he cannot remember it, read him the first sentence of the narration ONLY ONCE. Tell the student to repeat the sentence to himself, and then to say it out loud to himself as he writes it down on Evaluation Page 3.

Give all necessary help in spelling and punctuation.

Pull out Evaluation Page 4. Ask the student to write his name and the date.

Tell the student that today's dictation sentences are from *Rabbit Hill.* Before Georgie sets off on his journey, his father wants to make sure that he knows how to cross over a bridge safely. He asks Georgie, "What do you do when you come to a bridge?" This is Georgie's response.

Dictate the following sentences to the student three times. Before you read, tell the student that you will read the sentences only three times before asking him to write, and will not repeat them afterwards. Be sure to indicate the periods and commas with appropriate pauses. Use inflection to indicate the ends of sentences, and use a different voice for Georgie's exact words.

"I hide well," answered Georgie, "and wait a good long time. I look all around for dogs. I look up the road for cars and down the road for cars."

Now ask the student to repeat the sentences back to you before he writes. He should not need you to prompt him with single words.

Allow the student to write without interruption. You may help him spell "Georgie," but he should not need any other assistance with spelling or punctuation.

THE COMPLETE WRITER

Level Three
Workbook for Writing with Ease

STUDENT PAGES

By

Susan Wise Bauer

$14.95

ISBN 978-1-933339-42-9

51495>

9 781933 339429

WELL-
TRAINED
MIND
PRESS

www.welltrainedmind.com

PHOTOCOPYING AND DISTRIBUTION POLICY

The illustrations, reading lists, and all other content in this Workbook are copyrighted material owned by Well-Trained Mind Press. Please do not reproduce reading lists, etc., on email lists or websites.

For families: You may make as many photocopies of the Student Pages as you need for use WITHIN YOUR OWN FAMILY ONLY. Photocopying the pages so that the book can then be resold is a violation of copyright.

Schools and co-ops MAY NOT PHOTOCOPY any portion of the Workbook. Smaller schools usually find that purchasing a set of the pre-copied Student Pages for each student is the best option. Other schools may purchase a license that allows school and co-op duplication. For more information, please contact Well-Trained Mind Press: email support@welltrainedmind.com; phone 1.877.322.3445.

"The Straw, the Coal, and the Bean"

by Jacob and Wilhelm Grimm

This story is a very old fairy tale, written down almost two hundred years ago by two brothers named Jacob and Wilhelm Grimm who wanted to collect ancient stories and keep them alive.

In a village there lived a poor old woman, who had gathered together a dish of beans and wanted to cook them. So she made a fire on her hearth, and so that it might burn the quicker, she added a handful of straw. When she was emptying the beans into the pan, one dropped without her observing it, and lay on the ground beside a straw, and soon afterwards a burning coal from the fire leapt down to the two.

Then the straw said, "Friends, where do you come from, and how did you get here?"

The coal replied, "I sprang out of the fire, and if I had not escaped by sheer force, my death would have been certain. I would have been burnt to ashes."

The bean said: "I too have escaped with a whole skin, but if the old woman had got me into the pan, I would have been made into soup without any mercy, like all of the others."

"Nothing good would have happened to me either!" said the straw. "The old woman has destroyed all my brothers in fire and smoke; she seized sixty of them at once, and took their lives. I luckily slipped through her fingers."

"But what are we to do now?" said the coal.

"I think," answered the bean, "that since we have so fortunately escaped death, we should keep together like good companions, and go on a journey to a foreign country."

The coal and the straw agreed, and the three set out on their way together. Soon, however, they came to a little brook, and as there was no bridge, they did not know how they were to get over it.

The straw said: "I will lay myself straight across, and then you can walk over on me as on a bridge." So the straw stretched itself from one bank to the other, and the coal tripped quite boldly on to the newly-built bridge. But when she had reached the middle, and heard the water rushing beneath her, she was afraid. She stood still, and did not dare go any farther. The straw began to burn, broke in two pieces, and fell into the stream. The coal slipped after her, hissed when she got into the water, and breathed her last.

The bean, who had prudently stayed behind on the shore, could not but laugh at the event. She was unable to stop, and laughed so heartily that she burst.

It would have been all over with the bean, but by good fortune a tailor, who was travelling in search of work, sat down to rest by the brook. As he had a kind heart, he pulled out his needle and thread, and sewed her together.

The bean thanked him most prettily. And, because the tailor used black thread, all beans since then have a black seam.

—Trans. Edgar Taylor and Marian Edwardes, 1823;
some archaic language has been clarified by Susan Wise Bauer

Narration Exercise

From "The Straw, the Coal, and the Bean" by the Brothers Grimm

Date _____

Name _____

Dictation Exercise

"Cat and Mouse in Partnership"
by Jacob and Wilhelm Grimm

A cat became friends with a mouse, and the two decided to keep house together.

"We must store up some food for winter," said the cat. The mouse agreed, and together the two bought a little pot of bacon fat. But they did not know where to put it.

Finally, after much thought, the cat said, "We should store it in the church, for no one dares steal anything from there. We will set it beneath the altar, and not touch it until we are really in need of it."

So the pot was placed in safety. But it was not long before the cat had a great yearning for it, and said to the mouse: "My cousin has brought a little son into the world. He is white with brown spots, and I must go to the christening."

"Yes, yes," answered the mouse, "by all means go."

But the cat had no cousin. She went straight to the church, stole to the pot, and licked the top of the fat off. Then she took a walk upon the roofs of the town and stretched herself in the sun, and not until it was evening did she return home.

"Well, here you are again," said the mouse. "What name did they give the child?"

"Top-off," said the cat quite coolly.

"Top-off!" cried the mouse, "that is a very odd and uncommon name."

"It is no worse than Crumb-stealer," said the cat, "which is the name of your own little nephew."

Before long the cat was seized by another fit of yearning. She said to the mouse: "You must do me a favour, and once more manage the house for a day alone. Another cousin of mine has had a child."

The good mouse consented, but the cat crept behind the town walls to the church, and devoured half the pot of fat.

When she went home the mouse inquired, "And what was the child named?"

"Half-done," answered the cat.

"Half-done!" said the mouse. "I've never heard such a name in my life!"

The cat's mouth soon began to water for some more of the fat. "All good things go in threes," said she. "My third cousin has had a child—a beautiful black kitten with white paws. You will let me go to the christening, won't you?"

This time, the cat entirely emptied the pot of fat. When she returned home at night, the mouse at once asked what name had been given to the third child.

"It will not please you more than the others," said the cat. "He is called All-gone."

"All-gone!" cried the mouse, "that is the strangest name of all!"

After this, no one invited the cat to christenings, but when the winter had come and there was no longer anything to be found outside, the mouse thought of their provision, and said: "Come, cat, we will go and eat our pot of fat—we shall enjoy that."

"Yes," answered the cat, "just as much as sticking our tongues out the window."

They set out on their way. When they arrived, the pot of fat was still in its place, but it was empty.

"Alas!" said the mouse. "Now I see what has happened! You have eaten it all while you were pretending to see your nephews named! First top-off, then half-done, then—"

"One more word," cried the cat, "and I will eat you too!"

But "All-gone" was already on the mouse's lips. She had barely spoken it when the cat sprang on her, seized her, and swallowed her down. In truth, that is the way of the world!

— Trans. Edgar Taylor and Marian Edwardes, 1823;
some archaic language has been clarified by Susan Wise Bauer

Narration/Dictation Exercise

From "Cat and Mouse in Partnership" by the Brothers Grimm

Date _____

Name _____

Dictation Exercise

From *Mr. Revere and I*
by Robert Lawson

Mr. Revere and I is a story about the American revolution—told by Paul Revere's horse, Scheherazade! In the first chapter, we learn that Scheherazade used to be a horse in the British cavalry (mounted soldiers). When British soldiers were sent to the colonies to fight against the American Revolution, Scheherazade and her rider were sent "to occupy the Port of Boston in the Massachusetts Colony" and to help put down the rebellion.

Scheherazade's rider belonged to a group of soldiers known as the 14th Regiment. All of the horses in the 14th Regiment were put on a ship and sent from England to America. This is Scheherazade's account of her journey.

Ajax is another horse, a "magnificent charger." The "artillery horses" were horses that belonged to another military division which was also being sent to America. A "transport" is a ship designed especially to move men and horses from one place to another; a "ship of the line" is a warship with cannons on both sides. To "pipe-clay" a belt meant to clean it with a very fine, white clay that removed dirt and stains from the leather. "Gaols" is an old-fashioned way to spell "jails." An "Accoutrement" is part of a military uniform that isn't a weapon—like a belt, or a bag for carrying food.

I will not dwell long on the horrors of that trip. It was my first sea voyage, but Ajax, who had made several, said he had seen worse. What *they* could have been like I cannot imagine, for it is hard to conceive of any voyage being worse than ours.

We were quartered in the hold of an extremely old and leaky vessel misnamed the *Glorious*. There was no light and less air. Our hay was moldy, the grain mildewed and weevily, the water unspeakable. Rats were everywhere; they ate the food from under our very noses, they nibbled at our hoofs, they made sleep impossible. Our stalls were never cleaned, and of course currying and brushing were unheard-of.

Our grooms occupied the deck above us and a worse lot could scarce be imagined. They had been plucked from the gaols and prisons to fill out our ranks and fought and caroused unceasingly. Ajax and I were fortunate, for the thug assigned to us had been in prison for horse stealing, so at least he knew *something* of horses, and we fared a bit better than our less lucky companions.

How we envied the artillery horses who were stabled on the open deck of another transport, the *Unfathomable!* Of course they were exposed to the weather, and three were swept overboard in a storm; but I think I envied those three most of all.

From the conversation of the so-called grooms, we learned the make-up of the rest of the expedition. There were four transports for the troops, whose condition was not much better than ours, except that they were given rum three times a day and were allowed to go on deck now and then, weather permitting. They had to be closely watched, however, for many had shown a most unpatriotic tendency to jump overboard. A very fine ship, the *Thunderous*, was given over entirely to the Officers and their servants; and of course we had an escort of four great ships of the line: the *Implacable,* the *Incapable,* the *Impossible* and the *Implausible.*

Our passage consumed only a little more than one month—remarkably fast, Ajax said, but to me it seemed an endless horror. Had I been capable of any feeling at all I should have rejoiced when, on the last day of September, 1768, the everlasting motion stopped and the roaring of the anchor chains shuddered through the ship. As it was, I was too sick and weary to care. I could not be interested when the grooms stumbled below to throw us our horrid evening meal.

We were anchored in Boston Harbor, I gathered. Tomorrow we would land. All troops to be clean-shaven, belts pipe-clayed, arms and accoutrements polished, uniforms pressed, hair powdered....

There was no mention of us horses.

Narration Exercise

From *Mr. Revere and I* by Robert Lawson

Name _____

Date _____

Dictation Exercise

From *Mr. Revere and I*
by Robert Lawson

After Scheherazade comes to Boston, the soldier who owns her loses her in a game of dice to the owner of a glue factory, a man named Nat Sime. The white glue you use for projects is made from special chemicals that dry when they are squeezed out into the open air. But in those days, glue was made in factories that boiled up animal hides, bones, and joints. The hides and bones have a sticky protein in them that acts just like your glue does today.

Scheherazade isn't made into glue—but she is forced to pull a cart that collects the hides and bones. In the mornings, she is driven down the fish market to collect fish heads, skins, and bones. This passage describes the rest of her daily routine. Hezekiah is the man who takes care of Scheherazade; Mildred is another horse in the 14th Regiment, and Scheherazade does not like Mildred at all.

There are some unfamiliar words in the story. "Gurry" is an old word for fishheads and bones, all piled together. The "van" of an army division is the group of soldiers right at the front of the division, leading the way. A "wain" is a large farm wagon.

In the afternoon we drove to the slaughterhouse, whence we fetched an equally offensive load of hoofs and horns. Then, apparently, my duties for the day were done. I was fed, rather poorly watered and bedded down for the night. This was to be my daily routine for many months.

While the work was not unduly hard the humiliation was almost too dreadful to bear. In the first place, for a horse of my background and attainments to be put in harness at all was unthinkable. Had I my old strength and spirits, I would have kicked cart and harness to bits before submitting to such an indignity. Then to be hitched to a *cart,* and *such* a cart—its unsavory loads the butt of jeers and insults whenever it appeared on the streets!

Also there was my appearance, which grew steadily more pitiful. Nat Sime was not one to waste money on fancy feed, so mine was both atrocious and scanty. I was always half shod, my coat grew long and matted. Hezekiah, although kindly enough, knew nothing of the care of horses. My stable was seldom cleaned; often he forgot to water me or give me bedding. I developed two collar sores which he did not know how to treat. They became more painful and hideous daily.

Worst of all was the constant dread that someday I would come face to face with my old Regiment. Changed though my appearance was, every horse would surely recognize me, and that would be the last straw; the very thought of it chilled me. I could picture the dismay of Ajax and the sneers of that nasty little

Mildred. I resolved firmly that rather than undergo that ordeal I would first drown myself in the Harbor.

Of course in a town as small as Boston it was inevitable that someday I must encounter my old comrades in arms and one morning the very thing that I had been so dreading came to pass.

We were toiling up Milk Street from the wharfs with our usual load of gurry when I suddenly became aware of the familiar rattle of drums and the squealing of fifes. Raising my drooping head I beheld the proud van of the glorious 14th advancing down the hill in all its majesty. The morning sun winked and glittered on bayonet and buckle, the scarlet coats glowed hotly, the white-gaitered legs rose and fell rhythmically....

For the first time in my life I ran away.

Wheeling sharply I plunged into the first side street, my one thought to regain the docks and hurl myself into the Harbor waters. I did not get very far.

The street was a narrow one and almost blocked by a huge wain toiling up the hill. Cart and wagon locked wheels, then with a great crash the cart, I, Hezekiah and our horrid load piled up in a tangled mass on the sidewalk.

The crash turns out to be a good thing for Scheherazade—she is rescued from the glue factory by the colonial leader Sam Adams, who gives her to Paul Revere so that he can learn how to ride. That's only the beginning of Scheherazade's adventures.

Narration/Dictation Exercise

From *Mr. Revere and I* by Robert Lawson

Name _____

Date _____

Dictation Exercise

From *And Then What Happened, Paul Revere?*

by Jean Fritz

Last week, you saw what Boston looked like in colonial days—to a horse. Although the story Mr. Revere and I *has many accurate facts in it about the Revolutionary War, the story itself is imaginary. It is "historical fiction"—"historical" because the story takes place during a real time in the past and happens in a real place, "fiction" because the story itself is made up.*

This week, you will read about Paul Revere's Boston from a nonfiction book—one with no made-up stories in it. Nonfiction books that describe the lives of real people are called biographies; this selection comes from the beginning of a biography written by Jean Fritz, called And Then What Happened, Paul Revere?

You will see a series of periods in the middle of the selection, like this:.... These are called "ellipses." Ellipses show you where text has been left out. We shortened this selection so that it would fit more easily into this book by cutting out several paragraphs in the middle.

A "Day Book" was a diary or journal. A "ewer" was a vessel for pouring water, and a "porringer" was a food dish.

In Boston, there was always plenty to see. Ships were constantly coming and going, unloading everything from turtles to chandeliers. Street vendors were constantly crying their wares—everything from fever pills to hair oil to oysters. From time to time there were traveling acrobats, performing monkeys, parades, firework displays, and fistfights.

Once there was a pickled pirate's head on exhibit; once there was a polar bear.

And there was plenty for Paul to do. When he was fifteen years old, his father died, and Paul took over the silversmithing business. He made beads, rings, lockets, bracelets, buttons, medals, pitchers, teapots, spoons, sugar basins, cups, ewers, porringers, shoe buckles, and candlesticks.

Once he made a silver collar for a man's pet squirrel.

To make extra money, he took a job ringing the bells in Christ Church. In Boston, church bells were rung not just on Sundays but three times a day on weekdays, at special hours on holidays and anniversaries, for fires and emergencies, whenever a member of the congregation died, and whenever there was especially good news or especially bad news to announce. Sometimes at a moment's notice word would come that the bells were to be rung, and off Paul would run, his hat clapped to his head, his coattails flying....

Paul had to find new ways to make money. So he engraved portraits, produced bookplates, sold pictures, made picture frames, brought out hymnbooks, and became a dentist. "Artificial Teeth. Paul Revere," he advertised. "He fixes them in such a Manner that they are not only an Ornament, but of real Use in Speaking and Eating."

You would think that with all Paul Revere did, he would make mistakes. But he always remembered to put spouts on his teapots and handles on his cups.

The false teeth that he whittled out of hippopotamus tusk looked just fine.

Generally when he did arithmetic in his Day Book, he got the right answers.

Of course, sometimes there were so many different things to do that he forgot what he was doing. In the beginning of a new Day Book, he wrote, "This is my book for me to—," but he never finished the sentence.

Narration Exercise

From *And Then What Happened, Paul Revere?* by Jean Fritz

Name _____

Date _____

Dictation Exercise

From *The Many Rides of Paul Revere*
by James Cross Giblin

This selection is from another biography, The Many Rides of Paul Revere *by James Cross Giblin. Paul Revere and other American colonists were angry because the British government had declared that only one British company, the East India Company, could sell tea in America, and all the money from selling tea would go directly to British merchants. No American merchant could sell tea. A group of colonists who called themselves the Sons of Liberty led the protests against the new British laws.*

Ships filled with cargoes of tea were already sailing toward American ports. The first to arrive in Boston was the *Dartmouth*. The Sons warned its owner not to unload the vessel "on his peril." Twenty-five members of the Sons, armed with muskets and bayonets, stood guard that night to make sure the owner obeyed the warning. Among them was Paul Revere.

The next day, the Sons decided that nearby seaports should be alerted that British tea ships might try to unload at their docks. In a time before the telegraph and telephone had been invented, the only means of speedy communication was a rider on a fast horse. So the Sons assigned five horsemen, including Paul, to carry their urgent message.

Paul must have been an excellent rider for this would be only the first of many rides he would make on behalf of the Revolution. We don't know where he was headed on that December day, or how long it took him to ride there and back. But he must have had to fight weariness all the way, since he'd had no sleep the night before.

In Boston, meanwhile, two more teaships joined the *Dartmouth* at Griffin's Wharf....

That night more than a hundred men, most of them Sons of Liberty, gathered at the wharf where the three tea ships were docked. The men wore ragged clothes and had darkened their faces with soot or lamp black so they would not be recognized. As part of their disguise, many of the men carried tomahawks like those used by Native Americans.

Hundreds of other Bostonians watched from the wharf as the men boarded the first of the ships. After getting the key to the hold, the men hauled the tea chests up onto the deck, broke them open, and hurled them into the water. Once all the tea from the first ship had been disposed of, the men moved on to the other ships and repeated the process. No one tried to stop them. By the time the men had finished, Boston Harbor was awash with tea.

Narration/Dictation Exercise

From *The Many Rides of Paul Revere* by James Cross Giblin

Name _____

Dictation Exercise

From *Homer Price*
by Robert McCloskey

This story happens about seventy years ago. Homer Price lives in the little town of Centerburg. He is going with his friend Freddy and Freddy's little brother Louis to see a movie about their favorite comic-book character, the Super-Duper. They have just heard that the Super-Duper himself is going to be there! Because this story happens a long time ago, Homer and his friends drive to the movie theater in a wagon pulled by their old horse Lucy. In those days, only rich people owned cars!

The Super-Duper's super-stream-lined car was standing in front of the theater. It was long and red, with chromium trimmings, and it had the Super-Duper's monogram on the side. After they had admired the car, they bought three tickets and went inside. There in the lobby was the *real honest-to-goodness* Super-Duper. He shook hands with Freddy and Homer and little brother Louis, and he autographed a card for Freddy, too.

"Mr. Super-Duper, would you please do a little flying through space for us, or mebbe just bend a few horse shoes?" asked Freddy.

"I'm sorry, boys, but I haven't time today," said the Super-Duper with a smile.

So Homer and Freddy and little Louis found three good seats, and ate doughnuts until the picture began.

The picture was called "THE SUPER-DUPER and the ELECTRIC RAY." That was because the villain had a machine that produced an electric ray, and every time he shined it on a skyscraper, or an airplane, the skyscraper or the airplane would explode! He turned the ray on Super-Duper too, but of course the Super-Duper was so tough that it didn't hurt *him.*

Little Louis got so excited, though, that he choked on a doughnut and Homer had to take him to the lobby for a drink of water. But finally the Super-Duper broke the villain's headquarters to bits, and lifted the ray-machine (which must have weighed several tons) and tossed it over a cliff. *Then,* he caught the villain and rescued the pretty girl. But at the very end, the villain stepped away again, and then these words appeared on the screen: "NEXT INSTALLMENT NEXT SATURDAY AFTERNOON!"

"Why did the Super-Duper let the villain get away again?" asked little Louis on the way out.

"I guess that's because he wants to chase him again next Saturday," said Homer.

Outside they admired the Super-Duper's car once more and then started home in the wagon.

It was evening by the time old Lucy, pulling the wagon with Freddy and little Louis and Homer on it, had reached the curve in the road just before you come to Homer's father's filling station.

A car honked from behind and Freddy pulled old Lucy over to the edge of the road. Then, "SWOOSH!" around from the rear sped a long red car with chromium trimmings.

"Gosh! it's the Super-Duper!" said Freddy.

"Well, he shouldn't drive so fast around this curve," said Homer, sort of doubtful like.

Almost before Homer had finished speaking there was a loud screech of brakes, and then a loud crash!

Narration Exercise

From *Homer Price* by Robert McCloskey

Date _____

Name _____

Dictation Exercise

From *Homer Price*
by Robert McCloskey

This selection continues the story you read last time.

Then Homer and Freddy and little Louis got out of the wagon and crept along the side of the road.

There, around the curve, was the Super-Duper's car, down in a ditch. All three boys stopped crawling along and lay down on their stomachs to watch.

"Oh, boy," whispered Freddy. "Now we'll get to see the Super-Duper lift it back on the road with one hand!"

There was a flash of light and little Louis cried, "Is that the electric ray?"

"It's only the headlights of a car," said Homer. "Come on, let's go a little closer."

They crept a little closer. They could see the Super-Duper now, sitting there in the twilight with his head in his hands.

"I wonder if he got hurt?" asked Homer.

"Naaw!" whispered Freddy. "Nothing can hurt the Super-Duper because he's too tough."

"Well, if he isn't hurt, why doesn't he lift the car back on the road?" asked Homer.

"Sh-h-h!" said Freddy, "he's an awful modest fellow." So they waited and watched from the bushes.

The Super-Duper sighed a couple of times, and then he got up and started walking around his car.

"Now watch!" said Freddy in a loud whisper. "Oh, boy! Oh, boy!" The Super-Duper didn't lift the car, no, not yet. He looked at the dent that a fence post had made in his shiny red fender, and *then,* the incredible happened. That colossal-osal, gigantic-antic, Super-Duper, that same Super-Duper who defied the elements, who was so strong that he broke up battleships like toothpicks, who was so tough that cannon-balls bounced off his chest, yes, who was *tougher* than steel, he stooped down and said..."Ouch!" Yes, there could be no mistake, he said it again, louder..."OUCH!"

The great Super-Duper had gotten himself caught on a barbed-wire fence!

"Well...well, for crying out loud!" said Freddy.

"What happened?" asked little Louis. "Did he get himself rayed by the villain?"

"Come on, Freddy, let's go and untangle him," said Homer. Then Freddy and little Louis and Homer unsnagged the Super-Duper and he sighed again and said,

"Thank you boys. Do you know if there's a garage near here? It looks as though it will take a wrecking car to get my car out of this ditch."

"Sure, my father has a garage down at the crossing," said Homer.

"And we have a horse right up there on the road. We can pull your car out of the ditch!" said Freddy.

"Well, now, isn't that lucky!" said the Super-Duper with a smile.

So they hitched old Lucy to the car and she pulled and everybody pushed until the car was back on the road.

Narration/Dictation Exercise

From *Homer Price* by Robert McCloskey

Date _____

Name _____

Dictation Exercise

"Jabberwocky"
from *Through the Looking Glass*
by Lewis Carroll

This poem is full of made-up words that Lewis Carroll invented just for this poem—like brillig, toves, mimsy, *and* borogoves. *Don't worry about whether or not you're pronouncing the invented words properly, as long as they sound good to you. Don't worry about the blanks and letters to the right of the poem; you will discuss these with your instructor after you read.*

'Twas brillig, and the slithy toves   A
    Did gyre and gimble in the wabe: B
All mimsy were the borogoves,   A
    And the mome raths outgrabe.   B

"Beware the Jabberwock, my son!   _____
    The jaws that bite, the claws that catch!   _____
Beware the Jubjub bird, and shun   _____
    The frumious Bandersnatch!"   _____

He took his vorpal sword in hand: A
    Long time the manxome foe he sought—   B
So rested he by the Tumtum tree,   C
    And stood awhile in thought.   B

And, as in uffish thought he stood,   _____
    The Jabberwock, with eyes of flame,   _____
Came whiffling through the tulgey wood,   _____
    And burbled as it came!   _____

One, two! One, two! And through and through _____
    The vorpal blade went snicker-snack!   _____
He left it dead, and with its head   _____
    He went galumphing back.   _____

"And, has thou slain the Jabberwock?   _____
    Come to my arms, my beamish boy!   _____
O frabjous day! Callooh! Callay!"   _____
    He chortled in his joy.   _____

'Twas brillig, and the slithy toves   _____
   Did gyre and gimble in the wabe;   _____
All mimsy were the borogoves,   _____
   And the mome raths outgrabe.   _____

Quatrain   A set of four lines that belong together
Rhyme scheme   The pattern of rhyming words within each quatrain

Syllable   Part of a word containing one vowel sound
Stress   Where you emphasize a word with your voice
Foot   A certain number of syllables that always fall into the
                  same pattern of stresses

One, **two!** One, **two!** And **through** and **through**
   The **vor**pal **blade** went **snick**er-**snack**!
He **left** it **dead**, and **with** its **head**
   He **went** ga**lumph**ing **back.**

Meter   The rhythm of a poem

Date ____________________

Name ____

Week 5
Day Two

Dictation Exercise

"Stegosaurus"
by Jack Prelutsky

This poem is from Jack Prelutsky's book Tyrannosaurus Was a Beast. *You will use the blanks at the ends of the lines later in this lesson.*

Stegosaurus was a creature uncontentious and benign,   _____

and the row of armored plates upon its back   _____

failed to guard its tender belly or protect its flimsy spine— _____

Stegosaurus often wound up as a snack.   _____

Stegosaurus blundered calmly through the prehistoric scene,   _____

never causing any other creature woe,   _____

its brain was somewhat smaller than the average nectarine—   _____

Stegosaurus vanished many years ago.   _____

1. _____

Stegosaur**us** **blund**ered **calm**ly **through** the **pre**his**tor**ic **scene,**
never **caus**ing **an**y **oth**er **crea**ture **woe.**

2.   unstress **stress**   _____

3.   **stress** unstress   trochaic

Name _____

Dictation Exercise

From *Time Cat*
by Lloyd Alexander

In Time Cat, *a boy named Jason discovers that his black cat, Gareth, can travel back in time—and can take Jason with him. The first time the two travel in time together, they end up back in ancient Egypt. They meet the Chief Scribe of the Pharaoh, who offers to take them to the royal residence, the Great House, to meet the king of the Egyptians. But Jason doesn't realize that the Chief Scribe intends to take Gareth for the Pharaoh. In this story, Jason and Gareth have just finished travelling by boat to the Great House.*

At last, the oarsmen docked at the riverbank. The Great House, Jason realized, was a whole city in itself, with bakers, carpenters, brickmakers, weavers. Holding Gareth tightly, Jason followed the Chief Scribe to the biggest building of all. They stopped in one hall filled with nothing but men marking on clay tablets. Here, messengers never ceased hurrying in and shouting commands from King Neter-Khet.

In the space of a few minutes, from what Jason could hear, Neter-Khet had declared five wars, signed three peace treaties, and ordered eight thousand stonemasons to begin a new pyramid. There was also a constant procession of slaves dragging in goods of all kinds. The scribes made a great ceremony of scratching down their tallies. The Egyptians, Jason decided, loved to count things. Nobody, so far as he saw, could do anything without mentioning quantities, writing them down, comparing, adding, and marveling at the totals.

The Chief Scribe approached one of the clerks. "In the records of the Great House make this notation: this day, to the possessions of Pharaoh—life, health, strength—there shall be added forty thousand bushels of grain, seventy thousand jars of oil, three thousand ounces of gold, and one black cat."

"So it was spoken," said the clerk, "so it is written!"

"Oh no it won't!" Jason cried. "My cat isn't one of Pharaoh's possessions!"

"It would seem," said the Chief Scribe, with a cold smile, "that he is now."

Before Jason could turn and race from the hall, the Chief Scribe scooped the bristling, spitting Gareth from his arms. Jason himself was seized from behind, hustled down a corridor, and most unceremoniously shoved into a tiny room.

The heavy stone door swung shut behind him. Jason beat at it with his fists. He had never trusted the oily words of the Chief Scribe. How, Jason thought furiously, had he let himself be tricked so easily? He threw himself against the unyielding door; then, exhausted, dropped to the ground. Now Gareth was gone. Jason would spend the rest of his life in a stone cell in Neter-Khet's palace. The boy hid his face in his hands and his shoulders shook with sobbing. At least, he consoled himself, the Egyptians loved cats and Gareth would be well looked after.

To Jason's surprise, a little while later the door opened and a Sub-minor Scribe peered in. Jason scrambled to his feet. Behind the Sub-minor Scribe were two guards, who took him by the arms and marched him from the cell down one hall of columns after the other, until Jason lost track of them all. In a huge room at the end of one corridor, on a platform topped by a carved and decorated throne, sat King Neter-Khet.

Beside the King stood slaves with fly whisks and feathered fans on jeweled poles, musicians with trumpets and cymbals, and the Chief Scribe himself, looking sour. In front of the throne sat Gareth.

Name _____

From *Time Cat* by Lloyd Alexander

Name _____

Date _____

Dictation Exercise

From *Time Cat*

by Lloyd Alexander

Jason soon finds out that King Neter-Khet has sent for him because the king has a problem. He likes the cat, Gareth, but he can't get Gareth to do anything he says. He wants Jason to make Gareth obey the royal orders.

"I COMMAND THIS CAT TO PLAY AND ENTERTAIN PHARAOH!" shouted King Neter-Khet at the top of his voice.

The musicians clashed their cymbals. The slaves cried "Life! Health! Strength!" and the fly-whisker whisked as fast as he could.

Gareth did not move.

"Well, go ahead, boy!" hissed the Chief Scribe. "Make the cat be entertaining!"

Jason hesitated, then knelt on the floor beside Gareth. One of the slaves tossed down a toy, a bejeweled mouse on a golden chain. Jason pulled it back and forth in front of the cat, but he could tell from the set of Gareth's ears and whiskers that he was in no mood for games.

Jason dropped the toy and shook his head. "He doesn't want to," he said. "I'm afraid there isn't anything I can do."

Neter-Khet looked angrier than ever.

"I COMMAND THIS CAT TO PURR AND MAKE HIMSELF AGREEABLE TO PHARAOH!" he shouted.

Once again there was a clashing of cymbals and cries of "Life! Health! Strength!"

The Chief Scribe took out a clay tablet. "So it is ordered," he said, "so it is written, and so it shall be done!"

Gareth still did not move. Jason shrugged hopelessly, then picked up Gareth and put him on Neter-Khet's lap. The King began stroking him, but Gareth put down his ears and squinted his eyes. He wriggled out of Pharaoh's arms and leaped to the floor.

"Aiee!" Neter-Khet put his thumb to his mouth. One of Gareth's claws had accidentally scratched the King, and Pharaoh's braided beard shook with rage.

"I'm sorry," Jason said. "He doesn't feel like playing or being agreeable right now. It's nothing personal," he added quickly, "it's the way cats are."

"It's obvious," said the Chief Scribe, "the boy is useless."

"Return the cat to Bubastis," ordered Neter-Khet. "He does not please me. Continue your search."

"And the boy?" asked the Scribe. "The sacred crocodiles are always hungry," he suggested cheerfully.

Neter-Khet closed his eyes and nodded.

"So it is ordered," said the Chief Scribe, making another note on his tablet, "so it shall be done."

Narration/Dictation Exercise

From *Time Cat* by Lloyd Alexander

Dictation Exercise

From *The Story of the World, Volume 1: Ancient Times*
by Susan Wise Bauer

This excerpt describes one of the great accomplishments of Qin Zheng, a warrior who conquered the battling states of China and made them into one country. These battling states were known as "The Warring States" before Qin Zheng unified them. The word "China" comes from the word "Qin."

When Qin Zheng became the emperor of all China in 221 BC/BCE, he changed his name. From now on, he would be known as "Shi Huangdi." In Chinese, this name means "First Emperor." Qin Zheng, now called Shi Huangdi, wanted his subjects to remember his power every time they spoke his name.

One day Shi Huangdi sat on his throne, thinking about his new empire. He had been careful to stamp out rebellion inside his borders. All of his enemies lived near his palace, and Shi Huangdi had sent his soldiers to guard them and to report on all their activities. He had burned the books that might encourage his people to rebel. He was safe from revolt.

But his kingdom wasn't secure yet. Outside the borders of China, ferocious tribes roved through the wild mountains and plains of the north. For years, these northern barbarians had attacked the Warring States, trying to take over their land. They were the earliest of the tribes which were later called Mongols.

The Mongols rode swift horses and shot arrows with deadly precision. So some of the Warring States had built walls to keep the Mongols out. These walls were still standing, but parts of them had crumbled away into dust. And between the walls were huge gaps.

"The Mongols could come through those gaps at any time," Shi Huangdi thought. "They could sweep down and take over parts of my empire. How can I protect China from the Mongols? If only I could build a wall along the whole northern side of my empire!"

Then Shi Huangdi had an idea: a stupendous, incredible idea. "Perhaps I *can* build a wall along China's northern border," he exclaimed. "A wall thousands of miles long! A *Great* Wall!"

So Shi Huangdi summoned his architects and builders. "All along the northern part of my empire," he told them, "old walls are falling down. I want to repair these walls. And then I want to build a new wall, connecting all the old walls together into one huge barrier that will keep the Mongols out of my kingdom."

"But, Emperor," the architects and builders protested, "there is not enough stone in the far reaches of your kingdom to build a Great Wall!"

"Then think of another way to do it," Shi Huangdi ordered.

The builders and architects labored for weeks trying to think of a way to build the wall in places where stone was scarce. Finally, they discovered a way. The builders made a wooden frame, as high as a man's waist and as wide as a wall. They set this frame upon the ground and filled it with loose dirt. Then workers stamped and packed the earth until it was only four inches high and as hard as concrete. They lifted the frame up, set it on top of the packed dirt, and filled it again. They could build a dirt wall as hard as stone, four inches at a time!

Narration Exercise

From *The Story of the World, Volume 1: Ancient Times* by Susan Wise Bauer

Name _____

Date _____

Dictation Exercise

From *The Story of the World, Volume 2: The Middle Ages*
by Susan Wise Bauer

This excerpt, from the second volume of The Story of the World, *describes the Mongols more than a thousand years after the building of the Great Wall.*

The Mongols came from the wild, cold mountains north of China. They lived in felt tents which they took down each morning, leaving nothing but the ashes from their campfires behind. They were nomads who swept over the countryside, conquering and killing. The bone-chilling cold of the north didn't stop them; they wore furs and leather and rubbed their skin with grease to keep the wind away. They never settled down and grew crops; instead they ate foxes, rabbits, and other small wild creatures. But they could go without food for days at a time. If they were in danger of starving, they would open the veins of their horses, drink some blood, and then close the vein and ride on.

The Mongol tribes raided Chinese villages on the northern edge of China. They killed merchants and stole their goods. But they never tried to invade China itself—until Genghis Khan became their leader.

Genghis Khan was born around 1167, into a small Mongol tribe called the Yakka. His father was the Yakka chieftain, or *khan*. But the Yakka was only one of many Mongol clans. And the Mongols fought with each other as often as they fought with the Chinese.

Genghis Khan had a better idea. He thought that the Mongols should all join together and attack China. Just on the other side of the Great Wall lay the rich Chinese city of Beijing, where people lived in warm houses, heated by fires, with soft beds, plenty of food, and bags of gold. Genghis Khan wanted to conquer this rich city.

But first he had to convince all the Mongol tribes to follow him. When his father died, Genghis became leader of the Yakka. He set out at once to conquer the other Mongol clans as well. He fought savagely against them, forcing their leaders to swear allegiance to him. He promised, "Anyone who doesn't follow me will be killed. I will flatten his tent far into the ground, so that a horse galloping across it at midnight won't even stumble. The greatest joy in my life is to kill my rivals and steal their possessions!"

Would *you* surrender to a man who talked like that? Most of the Mongols did. And those who didn't were killed. After Genghis Khan killed one rival leader, he moved his tent to cover the body. Then he ordered his servants to remove the body through the tent's smoke hole, late at night, while everyone was watching the front of the tent. In the morning he announced that the gods had killed his rival and spirited the body away as punishment for defying Genghis Khan. After that, *everyone* followed Genghis.

Now it was time for Genghis Khan to lead the unified Mongols against China. They swarmed down out of the north, destroying every city they came across, leveling every building to the ground. They broke through the Great Wall, into China. And while King John was signing the Magna Carta over in England, Genghis Khan was conquering the city of Beijing.

Narration/Dictation Exercise

From *The Story of the World, Volume 2: The Middle Ages* by Susan Wise Bauer

Date _____

Name _____

Dictation Exercise

From *The Lion, the Witch and the Wardrobe*
by C. S. Lewis

Four children—Peter, Susan, Edmund, and Lucy—have been sent away from London during World War II to stay in the country, which is safer for them. The house where they stay is huge and mysterious. During a game of hide and seek, Lucy (who is the youngest) decides to hide in a wardrobe—a big closet made of wood.

You may not know what a moth-ball is. It is a small hard ball made of chemicals that moths dislike, and moth-balls put in with clothing will keep moths from eating holes in the fabric or fur. In Lucy's day, moth-balls were made from a very smelly chemical called naphthalene.

Looking into the inside, she saw several coats hanging up—mostly long fur coats. There was nothing Lucy liked so much as the smell and feel of fur. She immediately stepped into the wardrobe and got in among the coats and rubbed her face against them, leaving the door open, of course, because she knew that it is very foolish to shut oneself into any wardrobe. Soon she went further in and found that there was a second row of coats hanging up behind the first one. It was almost quite dark in there and she kept her arms stretched out in front of her so as not to bump her face into the back of the wardrobe. She took a step further in—then two or three steps—always expecting to feel woodwork against the tips of her fingers. But she could not feel it.

"This must be a simply enormous wardrobe!" thought Lucy, going still further in and pushing the soft folds of the coats aside to make room for her. Then she noticed that there was something crunching under her feet. "I wonder is that more moth-balls?" she thought, stooping down to feel it with her hands. But instead of feeling the hard, smooth wood of the floor of the wardrobe, she felt something soft and powdery and extremely cold. "This is very queer," she said, and went on a step or two further.

Next moment she found that what was rubbing against her face and hands was no longer soft fur but something hard and rough and even prickly. "Why, it is just like branches of trees!" exclaimed Lucy. And then she saw that there was a light ahead of her; not a few inches away where the back of the wardrobe ought to have been, but a long way off. Something cold and soft was falling on her. A moment later she found that she was standing in the middle of a wood at night-time with snow under her feet and snowflakes falling through the air.

Lucy felt a little frightened, but she felt very inquisitive and excited as well. She looked back over her shoulder and there, between the dark tree-trunks, she could still see the open doorway of the wardrobe and even catch a glimpse of the empty room from which she had set out. (She had, of course, left the door open, for she knew that it is a very silly thing to shut oneself into a wardrobe.) It seemed to be still daylight there. "I can always get back if anything goes wrong," thought Lucy. She began to walk forward, *crunch-crunch*, over the snow and through the wood towards the other light.

Narration Exercise

From *The Lion, the Witch and the Wardrobe* by C. S. Lewis

Date _____

Name _____

Dictation Exercise

From *The Lion, the Witch and the Wardrobe*
by C. S. Lewis

All four of the children have now gone through the wardrobe into the country Lucy has discovered: Narnia. There they meet two beavers who take them home to dinner. The oldest brother, Peter, and Mr. Beaver go fishing in the river, while the others help Mrs. Beaver get the rest of the meal ready.

"Gum boots" are rubber boots, and "oilskins" are like raincoats. A "marmalade roll" is a sweet cake with a jam filling.

Meanwhile the girls were helping Mrs. Beaver to fill the kettle and lay the table and cut the bread and put the plates in the oven to heat and draw a huge jug of beer for Mr. Beaver from a barrel which stood in one corner of the house, and to put on the frying pan and get the dripping hot. Lucy thought the Beavers had a very snug little home though it was not at all like Mr. Tumnus's cave. There were no books or pictures and instead of beds there were bunks, like on board ship, built into the wall. And there were hams and strings of onions hanging from the roof and against the walls were gum boots and oilskins and hatchets and pairs of shears and spades and trowels and things for carrying mortar in and fishing rods and fishing nets and sacks. And the cloth on the table tho' very clean was very rough.

Just as the frying pan was nicely hissing Peter and Mr. Beaver came in with the fish which Mr. Beaver had already opened with his knife and cleaned out in the open air. You can think how good the new-caught fish smelled while they were frying and how the hungry children longed for them to be done and how very much hungrier still they had become before Mrs. Beaver said, "Now we're nearly ready." Susan drained the potatoes and then put them all back in the empty pot to dry on the side of the range while Lucy was helping Mrs. Beaver to dish up the trout, so that in a very few minutes everyone was drawing up stools (it was all three-legged stools in the Beavers' house except for Mrs. Beaver's own special rocking chair beside the fire) and preparing to enjoy themselves. There was a jug of creamy milk for the children (Mr. Beaver stuck to beer) and a great big lump of deep yellow butter in the middle of the table from which everyone took as much as he wanted to go with his potatoes and all the children thought—and I agree with them—that there's nothing to beat good freshwater fish if you eat it when it has been alive half an hour ago and has come out of the pan half a minute ago. And when they had finished the fish Mrs. Beaver brought unexpectedly out of the oven a great and gloriously sticky marmalade roll, steaming hot, and at the same time moved the kettle on to the fire, so that when they had finished the marmalade roll the tea was made and ready to be poured out. And when each person had got his (or her) cup of tea, each person shoved back his (or her) stool so as to be able to lean against the wall and gave a long sigh of contentment.

Narration/Dictation Exercise

From *The Lion, the Witch and the Wardrobe* by C. S. Lewis

Name _____

Date _____

Dictation Exercise

From *C. S. Lewis: The Man Behind Narnia*
by Beatrice Gormley

At the beginning of The Lion, the Witch and the Wardrobe, *the four children are sent away from London because the city is being bombed.* The Lion, the Witch and the Wardrobe *takes place during World War II. The author of the book, C. S. Lewis, knew what life during wartime was like. When he was a young man, he fought in World War I.*

This selection is from the biography C. S. Lewis: The Man Behind Narnia, *by Beatrice Gormley. (A biography is the true story of a real person's life.) In the biography, C. S. Lewis is called "Jack"—the name Lewis's friends and family used for him.*

When C. S. Lewis became a soldier, he was first sent to a training school called "officers' training corps." The "trenches" were deep, long ditches soldiers dug on the front lines of the battle. Soldiers stayed down inside the trenches for much of the fighting, since the trenches protected them from bullets fired by the other side. A "latrine" is an outhouse. (There were no warm comfortable bathrooms on the front lines of World War I!)

If you are not familiar with "enlisting" or "the draft," you should know that enlisting means joining the military, and that sometimes during wars governments required every healthy young man to join the military whether he wanted to or not. This was called "the draft." To be "exempt" from the draft meant that you would not be drafted, even if you were the right age.

While you are reading, you will see words inside brackets, like this: []. These show that extra words have been put into the original text to help you understand it better.

Since England was at war, every man over the age of eighteen was required to enlist for military service. Jack could have applied for an exemption from the draft, because his home residence was Ireland rather than England. To his father's distress, Jack refused to take the exemption. He was not at all enthusiastic about the war, but he felt it would be dishonorable not to serve.

During his spare time in the officers' training corps, perhaps spurred on by knowing that he might be killed in the war, Jack worked hard on a collection of poems. He intended to send it to a publisher.

On November 15 [1917], Jack heard alarming news: his battalion was ordered to the front lines of the war in France. They were given only two days' leave, not enough time for Jack to go home to Belfast and say goodbye....By November 29, his nineteenth birthday, Jack was in the trenches.

From there Jack wrote his father reassuring letters like this one:

This is a very quiet part of the line and the dug outs are much more comfortable than one imagines at home. They are very deep, you go down to them by a shaft of about twenty steps; they have wire bunks where a man can sleep quite snugly and brasiers [pans for holding burning coals] for warmth and cooking. Indeed, the chief discomfort is that they tend to get TOO hot, while the bad air makes one rather headachy. I had quite a pleasant time, and was only once in a situation of unusual danger, owing to a shell falling near the latrines while I was using them....

In his autobiography, Jack would describe a soldier's life on the front lines more vividly: "Through the winter, weariness and water were our chief enemies. I have gone to sleep marching and woken again and found myself marching still. One walked in the trenches in thigh gum boots with water above the knee; one remembers the icy stream welling up inside the boot when you punctured it on concealed barbed wire."

....On April 15, during the Battle of Arras in northern France, Second Lieutenant C. S. Lewis was wounded by an exploding artillery shell that killed his sergeant. Jack was taken to a mobile hospital in Etaples, on the coast of Normandy. There it was discovered that one of his wounds, caused by a piece of shrapnel lodged in his chest, was bad enough to put him out of combat permanently.

C. S. Lewis recovered from his wounds and went back to England, and back to his life as a reader and writer. The war ended in November 1918, a year after Lewis first went to fight in France.

Narration Exercise

From *C. S. Lewis: The Man Behind Narnia* by Beatrice Gormley

Name _____

Dictation Exercise

From *Everyday Life: World War I*
by Walter A. Hazen

World War I, which took place when C. S. Lewis was a young man, began in 1914. Germany and its friends were known as the Central Powers; they were fighting against Great Britain, Russia, and France, who were called the Allies. The Germans were planning on invading France, and the Russians were planning on invading Germany. The French and British were afraid that the war would last a long time.

The selection below tells how differently the Germans and Russians felt.

"Kaiser" is the title that the Germans used for their king; "czar" is the Russian word for king. The Boulevard is a street in the French city of Paris.

Most wars begin amid much excitement and expectations of quick victory, and World War I was no exception. Every nation expected its warriors to be home safely by the onset of winter. This was especially true in Germany. The confident Germans gave the war no more than four months. Kaiser Wilhelm II told his departing troops that they would be home "before the leaves had fallen from the trees." One German officer went further, telling friends that he fully expected to be eating breakfast at one of Paris's more elegant cafes within a matter of weeks.

Departing German soldiers held similar views, scribbling boastful messages, such as "On to Paris" and "See you again on the Boulevard," on the sides of their transport trains as they departed for battle. They hung out the windows of the cars, waving and shouting as their trains pulled out of stations throughout Germany.

Not to be outdone, German civilians also got into the act. One famous picture of the time shows a young woman marching alongside the troops as they departed for the front. The same picture shows a man who had discarded his straw hat for a German soldier's helmet and marched along with the soldier's rifle on his shoulder.

Similar scenes took place throughout Europe. Huge crowds gathered in European capitals and cheered, sang, and danced. Young men rushed to recruitment offices to enlist. Some actually worried that the fighting would be over before they had a chance to fight. Others saw the war as an opportunity to escape from routine jobs. Few seemed to realize the horrors they would soon face.

Nowhere were expectations of success higher than in Russia. Russians were convinced that they would win and argued only about how long it would take. Most said two or three months, and anyone who suggested six months was thought to be an extreme pessimist. One Imperial Guard officer asked the czar's private physician if he should go ahead and pack his full-dress uniform so he would have it for the Russians' triumphal entry into Berlin [in Germany]. How's that for confidence?

Narration/Dictation Exercise

From *Everyday Life: World War I* by Walter A. Hazen

Name _____

Date _____

Dictation Exercise

From *Farmer Boy*
by Laura Ingalls Wilder

Farmer Boy tells the story of a young boy named Almanzo Wilder who lives on a farm in upstate New York in 1866. Almanzo is eight years old, and after school every day he has farm chores to do in the family's three big barns.

You may have read the book Little House in the Big Woods, *which tells about Laura Ingalls Wilder's childhood. When Laura grew up, she married Almanzo Wilder.*

When Almanzo went into these great barns, he always went through into the Horse-Barn's little door. He loved horses. There they stood in their roomy box-stalls, clean and sleek and gleaming brown, with long black manes and tails. The wise, sedate work-horses placidly munched hay. The three-year-olds put their noses together across the bars; they seemed to whisper together. Then softly their nostrils whooshed along one another's necks; one pretended to bite, and they squealed and whirled and kicked in play. The old horses turned their heads and looked like grandmothers at the young ones. But the colts ran about excited, on their gangling legs, and stared and wondered.

They all knew Almanzo. Their ears pricked up and their eyes shone softly when they saw him. The three-year-olds came eagerly and thrust their heads out to nuzzle at him. Their noses, prickled with a few stiff hairs, were soft as velvet, and on their foreheads the short, fine hair was silky smooth. Their necks arched proudly, firm and round, and the black manes fell over them like a heavy fringe. You could run your hand along those firm, curved necks, in the warmth under the mane.

But Almanzo hardly dared to do it. He was not allowed to touch the beautiful three-year-olds. He could not go into their stalls, not even to clean them. He was only eight years old, and Father would not let him handle the young horses or the colts. Father didn't trust him yet, because colts and young, unbroken horses are very easily spoiled.

A boy who didn't know any better might scare a young horse, or tease it, or even strike it, and that would ruin it. It would learn to bite and kick and hate people, and then it would never be a good horse.

Almanzo did know better; he wouldn't ever scare or hurt one of those beautiful colts. He would always be quiet, and gentle, and patient; he wouldn't startle a colt, or shout at it, not even if it stepped on his foot. But Father wouldn't believe this.

So Almanzo could only look longingly at the eager three-year-olds. He just touched their velvety noses, and then he went quickly away from them, and put his barn frock over his good school-clothes.

Father had already watered all the stock, and he was beginning to give them their grain. Royal and Almanzo took pitchforks and went from stall to stall, cleaning out the soiled hay underfoot, and spreading fresh hay from the mangers to make clean beds for the cows and the oxen and the calves and the sheep.

They did not have to make beds for the hogs, because hogs make their own beds and keep them clean.

In the South Barn, Almanzo's own two little calves were in one stall. They came crowding each other at the bars when they saw him. Both calves were red, and one had a white spot on his forehead. Almanzo had named him Star. The other was a bright red all over, and Almanzo called him Bright.

Star and Bright were young calves, not yet a year old. Their little horns had only begun to grow hard in the soft hair by their ears. Almanzo scratched around the little horns, because calves like that. They pushed their moist blunt noses between the bars and licked with their rough tongues.

Narration Exercise

From *Farmer Boy* by Laura Ingalls Wilder

Date _____

Name _____

Dictation Exercise

From *Farmer Boy*
by Laura Ingalls Wilder

After chores, Almanzo and his brother Royal go into the house, where their mother and their sisters, Eliza Jane and Alice, have been getting dinner on the table. The schoolmaster, Mr. Corse, has come to dinner with the family.

You may not be familiar with some of the foods. "Headcheese" was made by cleaning the animal's head and boiling it until all of the remaining meat fell off. The bones were then taken out, and the liquid and bits of meat were poured into molds. This cooled and solidified, like Jello, because of the natural gelatin in the animal's meat and bones. Slices could then be cut off of it.

This may sound disgusting to you, but people have eaten headcheese since the Middle Ages. In fact, Susan (the author of this book) ate headcheese when she was little; her grandmother, who was a very traditional cook, made it on hog-killing days.

There were slabs of tempting cheese, there was a plate of quivering headcheese; there were glass dishes of jams and jellies and preserves, and a tall pitcher of milk, and a steaming pan of baked beans with a crisp bit of fat pork in the crumbling brown crust.

Almanzo looked at them all, and something twisted in his middle. He swallowed, and went slowly away.

The dining-room was pretty. There were green stripes and rows of tiny red flowers on the chocolate-brown wall-paper, and Mother had woven the rag-carpet to match. She had dyed the rags green and chocolate-brown, and woven them in stripes, with a tiny stripe of red and white rags twisted together between them. The tall corner cupboards were full of fascinating things—sea-shells, and petrified wood, and curious rocks, and books. And over the center-table hung an air-castle. Alice had made it of clean yellow wheat-straws, set together airily, with bits of bright-colored cloth at the corners. It swayed and quivered in the slightest breath of air, and the lamplight ran gleaming along the golden straws.

But to Almanzo the most beautiful sight was his mother, bringing in the big willow-ware platter full of sizzling ham.

Mother was short and plump and pretty. Her eyes were blue, and her brown hair was like a bird's smooth wings. A row of little red buttons ran down from the front of her dress of wine-colored wool, from her flat white linen collar to the white apron tied round her waist. Her big sleeves hung like large red bells at either end of the blue platter. She came through the doorway with a little pause and a tug, because her hoop-skirts were wider than the door.

The smell of ham was almost more than Almanzo could bear.

Mother set the platter on the table. She looked to see that everything was ready, and the table properly set. She took off her apron and hung it in the kitchen. She waited until Father had finished what he was saying to Mr. Corse. But at last she said,

"James, supper is ready."

It seemed a long time before they were all in their places. Father sat at the head of the table, Mother at the foot. Then they must all bow their heads while Father asked God to bless the food. After that, there was a little pause before Father unfolded his napkin and tucked it in the neckband of his frock.

He began to fill the plates. First he filled Mr. Corse's plate. Then Mother's. Then Royal's and Eliza Jane's and Alice's. Then, at last, he filled Almanzo's plate.

"Thank you," Almanzo said. Those were the only words he was allowed to speak at table. Children must be seen and not heard. Father and Mother and Mr. Corse could talk, but Royal and Eliza Jane and Alice and Almanzo must not say a word.

Almanzo ate the sweet, mellow baked beans. He ate the bit of salt pork that melted like cream in his mouth. He ate mealy boiled potatoes, with brown ham-gravy. He ate the ham. He bit deep into velvety bread spread with sleek butter, and he ate the crisp golden crust. He demolished a tall heap of pale mashed turnips, and a hill of stewed yellow pumpkin. Then he sighed, and tucked his napkin deeper into the neckband of his red waist. And he ate plum preserves, and strawberry jam, and grape jelly, and spiced watermelon-rind pickles. He felt very comfortable inside. Slowly he ate a large piece of pumpkin pie.

Narration/Dictation Exercise

From *Farmer Boy* by Laura Ingalls Wilder

Date _____

Name _____

Dictation Exercise

From *Tales of Ancient Egypt*
by Roger Lancelyn Green

This passage comes from the Egyptian story "The Treasure Thief." It is about the great Pharaoh Rameses III, who ruled Egypt around 1182–1151 B.C. According to this story, Rameses asked his Master Builder, Hor-em-heb, to built him a pyramid that would keep not only his body, but his treasures, safe. But Hor-em-heb tricked him.

This story was first written down by the Greek historian Herodotus around 425 B.C. An English writer named Roger Lancelyn Green took the Greek story and retold it in his book Tales of Ancient Egypt.

Under the care of the Master Builder the walls of the new building were reared and a pyramid was built over the whole, leaving a great treasure chamber in the middle. In the entrance he set sliding doors of stone, and others of iron and bronze; and when the untold riches of Pharaoh Rameses were placed in the chamber, the doors were locked and each was sealed with Pharaoh's great seal, that none might copy on pain of death....

Yet Hor-em-heb the Master Builder played Pharaoh false. In the thick wall of the Treasure House he made a narrow passage, with a stone at either end turning on a pivot that, when closed, looked and felt like any other part of the smooth, strong wall—except for those who knew where to feel for the hidden spring that held it firmly in place.

By means of this secret entrance Hor-em-heb was able to add to the reward which Pharaoh gave to him when the Treasure House was complete. Yet he did not add much, for very soon a great sickness fell upon him, and presently he died.

But on his death-bed he told his two sons about the secret entrance to the Treasure House; and when he was dead, and they had buried his body with all honour in a rock chamber among the Tombs of the Nobles at Western Thebes, the two young men made such good use of their knowledge that Pharaoh soon realized that his treasure was beginning to grow mysteriously less.

Rameses was at a loss to understand how the thieves got in, for the royal seals were never broken, but get in they certainly did. Pharaoh was fast becoming a miser, and he paid frequent visits to his Treasure House and knew every object of value in it—and the treasure continued to go.

At last Pharaoh commanded that cunning traps and meshes should be set near the chests and vessels from which the treasure was disappearing.

This was done secretly; and when next the two brothers made their way into the Treasure House by the secret entrance to collect more gold and jewels, the first to step across the floor towards the chests was caught in one of the traps and knew at once that he could not escape.

Narration Exercise

From *Tales of Ancient Egypt* by Roger Lancelyn Green

Name _____

Dictation Exercise

From *The Histories*

by Herodotus

trans. by Robin Waterfield

This is Herodotus' version of this same story about the Egyptian king Rameses.
"Depredations" are "acts of robbing or plundering."

He wanted to store his money in a safe place, so he built a stone chamber as
an extension off one of the outside walls of his residence. The builder, however,
came up with the following crafty scheme. He cleverly fitted one of the stones in
such a way that it would easily be removable from its wall by two men or even
one. Anyway, the chamber was finished and the king stored his money in it. Time
passed. At the end of his life, the builder summoned his sons (there were two of
them) and told them of the plan he had put into effect while building the king's
treasure-chamber, so that they would be comfortable for the rest of their lives. He
explained precisely to them how to remove the stone and described its position in
the wall. He told them that if they remembered his instructions, they would be
the stewards of the king's treasury.

He died, and his sons soon set to work. They went by night to the royal
residence and found the stone in the building. It was easy for them to handle, and
they carried off a lot of money. When the king happened to go into the chamber
next, he was surprised to see that the caskets were missing some money, but the
seals on the door were still intact and the chamber had been locked up, so he
could not blame anyone. But the same thing happened the next couple of times
he opened the door as well: his money was obviously dwindling all the time (for
the thieves had not stopped their depredations). So the king had traps made, and
set them around the caskets which held the money. The thieves came as usual and
one of them sneaked into the chamber, but as soon as he approached a casket he
was caught in the trap.

Name _____

Narration/Dictation Exercise

From *The Histories* by Herodotus

Name _____

Dictation Exercise

From "Ali Baba and the Forty Thieves"
by Jacob and Wilhelm Grimm

This story comes from an old collection of fairy tales called The Thousand and One Nights. *This version was retold by Jacob and Wilhelm Grimm.*

Once upon a time, in a distant Persian city lived two brothers called Ali Baba and Kasim. Ali Baba was terribly poor, and he lived with his wife in a mud hut. He picked up sticks in the woods and sold them in bundles at the market.

Kasim, however, had a rich wife, and he lived in a big fine house and sold carpets. He became richer than ever. One day, as Ali Baba was gathering sticks in a wood some way from the city he heard a band of horsemen gallop towards him. Scared that he might be in trouble for stealing wood, he scrambled up a tree and hid amongst the foliage, seconds before the men, armed to the teeth, rode underneath.

They were robbers, no doubt about that. Ali could tell by their evil looks, rough beards and bad language. But what made it perfectly clear to him was the booty they unloaded from their horses, obviously plundered in a raid. Their leader was a grim wicked-looking man. Followed by his men, he strode towards a rocky mountain nearby. Throwing wide his arms, he suddenly shouted, "Open Sesame!"

Ali Baba could hardly believe his eyes. For at the robber's words, the rock face swung open to become the entrance to a deep, dark cave. The robbers trooped inside, dragging their sacks. Ali Baba was struck dumb by this amazing sight, and he crouched in his tree, without moving a muscle. He could hear the robbers' voices echo in the cave, then out they came. Again opening his arms, the leader exclaimed loudly, "Close Sesame!" And the rock swung tightly shut, as they leapt onto their horses and galloped away.

Trembling with fear, Ali Baba climbed down the tree. He had just had the biggest shock of his life. Hardly aware of what he was doing, he muttered, "Open Sesame." But the mountain stood still.

Ali Baba said the words again, but this time he shouted them. Suddenly, the rock began to move. Ali Baba lit a flare and entered the cave. In front of his bulging eyes lay vast piles of treasure: pots of silver and gold, precious vases, weapons studded with rubies and emeralds, diamonds, carved plates and carpets, all heaped together.

The poverty-stricken stick-gatherer rubbed his eyes in disbelief. His hand was shaking like a leaf, as he picked up a gold coin.

"It's real!" he said in awe. Jabbering with excitement and stunned at the sight of such untold wealth, he told himself, "I'll take some coins. Nobody will ever know!" And he filled four bags full.

The second he reached home, Ali Baba locked the door and emptied the sacks in front of his astounded wife. "Count them," he ordered her triumphantly, before telling her what had happened. But there were far too many coins for these poor people to count.

"We can't count them all. Run to my brother's house and ask him for a corn measure. We'll use that," said Ali Baba.

When Kasim's wife heard this strange request, her curiosity was aroused. "I wonder what they want to measure," she thought. "It can't be corn, they're far too poor." And she quickly brushed a touch of tar across the bottom of the measuring pail. And when she got the pail back there was something stuck to it—as the clever woman had known there would be.

It was a gold coin.

Narration Exercise

From "Ali Baba and the Forty Thieves" by the Brothers Grimm

Name _____

Date _____

Dictation Exercise

From "Ali Baba and the Forty Thieves"
by Jacob and Wilhelm Grimm

In this passage, the story of Ali Baba and his brother Kasim continues.

Kasim's wife was immediately filled with envy. "What!" she said. "How did Ali Baba get so much gold that he has to measure it? Where did he get all this wealth?"

Kasim, her husband, was at his shop. When he came home, his wife said to him: "Kasim, I know you think yourself rich, but Ali Baba is infinitely richer than you. He does not even count his money. He measures it." Then she told him how she had discovered Ali Baba's wealth, and showed him the piece of money, which was so old that they could not tell in what prince's reign it was coined.

Instead of being pleased at his brother's good fortune, Kasim became more and more jealous of Ali Baba's prosperity. He could not sleep all that night, and went to him in the morning before sunrise. "Ali Baba," he said, "I am surprised at you. You pretend to be miserably poor, and yet you measure gold. My wife found this at the bottom of the measure you borrowed yesterday."

Ali Baba realized that Kasim and his wife had discovered their secret. Knowing that he could not hide the wealth, he told Kasim all about the cave, and offered his brother part of his treasure to keep the secret.

Kasim rose the next morning long before the sun, and set out for the forest alone, with ten mules bearing ten great chests which he intended to fill. He followed the road which Ali Baba had told him about. It was not long before he reached the rocky mountain. When he reached the entrance of the cavern, he shouted, "Open, Sesame!"

The door immediately opened, and when he was in, closed upon him. He looked around the cave and saw rich bales of silk, embroideries, gold and silver in great heaps, and money in bags. He quickly laid as many bags of gold as he could carry at the door of the cavern; but his thoughts were so full of the great riches he should possess, that he could not think of the word to make it open. Instead of "Open, Sesame!" he said, "Open, Barley!" and was surprised to find that the door remained fast shut.

He named several sorts of grain, but still the door would not open. The more he tried to remember the word "Sesame," the more confused he became. Soon his memory had lost the word altogether, as if he had never heard it mentioned. He threw down the bags he had loaded himself with, and walked up and down the cave in great fear, without even looking at the riches around him.

Narration/Dictation Exercise

From "Ali Baba and the Forty Thieves" by the Brothers Grimm

Name _____

Dictation Exercise

From *The Four-Story Mistake*
by Elizabeth Enright

In The Four-Story Mistake, *the four Melendy children, their father, and their housekeeper, Cuffy, have just moved from New York City into a big house in the country. Although they were sad to leave their old house in the city, the new house is filled with secrets—and the country is filled with adventures.*

The youngest boy, Oliver, is exploring the house and has just discovered two doors, down in the basement. The "Cassidy children" are the children who lived in the house before the Melendy family bought it. "The Office" is what the Melendy children call their playroom. Its walls are covered with pictures of olden times.

From the furnace room two other chambers opened out. In the first one Oliver found an old bedspring, an empty barrel, and a Mason jar high up on the windowsill containing nothing but a large, hairy spider which he did not disturb. The spider's web was laced across the window, and was hung with dried fragments of moth wings, and the husks of beetles and houseflies.

The second room had a wooden door which was shut. Oliver had a hard time getting it open: it was stuck in its casing as though it had not been opened for a very long time. But he pushed against it with all his weight and finally it flew open and he flew into the room with it.

He could hardly believe his eyes.

This room was smaller than the other, and it was to Oliver as the cave was to Ali Baba: a storehouse full of treasure.

The first things he saw were two sleds propped up against the wall on their hind legs. They were very old, with rusted runners, and one was red, and one was blue. Names were painted on them in fancy letters. "Snow Demon," said one; and "Little Kriss Kringle," said the other. They must have belonged to the Cassidy children, thought Oliver. And then he saw the bicycle. Upstairs in the attic there were pictures of boys riding bicycles like this one. The front wheel was taller than he was, though the back wheel was small; and the saddle and handlebars soared loftily atop the front wheel. If only my legs were longer, thought Oliver, impatiently, looking down at his short, fat underpinnings; this bike is much better than the kind they have nowadays; more dangerous.

Besides the bicycle and the sleds, there was an old-fashioned tin bathtub covered with rust and chipped paint of robin's-egg blue, and shaped like an armchair with a high back. And there were more Mason jars, with more spiders in them, and a doll carriage made of decaying leather, and a broken coffee grinder, and a cast-iron crib frame, and a set of big books. All the objects in the room were covered with a layer of fine, ashy, white dust. Oliver sat down on one of the books, took another on his lap, reveling in the dust, and began to look at it. It turned out to be the bound volume of a magazine called *Harper's Young People,* published in the year 1887. The book was mildewed, some of its pages were glued together by years of damp, and its green cover had been gnawed by mice, but it exuded the indescribably delicious odor of all ancient books; better still, it was full of the pictures and adventures of the children of that other world which he had already explored on the walls of the Office upstairs. A world where girls wore sashes and long hair, and boys wore long stockings and button boots, and the horses which pulled the trolley cars wore straw hats. In that world there were no automobiles, no airplanes, no streamline trains, and yet the children seemed to be almost the same kind of children there were now.

Overhead Cuffy's feet creaked to and fro across the kitchen floor boards. Outside the morning was clear and golden with Indian summer. But Oliver sat in the dim light of his cellar room; pale and happy as a mushroom in its native habitat.

Narration Exercise

From *The Four-Story Mistake* by Elizabeth Enright

Name _____

Date _____

Dictation Exercise

From *The Four-Story Mistake*
by Elizabeth Enright

Later in the year, the Melendy children experience their first snowstorm in the country. Oliver and his older brother, Rush, along with their two sisters, Mona and Randy, and their dog, Isaac, head out to try the sleds Oliver found in the cellar room.

The sleds turned out to be all right, though not greased lightning by any means. Rush had an inspiration, too, and went and got two large dishpans from the house; so each of them had a suitable vehicle for traveling down a snowy hill. The dishpans were particularly exciting, because they not only descended rapidly, but spun round and round while doing so. At the bottom of the slope you rose with difficulty, staggered, and discovered that you were the exact center of a world that revolved about you like a mammoth merry-go-round. Oliver was the only one who didn't care for this. His stomach resented the spinning of the dishpan, though for some reason it did not resent being slammed down belly-whopper on a sled over and over again....

"I know what let's do," Mona said, when they were all exhausted and hot and red-cheeked. "I read about it in a book. They made snow ice cream in this book. Why don't we make some?"

"How do we do it?"

"Well, first we have to beg a bottle of milk and some sugar from Cuffy. You do it, Rush. You're best at it."

"Okay," said Rush, who was hungry, trotting obediently toward the house.

"And some cups," called Mona, "and some spoons!"

Then she and Randy and Oliver went looking for the cleanest, purest patch of snow they could find, which was in the middle of the front lawn; untouched, unmarked, it looked as though it had been created to be eaten.

It tasted very good, too, though rather flat, later on when Rush had brought sugar and milk to mix with it. Oliver ate so much that his alert and responsive little stomach felt strange again, and he retired to the house.

Mona and Randy gathered up cups and spoons and went back to the house, too. But Rush left them and took a walk up into the woods. It was dusk, but the snow lent a strange radiance to the world. Flakes still fell, melting cold on his cheek, whispering with a feathery sound. There was no sound but their whisper, and his boots crunching softly. Isaac bounded at his heels with a white beard and ear-fringes.

"Just think," Rush said, "almost a year ago I found you. And in a snowstorm like this." He leaned down and patted Isaac, who looked up at him lovingly with one cold paw raised out of the snow. "Let's go back," Rush said. The woods were beautiful and mysterious; but suddenly he was cold; he longed for noise, and warmth and light. Isaac understood; he turned with a little yelp of joy and galloped beside his master down the hill toward the bright windows of the kitchen.

Narration/Dictation Exercise

From *The Four-Story Mistake* by Elizabeth Enright

Name _____

Dictation Exercise

From *The Moffats*
by Eleanor Estes

The four Moffat children live in a yellow house on Dollar Street. Sylvie, the oldest, is fifteen; Joey is twelve; Janey is nine; and the youngest, Rufus, is five and a half. Their cat Catherine has just had four kittens, and the children are getting ready to play a game that will help each one of them choose a kitten as a pet.

The children looked the kittens over and decided on temporary names for them. The little gray one they called Boots because of her truly extraordinary feet. Another kitten they named Mask. This one was black all over except for its face, which was white. It was Rufus who thought up the name Mask for it. Another they called Whiskers and the last one they named Funny because she had one green eye and one blue eye. Next Sylvie wrote each of these four names on four pieces of paper. These she dropped into Mama's hat.

"Now, who will be the one to draw out the names?" Sylvie asked.

"Rufus! Rufus!" cried Joe and Janey. "Because he is the littlest."

"All right," said Sylvie. "Whichever cat has his name drawn by Rufus will be set in the middle of the room. Then we will all go to the four corners of the room and call, Kitty, Kitty. Whichever person that kitten goes to, why, that person will be the winner of that kitten."

Sylvie had thought this game up years ago and they all loved it.

So now Rufus closed his eyes, put his chubby fist into the hat, and drew out the first name. They waited with bated breath while Sylvie read the name.

"Funny!" she said.

A cheer went up as Funny was put in the middle of the room.

"Kitty, kitty, kitty," the children called from the four corners of the room. In this game it was possible that you might have a preference for one or another of the four kittens. But this must never be evident. You must call as fervently for this one as that one.

"Kitty, kitty, kitty," they called to the little one named Funny.

"Muu-u-r-r." A very feeble, wistful cry came from Funny. She turned around with difficulty. She was feeling terribly alone in a strange world. Suddenly she rushed as fast as she could towards Jane. However, walking in a straight line was utterly impossible for her and it was Sylvie's corner she finally ended up in. So Sylvie and Funny were out of the game.

Rufus scrunched up his face, put his hand in the hat again. The name was— Whiskers!

Whiskers! Cheers again. But Whiskers didn't care. He just sat there with his head nodding on his shoulders, looking as though he were going to fall asleep at any moment.

"Kitty, kitty, kitty," Joe, Jane, and Rufus coaxed.

Whiskers just sat there and looked around the room with a pleasant though simple expression.

"Come, Whiskers. Come, kitty," they pleaded again.

But Whiskers just sat there, swaying gently to and fro.

"We shall have to go nearer this one," said Joey in the manner of a patient parent.

Joey, Jane, and Rufus drew nearer, to within a few feet of Whiskers. Still he just sat.

"He doesn't want to play," said Rufus in disgust.

Now the three went right up close to him. Just a kitten's length away. At this, Whiskers stood up on his shaky legs and staggered nonchalantly over to Rufus. He nestled comfortably on his sleeve and was asleep in a second. So Rufus and Whiskers were out of the game too.

Name _____

Date _____

Narration Exercise

From *The Moffats* by Eleanor Estes

Name _____

Dictation Exercise

From *The Moffats*
by Eleanor Estes

Boots, a gray kitten who springs happily around on enormous feet, is Jane's favorite kitten, and Jane is desperate to get her. But Jane thinks to herself that she really doesn't deserve Boots. She is feeling guilty because a neighbor gave her money to buy candy earlier in the day, and instead of sharing the money with her sister and brothers, Jane bought herself an ice-cream cone and ate the whole thing herself.

Now just Boots and Mask were left. And Joe and Jane.

"Oh, please let Boots be mine," Jane prayed again and again. "Although of course I know I don't deserve it," she added.

Rufus drew again. This time the name was—Boots.

Boots! The children all cheered lustily. Boots herself seemed full of excitement. All the while the game had been going on, she had been clawing at the soap box and miaowing madly to get out. Now she was out!

"Oh, be mine, be mine," breathed Jane.

"Look at the big toes on her," Joe marveled. "Boy, oh, boy, I hope I win her."

Of course Joe was just as anxious for Boots as Jane was. And why shouldn't he be? Of these four sweet kittens she alone showed marks of personality that lifted her above the usual run of cats and kittens. She paid no attention to Joe or to Jane. Instead she raced madly around the room. She whacked at a tassel that was hanging from the red plush chair. This caused her to lose her balance and she rolled over and over. Up again. She resumed her swift, though wobbly, adventuring through the sitting-room, the new world.

"Oh, pussy, come. Come, pussy," Jane begged.

Boots ran right over to Jane's corner but then, just as she was within a cat's length of her, she backed off to the middle of the room. What a kitten!

"Come, kitty, come, kitty," said Joey in that gentle voice of his that surely Boots would not be able to resist.

Now Boots teetered over towards Joe. She sat down not far from him and stared at him with her big blue eyes. Her little pink tongue was hanging out and she was thoroughly irresistible. Suddenly she began to purr. She was the first one to purr and she sounded like a little engine.

"She's going to Joey," mourned Jane. "Well, of course I don't deserve her."

But at this moment Boots suddenly turned right about again. She jumped wildly into the air a couple of times and then, in a series of little sideways leaps, she landed right in Jane's lap. Tears came into Jane's eyes. "She's mine. She's mine," she cried, burying her nose in Boots' sweet-smelling fur.

So Mask went to Joey and he immediately found many engaging things about this kitten that they had not yet discovered. For instance, he had the longest fur, the prettiest markings, the longest tail, and many other unusual qualities. Moreover he was the smallest of the four and would need special attention.

At this moment Catherine-the-cat came in. She looked around the room disdainfully. Then she jumped into the soap-box and whirrupped for her kittens. Jane gave Boots one last hug. She already loved this little kitten so much it was almost more than she could bear. She put the kitten carefully back into the soap-box as the other children were doing with theirs. And the choosing game was over.

Narration/Dictation Exercise

From *The Moffats* by Eleanor Estes

Name _____

Date _____

Dictation Exercise

From *The Lemonade Trick*
by Scott Corbett

Kerby has a mysterious chemistry set. It was given to him by a strange old lady named Mrs. Graymalkin. He's not sure what the chemicals do—but he decides to try out an experiment, just for fun.

Waldo is Kerby's dog. Dr. Jekyll and Mr. Hyde *is a famous book by Robert Louis Stevenson.*

Kerby took a beaker to the bathroom and filled it half full of water. Returning to his room, he placed it in a wire stand that came with the set. Next he opened the same tube again and thrust an eyedropper into it. Holding the eyedropper and tube high where he could watch closely, he carefully pulled a tiny amount of liquid into the eyedropper.

Kerby felt very scientific.

"That ought to be about two drops," he said to Waldo, forgetting that Waldo had left.

He turned to the beaker half full of water. Carefully, holding his breath, he squeezed the chemical into the water.

Nothing happened.

No bubbling.

No boiling.

No steaming.

The water just sat there doing nothing. It was very disappointing. Kerby flopped down on his bed with an angry bounce.

"Aw heck! Might know her old chemistry set would be a fake!" he muttered, thinking hard thoughts about Mrs. Graymalkin.

After brooding for a moment, he sighed and decided to empty the beaker in the bathroom. After that he would try a couple of the other tricks, just to see if any of them would work. Probably the chemicals were old and had lost all their fizz, but maybe some of them were still good. He might as well try. While he was experimenting with the chemistry stuff, he could think of some excuse for not mowing the lawn.

As he walked down the hall he held the water up to the strong light pouring through the window at the end of the hall. The water was clear and not smoking or bubbling or boiling or steaming even a little bit. He sniffed it to see if the chemical gave it any smell.

Kerby stopped. The water had a strangely delightful, irresistibly tempting scent. Before he knew what he was doing, he obeyed a powerful urge.

He lifted the beaker to his lips and drank its contents.

The instant he did this, Kerby was scared.

He remembered all about *Dr. Jekyll and Mr. Hyde*, and what had happened to Dr. Jekyll when he got to messing around with *his* chemistry set. Dr. Jekyll had drunk some stuff he mixed up, and the next thing he knew he had changed into a horrible, hairy man who went out and did all sorts of terrible things. It made him bad, very bad.

With a scared cry, Kerby rushed into the bathroom and looked at himself in the mirror. Would he change into a monster before his very own eyes? Would his face get all hairy and his teeth turn into great fangs?

Narration Exercise

From *The Lemonade Trick* by Scott Corbett

Name _____

Date _____

Dictation Exercise

From *The Lemonade Trick*
by Scott Corbett

This is the story of Kerby's experiment, continued. It begins with what happens right after he drinks the good-smelling water.

Then all at once his eyes rolled in circles, twice, and a strange feeling overcame him.

He felt good.

That was the only way to describe it. Good. Very good.

When Waldo had heard Kerby's scared cry, he must have thought his master was really in trouble, because he came running loyally to see what was the matter.

By the time he arrived that good feeling had come over Kerby. He was rinsing out the beaker and drying it on a paper towel. Waldo stared up at him inquiringly. Kerby gave him a kind and affectionate smile. He stooped and patted his best friend gently on the head.

"Waldo, I want to apologize for dragging you down the hall by the tail," he said. "That is a mean thing to do, and I won't do it again. Besides, your nails scratch Mom's floors. In fact, they may already have done so from time to time. Later on I must remember to polish the floors for her."

Waldo reared back and gave his master a worried look. Kerby threw the paper towel in the wastebasket, being careful to see that it dropped in and did not litter up the bathroom floor. Then he returned to his room, with Waldo padding after him.

"I must put away my chemistry set now and not try any more experiments with it up here in my room," he told Waldo as he put away the beaker and closed the box. "After all, this is no place to play with chemicals—I might spill some and mark my furniture. Why, I didn't even spread any newspapers on my desk before I started! Besides, this is no time to be fooling around playing. I have work to do."

So saying, Kerby went outside and finished mowing the lawn. After he had finished mowing, he trimmed the grass around the trees and along the back fence. Then he raked up all the grass and put it on the compost heap.

When his mother came home, she found him down in the cellar finishing up his cleaning job there.

"What a wonderful job you did on the lawn!" she said, coming downstairs to stare at him in amazement. "I never saw such a job!"

"I was glad to do it, Mom," said Kerby.

"And now, to find you working down here—Kerby, do you feel all right?"

"I feel good, Mom," he said. "Very good."

"Well..." His mother still looked doubtful, but she rose and started upstairs. "I'll fix some lunch, and—"

"It's already fixed, Mom," said Kerby, causing his mother to stumble on a step and nearly fall on her face, she was so surprised. "I thought I'd have it all ready for you when you came home."

After lunch he worked in the basement again all afternoon. Every once in a while his mother called down in an anxious tone to make sure he was all right. Around three o-clock she even telephoned his father and had a long conversation in a low voice with him.

Name _____

Narration/Dictation Exercise

From *The Lemonade Trick* by Scott Corbett

Name _____

Date _____

Dictation Exercise

From *Magic...Naturally! Science Entertainments and Amusements*
by Vicki Cobb

Last week you read about a chemistry set that does real magic. Today, you're going to read about a "magic trick" done through chemistry. The trick: you place a coin in a dish, cover it with water, and then announce that you're going to get it out without wetting your fingers, using only a match, a birthday candle, and a glass.

YOU WILL NEED
    a small piece of clay to act as a candleholder
    a birthday candle
    a coin
    a shallow dish (such as a glass pie plate)
    water
    red or blue food coloring
    matches
    an 8-ounce glass or small glass jar

You can set this trick up right in front of your audience. Make a candleholder out of clay and place the candle in it.

Place the coin in the dish and pour in enough water to completely cover the coin. Add a few drops of food coloring to make the water more visible. Challenge anyone to remove the coin without tilting the dish, pouring out the water, or using an instrument to touch the coin—and without getting wet fingers.

When your audience has run out of ideas, announce that you will accomplish this feat with the aid of a candle, a match, and a glass. Place the candle in its holder in the dish as far from the coin as possible. Light the candle. Cover the lit candle with the glass. When the candle goes out (having used up all the oxygen in the glass) the water will be pushed by air pressure up into the glass (where there is a partial vacuum). The dish is now dry and you simply reach in and pick up the coin.

Here's how it works: If you empty a pail of water onto the floor, the water quickly spreads, flowing into even the smallest cracks in the floor. Air also flows into spaces not already occupied by air. The sound you hear when you open a vacuum-packed jar of coffee or peanuts is made by air rushing in as the seal is broken. The motor of a vacuum cleaner creates a partial vacuum in the bag. As air rushes in to fill this space, it sweeps up solid material in its path.

In this trick you create a partial vacuum by burning a candle in a closed space. When a candle burns it uses oxygen, which makes up about 20 percent of the gases in the air. (Most of the rest of air is another gas called nitrogen.) The flame goes out when all the oxygen has been used. The pressure of the air left in this closed space is less than the pressure outside. The water you want to remove from the coin is between this partial vacuum and the outside air. Like dirt being swept into a vacuum cleaner, the water can be pushed up into the closed space by the pressure of outside air.

Narration Exercise

From *Magic...Naturally!* by Vicki Cobb

Date _____

Name _____

Dictation Exercise

Adapted from *Magic Through Science*
by Robert Gardner

The "magic" trick that you read about earlier this week was actually a scientific experiment. Other magic tricks are done by deceiving the audience. This is one example of a way that magicians often deceive their audience.

Tell your audience that you can read minds! Ask someone to volunteer to help you. After you have chosen your volunteer, tell the audience that you will leave the room. While you are gone, the audience will choose an object. When you return to the room, your volunteer will then point to different objects in the room. You will read the volunteer's mind, and choose the correct object.

When you return, the volunteer points to several objects. None of these are the objects selected, so each time, you answer, "That's not it." Then the volunteer points to the object selected by the audience. You say, "I can read your mind. That is the correct object!"

Explanation: Your volunteer is actually your partner. Ahead of time, select your volunteer and tell him or her that you need to establish a set of signals. The correct object will be the object which the volunteer points to right after pointing to something *red*. If the object *is* something red, you need an additional signal. Tell the volunteer that he or she should use the *right* hand for pointing—*unless* the selected object is red. If the selected object is red, the volunteer will use his or her *left* hand to point. The volunteer will also point to a *black* object right before pointing to the correct object.

Practice this together a number of times, until you can always identify the correct object. Then, make sure that you choose your partner from the volunteers at the magic show! Most "mind reading" tricks in magic shows involve a volunteer who is actually a partner of the magician.

Narration/Dictation Exercise

From *Magic Through Science* by Robert Gardner

Name _____

Date _____

Dictation Exercise

From *Harry Houdini, Young Magician*
by Kathryn Kilby Borland

Harry Houdini was a famous magician who tricked his audience into believing that he had special powers. This selection is from a book about Houdini's childhood. Houdini's real name was Ehrich Weiss. Later, he changed his name to Harry Houdini because he thought it would sound better on stage.

In this story, young Houdini sees his very first magic trick—a man at a fair picks coins out of the air and fills a bucket with them. Houdini's family is very poor, so Houdini watches the man all day. He wants to learn how to make a bucket full of money so that he can take it home to his mother and father.

"Hey, kid!" the magician said, "why don't you go home like everybody else? You make me nervous watching, watching all day."

Ehrich looked around. It was true. He was the only one watching now. "I'm sorry, sir," he said. "I didn't think you'd notice me. It's just that I need to know how to fill the bucket with money, and I don't think I can quite do it yet. Could you—" Ehrich hesitated. The magician had sounded pretty cross.

The magician stared at him. "Are you pulling my leg, kid? Do you think I really pull money out of the air?"

"You don't really?" Ehrich asked. He was so pleased that the magician was actually talking to him that he almost forgot to be disappointed about not taking a bucket of money home. "Then where did it come from?"

Suddenly the magician smiled. "Look here, kid," he said. "I'm going to show you something. It's not what you really do in this business that counts. It's what people think you do. Now, when I show the empty bucket I hold it in my left hand, see? And in my left hand I also have a bunch of coins that nobody sees. They're too busy looking at the empty bucket. Now, in my right hand I have just one coin. See?"

Ehrich nodded. "But I saw you pick the coins out of the air."

"Aha! That's what you thought you saw. Here's what you really saw."

The man showed Ehrich that he was holding the coin behind his hand between his thumb and first finger. When he held his hand up, the coin did not show at all. Then he moved his fingers quickly. Now the coin could be plainly seen. Even though Ehrich saw him do the trick, it was hard to believe the man hadn't picked that coin out of the air.

"But how do you get another one after you throw that one in the bucket?"

"I don't throw it in."

"But I saw you do it every time."

"You thought you saw me. I acted as if I was throwing it in, but I slipped it in back of my hand again. At the same time I slipped a coin into the bucket out of my other hand. See how it's done? Come on up and try it."

"I don't think I could." But Ehrich's fingers were itching to try. He'd forgotten everything except the magician, the bucket, and the coins.

The first time he tried it the coins in his left hand fell to the floor. It was a hot day, and the coin in his right hand stuck between his fingers. He made every kind of mistake, but at last the magician said, "You're not doing badly, kid. You've got the fingers for it."

Narration Exercise

From *Harry Houdini, Young Magician* by Kathryn Kilby Borland

Name

Date _____

Dictation Exercise

From *Harry Houdini*
by Rita Thievon Mullin

When he began doing magic in front of audiences, Houdini often escaped from handcuffs. He grew expert at picking locks with tiny pieces of metal or hidden keys which he would conceal in his clothing. But soon he wanted to add a new challenge to his act. This excerpt from the biography Harry Houdini *by Rita Thievon Mullin tells how he escaped from wooden boxes.*

As Harry continued to welcome handcuff challenges, he added a new element: the box challenge. In city after city, local carpenters would build more and more elaborate packing boxes from which the great Houdini would escape. Often the box would be displayed in the theater lobby for days before a big performance so that audiences could see how sturdy it was.

After the box was carried on stage, Houdini would be handcuffed, chained, and lifted into the box. The carpenters would put the top on the box and seal it shut with plenty of nails. Then the tall drapery cabinet would be placed around it to hide what was happening inside from the audience. The theater band played faster and louder with each passing minute, as Houdini worked to escape first from his bonds and then from the box. When he emerged from the cabinet and the drapery was opened, the box stood there, just as it had, with all the sides—and all the nails that had sealed it—still in place.

So amazing were his feats that some people in Europe claimed Houdini had supernatural powers. Houdini was always quick to say that his skills were all based in the natural world. In the case of his many box escapes, the trick was simple: Before the performance Harry and [his assistant] Franz would replace the long nails holding one side of the box with shorter nails that Harry could easily push out from the inside. Then, once Houdini was out, he could tap the long ones back in while the band played louder and faster.

As the box challenge became more popular, Houdini developed new ways to amaze audiences. Sometimes the box was actually built onstage in front of the audience, so substituting short "dummy nails" was impossible. In that case, Houdini might use a simple steel jack that worked like the ones used to raise a car for changing a tire. He would hide the parts of the jack in his clothing and assemble them after he was sealed in the box. The jack would apply pressure to one side of the box until the nails slipped out. After he was outside, he would take the jack apart again, hide the parts, and tap the nails back in place while the house band played the ear-blasting "Storm King" for the audience to hide the noise.

During the nearly five years Harry and [his wife] Bess traveled through Europe, they became the most popular vaudeville performers there. They played to packed houses and received reviews in newspapers that any performer would envy. Although they had made two trips back to the U.S. to visit family during their time in Europe, by 1905 they were homesick and ready to move back to take on American vaudeville....

On the new tour, Harry expanded the box challenge that had been so popular in Europe. This time, he invited people to dare him to escape from just about anything. The challengers were very creative! During his tour he escaped from the world's largest envelope (without tearing the paper), a clear-glass box, a coffin with the top screwed down, a man-sized sausage skin, and a giant-sized football carried onstage by the University of Pennsylvania football team.

Narration/Dictation Exercise

From *Harry Houdini* by Rita Thievon Mullin

Name _____

Date _____

Dictation Exercise

From *Paul Bunyan Swings His Axe*
by Dell J. McCormick

Paul Bunyan is a legendary woodsman who is said to have been born in the woods of Maine. When he was grown, he was a giant of a man. He went west with a crew of lumberjacks to open his own logging camp. He took two cooks, nicknamed Hot Biscuit Slim and Cream Puff Fatty, with him. Stories say that everything Paul Bunyan owned was big—including his logging camp.

The Red River Valley stretches from the northern United States (North Dakota and Minnesota) into the Canadian territory of Manitoba.

When Paul moved his camp into the Red River country, he found that the dining room was too small to hold all his men. The kitchen was too small, too. Every day dinner would be from two to three hours late.

One day Paul got angry when dinner was late and shouted, "Hot Biscuit Slim, come here!"

Three men who were standing beside Paul were blown over by the force of his voice. They rolled over and over and landed on their feet. They started running and did not stop until they were well out of the reach of his voice.

Hot Biscuit Slim came on the run, and Paul said to him, "Slim, I want a larger kitchen where two hundred cooks can work at the same time. Also build a larger dining room. Make the tables six miles long! Yesterday the men sat down, and by the time the biscuits got there, they were cold. Nobody wants to eat cold biscuits!"

Slim had the men clear the forest for miles around and build a huge kitchen and dining room. Ole, the blacksmith, made a huge black kettle that held eleven hundred gallons of soup.

When Hot Biscuit Slim made soup, he rowed in the boiling water to the center of the big kettle with boatloads of cabbages, turnips, and potatoes. He shoveled the vegetables into the water, and in a few hours a wonderful soup was ready.

Ole also made a ten-acre hot-cake griddle. To grease the griddle, Hot Biscuit Slim strapped flat sides of bacon on the feet of the cookhouse boys and told them to skate back and forth over the huge griddle.

The boys had fun playing tag and crack-the-whip on the hot griddle. Sometimes they fell off and burned their trousers. When that griddle began to steam, no one could see across it because the fog was so thick.

For Sunday morning breakfast Hot Biscuit Slim tried to make his finest hot cakes. They were so large that it took five men to eat one. Paul himself often ate twelve to fourteen of the big cakes. The cookhouse boys worked all day Saturday mixing dough and bringing in huge barrels of maple syrup for the hot cakes.

The biggest meal of the week was Sunday dinner. Hot Biscuit Slim would cook the very best soup, the finest vegetables, and the nicest spring chicken of all for this meal.

One Saturday Slim said to Ole, "Tomorrow I am going to have the best Sunday dinner of the year. When the men are through eating my hot biscuits with jelly, my spinach, cucumbers, young red radishes, and my chicken pie, they won't be able to eat a mouthful of dessert."

Cream Puff Fatty overhead this big talk, and his pride was hurt. He made the desserts, and he thought such talk was running down his good name.

He said to himself, "So Hot Biscuit Slim thinks the boys won't eat any dessert? Well, we'll see about that."

Cream Puff Fatty called the dessert boys together and said, "We will make cream puffs that will melt in their mouths. Light creamy ones with whipped cream a foot high! We'll see if they refuse to eat dessert."

The Sunday dinner hour arrived, and then men sat down to eat. Soup, vegetables, and salads disappeared, and the men were almost full. Then they saw the chicken pie coming.

"Oh, look! Chicken pie!" they shouted. They knew Slim's chicken pie was the finest in the world, and they had to make room for it. The cookhouse boys on roller skates kept right on bringing in large platters of food.

"Hot biscuits and jelly! Hurrah!" the men cried, although they didn't seem to have room for another mouthful.

Cream Puff Fatty was in despair. He looked down the long dining room and saw that the men were slower and slower in lifting the food to their mouths. It looked as though they couldn't eat another bite.

"It's now or never, boys!" cried Cream Puff Fatty. The dessert boys had their roller skates strapped on, and they started down the long tables.

The men saw them coming and cried out, "Cream puffs! Cream puffs!" They started reaching for the fluffy white cakes piled full of rich custard cream. Not a man left the dining room until every cream puff was eaten.

Narration Exercise

From *Paul Bunyan Swings His Axe* by Dell J. McCormick

Name _____

Dictation Exercise

From *The Story of Canada*

by Janet Lunn and Christopher Moore

It took many pairs of hands to cut and haul trees. Many newcomers to North America, immigrants from other countries, went to the lumber camps to find work. This selection from The Story of Canada *describes life in the lumber camps.*

Immigrants poured into British Canada like a flood. Sometimes ten thousand landed in a single week. Families laboured to clear the forests and plant new farms, to build up the cities and towns. Gangs of young men known as "navvies" slaved to cut canals around the rapids and waterfalls. They hauled timber from the Canadian woods, salted down codfish in Newfoundland, and launched trim sailing ships from Atlantic Canada's shipyards.

Most of the immigrants came from Britain. There were Scottish highlanders, driven from their glens by cruel landlords who wanted the land to raise sheep.... Families also came from overcrowded Ireland, or to escape teeming cities in England. They settled all over British America....The newcomers called British North America "a good poor man's country," meaning that anyone willing to work hard could do well. "In England there is too many men. Here there is not enough," wrote one young man in a letter to his family.

....Winter meant woodcutting. Men tramped off to timber shanties in the pine forests. They lived on pork and beans, swinging their broadaxes and hauling the timber over the snow to the riverbanks. When the spring runoff swelled the rivers, the lumberjacks became *draveurs*, or raftsmen, riding the logs down the rapids to the sawmills and timber ships. Only the strongest stayed with it: men like Joseph Montferrand.

For thirty years of the early 1800s, Montferrand was the greatest lumberjack on the Ottawa River. People said he was so strong that no boxer could beat him, so agile that he could plant his bootmarks on a tavern ceiling and land on his feet. He was a legend, maybe the most famous man in French Canada.

The lumber camps of the Ottawa Valley were rough and rowdy places. Montferrand led French-Canadian loggers in battles against the Irish loggers. Yet even his English-speaking rivals bragged that "Joe Mufferaw" could drink a lake dry, dig out a river channel by dragging his axe, and comb his hair with a tall pine tree. Wherever lumber jacks went in the north woods, they spread his name and fame.

Narration/Dictation Exercise

From *The Story of Canada* by Janet Lunn and Christopher Moore

Name _____

Date _____

Dictation Exercise

From *The Story of the Declaration of Independence*
by Norman Richards

This excerpt from The Story of the Declaration of Independence *tells the story of the British colonies in North America, from their beginnings in 1620 up to the decision by those colonies in 1776 to rebel. The Continental Congress was a gathering of the colony leaders, who met together in Philadelphia to decide whether or not they would remain loyal to the British king.*

"Absolute rule" means that a king has power over every part of his subjects' lives—and the subject has no choice but to submit.

Ever since the Pilgrims had signed the Mayflower Compact, Americans had believed that absolute rule was wrong. In Europe kings ruled whether the people wanted them or not. Kings believed that it was their divine right to rule.

Americans had been living as free men, making their own laws for one hundred and fifty years. They would never surrender this precious freedom.

Richard Henry Lee of Virginia said in the Continental Congress: "These United Colonies are, and of right ought to be, free and independent states."

The members of the Continental Congress saw now that it was their duty to follow the people's wishes and declare the American colonies independent. They wanted officially to tell the world about the new union of the thirteen United States of America. They also wanted to tell the world why they were breaking away from Great Britain. Five men were chosen to work on the document—John Adams, Thomas Jefferson, Benjamin Franklin, Robert Livingston and Roger Sherman.

They chose young Thomas Jefferson from Virginia to write this official declaration. He was a smart man, and he could express ideas clearly. And they wanted this declaration understood by everybody.

Thomas Jefferson worked for two weeks writing the declaration. He stood at a desk in the second-floor parlor of a house belonging to a Philadelphia bricklayer whom he knew. He wrote on large paper with a quill (a feather) dipped in ink. He would study the sentences he had written the day before. If he didn't like them he would cross them out and write them again.

Jefferson, with four other men, was to present the declaration to the members of Congress. When he had finished writing the declaration he showed it to John Adams, Benjamin Franklin and the other members of the committee, and they made a few changes.

The Declaration of Independence has two main parts. The first part explains the beliefs of Americans about democracy. It tells that men have certain rights that can't be taken away from them. The signers declared these...truths to be understood by everyone: that all men are created equal; that all men are born with rights that no one can take away from them; that some of these rights are life, liberty, and the right to try to be happy; that the purpose of a government is to preserve these rights for all men....

The second part of the Declaration of Independence tells how the king refused to grant these rights to Americans. It contains a long list of examples of tyranny by the king. It tells the world why the colonies broke away from his rule and became the United States of America.

This document was presented to the members of the Congress. They debated about it for almost three days. It was approved on July 4, 1776, although the New York delegates did not accept it until eleven days later.

Name _____

Date _____

Narration Exercise

From *The Story of the Declaration of Independence* by Norman Richards

Name _____

Date _____

Dictation Exercise

From *The Young Oxford History of Britain & Ireland*
by Mike Corbishley and Kenneth O. Morgan

The Declaration of Independence was not the first document to tell a king that his subjects have rights. Five hundred years earlier, the people of England had forced their king, King John, to sign a document that spelled out their rights. King John had been fighting a war against France, and he had been forcing his people to pay higher and higher taxes so that he could spend more and more money on his war. When his army was defeated by the French, John's subjects rebelled against the taxes—and against John's tyranny.

This excerpt from The Young Oxford History of Britain & Ireland *begins with John inheriting the throne of England after the death of his brother, Richard the Lionhearted.*

Richard and his wife, Berengaria of Navarre, had no children, so the next king was his brother John (1199–1216). John's claim was disputed by his young nephew, Arthur of Brittany. In 1202 John captured Arthur who disappeared and was never seen again. Everyone believed that John had ordered his murder. So when King Philip of France attacked John's French lands in Anjou and Normandy, few were willing to fight for him. As a result he quickly lost them to the king of France, and from then on he was known as "Softsword."

John spent the next ten years taxing his subjects heavily, especially his richer ones, to raise the huge sums he needed to pay for a grand military alliance against France. Unfortunately for John, the allied army was defeated at the battle of Bouvines in 1214. The English people, led by the barons, had had enough of high taxes. They rebelled and the citizens of London opened their gates to the rebels. This forced John to meet their leaders at Runnymede by the river Thames in 1215. There they forced him to make promises which were written in the treaty later known as Magna Carta.

John promised to treat everyone more fairly, and agreed to have a committee of twenty-five barons to whom people could complain if they thought he was failing to keep his promises. In fact, as everyone had suspected, John did not keep his promises. Many barons then chose Louis, the son of Philip of France, to be king of England and in May 1216 a French army held London and Winchester. When John died in 1216 the country was divided by civil war. As a king John had turned out to be a failure. He had lost Normandy and Anjou, and much of England too. Although he had many enemies, he almost never dared face them. A song-writer of the time wrote,

No man may ever trust him,

For his heart is soft and cowardly.

John's eldest son, Henry, was only nine and therefore a "minor," so a number of barons formed a council to defeat Louis and to govern until Henry III was old enough to rule for himself. The leader of the "minority council" was William Marshal, now Earl of Pembroke and a famous old warrior. William beat the French in battle. The council reissued Magna Carta to show that they intended to govern the country better than John had done. From now on Magna Carta became a symbol of good government. For the next hundred years, whenever people thought a king was being tyrannical they reminded him of Magna Carta.

Narration/Dictation Exercise

From *The Young Oxford History of Britain & Ireland* by Mike Corbishley and
Kenneth O. Morgan

Name _____

Date _____

Dictation Exercise

"The Garden of Live Flowers"
from *Through the Looking-Glass*
by Lewis Carroll

This passage is from the sequel to Alice in Wonderland. *Alice has gotten through the mirror in her sitting-room and has found herself in a magical land behind it. As she walks along through this land, she finds herself walking through a flower-garden.*

When you read, remember that "ough" in "bough" is pronounced like "ow" as in "now."

"O Tiger-lily," said Alice, addressing herself to one that was waving gracefully about in the wind, "I *wish* you could talk!"

"We *can* talk," said the Tiger-lily, "when there's anybody worth talking to."

Alice was so astonished that she could not speak for a minute: it quite seemed to take her breath away. At length, as the Tiger-lily only went on waving about, she spoke again, in a timid voice—almost in a whisper. "And can *all* the flowers talk?"

"As well as *you* can," said the Tiger-lily. "And a great deal louder."

"It isn't manners for us to begin, you know," said the Rose, "and I really was wondering when you'd speak! Said I to myself, 'Her face has got *some* sense in it, thought it's not a clever one!' Still, you're the right colour, and that goes a long way."

"I don't care about the colour," the Tiger-lily remarked. "If only her petals curled up a little more, she'd be all right."

Alice didn't like being criticised, so she began asking questions. "Aren't you sometimes frightened at being planted out here, with nobody to take care of you?"

"There's the tree in the middle," said the Rose. "What else is it good for?"

"But what could it do, if any danger came?" Alice asked.

"It says 'Bough-wow!' cried a Daisy. "That's why its branches are called boughs!"

"Didn't you know *that*?" cried another Daisy, and here they all began shouting together, till the air seemed quite full of little shrill voices.

"Silence, every one of you!" cried the Tiger-lily, waving itself passionately from side to side, and trembling with excitement. "They know I can't get at them!" it panted, bending its quivering head towards Alice, "or they wouldn't dare to do it!"

"Never mind!" Alice said in a soothing tone, and stooping down to the daisies, who were just beginning again, she whispered, "If you don't hold your tongues, I'll pick you!"

There was silence in a moment, and several of the pink daisies turned white.

"That's right!" said the Tiger-lily. "The daisies are worst of all. When one speaks, they all begin together, and it's enough to make one wither to hear the way they go on!"

"How is it you can all talk so nicely?" Alice said, hoping to get it into a better temper by a compliment. "I've been in many gardens before, but none of the flowers could talk."

"Put your hand down, and feel the ground," said the Tiger-lily. "Then you'll know why."

Alice did so. "It's very hard," she said, "but I don't see what that has to do with it."

"In most gardens," the Tiger-lily said, "they make the beds too soft—so that the flowers are always asleep."

This sounded a very good reason, and Alice was quite pleased to know it. "I never thought of that before!" she said.

Narration Exercise

From "The Garden of Live Flowers" by Lewis Carroll

Name _____

Dictation Exercise

"Queen Alice"
from *Through the Looking-Glass*
by Lewis Carroll

This chapter is near the end of the book. Alice has found herself in the middle of a life-size chess game and has unexpectedly been made a queen. The other two queens, the Red and White Queens, have invited her to a dinner party in her honor.

Alice glanced nervously along the table, as she walked up the large hall, and noticed that there were about fifty guests, of all kinds: some were animals, some birds, and there were even a few flowers among them. "I'm glad they've come without waiting to be asked," she thought. "I should never have known who were the right people to invite!"

There were three chairs at the head of the table; the Red and White Queens had already taken two of them, but the middle one was empty. Alice sat down in it, rather uncomfortable in the silence, and longing for some one to speak.

At last the Red Queen began. "You've missed the soup and fish," she said. "Put on the joint!" And the waiters set a leg of mutton before Alice, who looked at it rather anxiously, as she had never had to carve a joint before.

"You look a little shy; let me introduce you to that leg of mutton," said the Red Queen. "Alice—Mutton; Mutton—Alice." The leg of mutton got up in the dish and made a little bow to Alice; and Alice returned the bow, not knowing whether to be frightened or amused.

"May I give you a slice?" she said, taking up the knife and fork, and looking from one Queen to the other.

"Certainly not," the Red Queen said, very decidedly. "It isn't etiquette to cut any one you've been introduced to. Remove the joint!" And the waiters carried it off, and brought a large plum-pudding in its place.

"I won't be introduced to the pudding, please," Alice said rather hastily, "or we shall get no dinner at all. May I give you some?"

But the Red Queen looked sulky, and growled "Pudding—Alice; Alice—Pudding. Remove the pudding!" and the waiters took it away so quickly that Alice couldn't return its bow.

However, she didn't see why the Red Queen should be the only one to give orders, so, as an experiment, she called out "Waiter! Bring back the pudding!" and there it was again in a moment like a conjuring-trick. It was so large that she couldn't help feeling a LITTLE shy with it, as she had been with the mutton;

however, she conquered her shyness by a great effort and cut a slice and handed it to the Red Queen.

"What impertinence!" said the Pudding. "I wonder how you'd like it, if I were to cut a slice out of YOU, you creature!"

It spoke in a thick, suety sort of voice, and Alice hadn't a word to say in reply: she could only sit and look at it and gasp.

"Make a remark," said the Red Queen: "it's ridiculous to leave all the conversation to the pudding!"

Name _____

Narration/Dictation Exercise

From "Queen Alice" by Lewis Carroll

Name _____

Date _____

Dictation Exercise

"Stopping by Woods on a Snowy Evening"
by Robert Frost

Whose woods these are I think I know.　　　_____

His house is in the village though;　　　_____

He will not see me stopping here　　　_____

To watch his woods fill up with snow.　　　_____

My little horse must think it queer　　　_____

To stop without a farmhouse near　　　_____

Between the woods and frozen lake　　　_____

The darkest evening of the year.　　　_____

He gives his harness bells a shake　　　_____

To ask if there is some mistake.　　　_____

The only other sound's the sweep　　　_____

Of easy wind and downy flake.　　　_____

The woods are lovely, dark and deep.　　　_____

But I have promises to keep,　　　_____

And miles to go before I sleep,　　　_____

And miles to go before I sleep.　　　_____

Whose **woods** these **are** I **think** I **know.**
His **house** is **in** the **vill**age **though**;

meter (unstress **stress**):　　_____

Dictation Exercise

"The Listeners"
by Walter de la Mare

"Is there anybody there?" said the Traveller,

Knocking on the moonlit door;   A

And his horse in the silence champed the grasses

Of the forest's ferny floor: A

And a bird flew up out of the turret,

Above the Traveller's head: _____

And he smote upon the door again a second time;

"Is there anybody there?" he said.   _____

But no one descended to the Traveller;

No head from the leaf-fringed sill   _____

Leaned over and looked into his grey eyes,

Where he stood perplexed and still.   _____

But only a host of phantom listeners

That dwelt in the lone house then   _____

Stood listening in the quiet of the moonlight

To that voice from the world of men: _____

Stood thronging the faint moonbeams on the dark stair,

That goes down to the empty hall,   _____

Hearkening in an air stirred and shaken

By the lonely Traveller's call.   _____

And he felt in his heart their strangeness,

Their stillness answering his cry,   _____

While his horse moved, cropping the dark turf,

'Neath the starred and leafy sky;   _____

For he suddenly smote on the door, even

Louder, and lifted his head:—   _____

"Tell them I came, and no one answered,

That I kept my word," he said.   _____

Never the least stir made the listeners,

Though every word he spake   _____

Fell echoing through the shadowiness of the still house

From the one man left awake: _____

Ay, they heard his foot upon the stirrup,

And the sound of iron on stone,   _____

And how the silence surged softly backward,

When the plunging hoofs were gone.   _____

"Is there anybody there?" said the **Traveller**,

Knocking on the moonlit door;   A

And his horse in the silence champed the **grasses**

Of the forest's ferny floor: A

And a bird flew up out of the **turret,**

Above the Traveller's head: B

And he smote upon the door again a second **time;**

"Is there anybody there?" he said.   B

But no one descended to the **Traveller;**

No head from the leaf-fringed sill   C

Leaned over and looked into his grey **eyes,**

Where he stood perplexed and still.   C

But only a host of phantom **listeners**

That dwelt in the lone house then   D

Stood listening in the quiet of the **moonlight**

To that voice from the world of men: D

Stood thronging the faint moonbeams on the dark **stair,**

That goes down to the empty hall,   E

Hearkening in an air stirred and **shaken**

By the lonely Traveller's call.   E

And he felt in his heart their **strangeness,**

Their stillness answering his cry,   F

While his horse moved, cropping the dark **turf,**

'Neath the starred and leafy sky;   F

For he suddenly smote on the door, **even**

Louder, and lifted his head:—   B

"Tell them I came, and no one **answered,**

That I kept my word," he said.   B

Never the least stir made the **listeners,**

Though every word he spake   G

Fell echoing through the shadowiness of the still **house**

From the one man left awake: G

Ay, they heard his foot upon the **stirrup,**

And the sound of iron on stone,   H

And how the silence surged softly **backward,**

When the plunging hoofs were gone.   H

Knocking **on** the **moon**lit **door**;

stress unstress **stress** unstress **stress** unstress **stress**

And his **horse** in the **silence champed** the **grass**es

unstress unstress **stress** unstress unstress **stress** unstress **stress** unstress **stress** unstress

And a **bird** flew **up** out **of** the **tur**ret,

unstress unstress **stress** unstress **stress** unstress **stress** unstress **stress** unstress

But **no** one de**scen**ded **to** the **Trav**eller;

unstress **stress** unstress unstress **stress** unstress **stress** unstress **stress** unstress

Their **still**ness **an**swering his **cry**,

unstress **stress** unstress **stress** unstress unstress unstress **stress**

Never the **least stir** made the **list**eners,

stress unstress unstress **stress stress** unstress unstress **stress** unstress unstress

And the **sound** of **ir**on on **stone**,

unstress unstress **stress** unstress **stress** unstress unstress **stress**

Name _____

Dictation Exercise

From *The Furious Flycycle*
by Jan Wahl

The hero of this book, Melvin Spitznagle, is going to invent a contraption that will make his bicycle do something unusual. Can you guess what it is? (Hint: look at the title of the book.)

"Orphan Asylum" is an old name for an orphanage, a place where children without parents lived.

The house in town that had the most shutters, a spooky turret, a cat named Tweet about to have babies, an ancient spreading apple tree with lots of red apples, and a barn in back with spires sticking up and fancy woodcarving, was the house on Bean Road in which lived Melvin Spitznagle.

Melvin was considered lucky; his father owned the Ice Cream Works on Radish Street, where they wholesaled and manufactured Spitznagle's Ice Cream. There was a freezer with a capacity of six tons a day; and the business included a fifteen horsepower engine. The annual output was between twenty thousand and thirty thousand gallons. It was the most important ice cream works in the County. Melvin liked to walk past the big plant and read the sign, with letters in faded gold and blue, that said:

SPITZNAGLE'S ICE CREAM

"Better than it sounds"

Because his father was the ice cream maker, Melvin grew pretty popular at school. His father brought home, in five-gallon containers, the ice cream not sold to stores within a week. So Melvin's schoolmates trooped hungrily off to Bean Road after school, and they would sit on the white-painted benches and lawn chairs in the Spitznagle back yard politely but eagerly, wondering which flavor Emma Dudd, the maid, was going to bring out. It was vanilla most often.

But with jams and sauces and different syrups (which they brought with them) added, Melvin's schoolmates could vary the flavors as they chose. Emma Dudd was kept busy zipping back and forth from the kitchen, and usually her linen maid's cap fell over her eyes as she hurried.

Thus Melvin never lacked for company. However, in his heart, he wished he were enjoyed for himself alone; with the result that suddenly one day he asked his father to give the unsold ice cream, in its five-gallon containers, to the county Orphan Asylum instead. Nobody much came to the back yard after that, except two fat little girls, the Sprenger sisters, Mavis and Edna—who wanted to play croquet.

Melvin said "Pooh Pooh!" to everybody and decided to spend his time becoming a scientific mechanical wizard.

He was handy at repairing bicycles. And people soon began showing up with broken chains and sprung sockets for him to fix. Again, however, Melvin began to feel he was not being appreciated for what he was himself.

So he pleaded with his parents and got them to let him use the unused barn for his private workshop.

He outfitted the place with wonderful tools—handdrills, wrenches, pronged and prongless hammers, pliers, vises, screwdrivers, files, saws, chisels, soldering irons, and other things.

On the door he put a sign:

BEWARE!! GROUCHY PERSON

Narration Exercise

From *The Furious Flycycle* by Jan Wahl

Dictation Exercise

From *The Furious Flycycle*
by Jan Wahl

This is the next part of The Furious Flycycle. *It tells what happens after Melvin establishes his mechanical workshop.*

When Emma Dudd was missing the eggbeater, she knew where it had gone. When Melvin's mother's sewing machine was missing some of its parts, she knew where they had disappeared to.

Yet always, when Melvin returned a thing (which he did, having learned its secret), it was better than new; he *was* a mechanical wizard. The eggbeater then became the fastest in town, the sewing machine stitched quicker and better than before.

One hot July day the freezer at his father's plant broke down. The ice cream came flooding out into a huge mound onto Radish Street.

The town fire department arrived, starting to work with shovels. Soon, all the dogs and cats in town heard about it and were there, licking up the rainbow-colored treat—the cherry, peach, lime, vanilla, strawberry, chocolate!

Melvin raced across town with his tool kit. He went straight to the source of the trouble—a loose rotary four-gauge Whirlogax—pulled out his #7 roman wrench, and, in a jiffy, had everything under control. The fire department stood there amazed. Mr. Spitznagle did not have to send his employees home.

A few days later a truck pulled up on Bean Road.

The expressman wheeled up to the door a dazzling object—a new Silver Zephyr bicycle. Attached to it was a tag reading IN GRATITUDE. YOUR FATHER.

Melvin took a few days off from his workshop to pedal the Silver Zephyr up and down the streets. He even went outside of town, trying country roads. There the riding got bumpy. Melvin wished he were able to ride as fast as a tornado. He drove everywhere with a dreamy look in his eyes, narrowly missing flocks of chickens and yipping dogs; Melvin was lost in thought.

Then Fate stepped into his life. Fate was an old, old man in battered top hat and shaggy beard.

Professor Mickimecki, with beard, top hat, with a red-bulb nose, with his hose torn, wearing worn carpet slippers in place of shoes, the great inventor Professor Mickimecki (formerly of Prague, Stuttgart, Liverpool, and Bombay) had shot through town on the Rapid Pearl Express, which came through once a week without stopping on its way to points West.

As the train raced through, Professor Mickimecki had pulled the emergency cord. "STOP THE TRAIN!" he shouted, tossing his valises out the window to the surprise of fellow passengers.

Then he scrambled out himself, holding onto his top hat.

"This is the town in which I want to spend the rest of my life. *Unnoticed!*"

That very same afternoon the Professor rented, with one hundred dollars down in two-dollar bills, the old Ketcham house.

Soon he painted the house green, so that it looked like grass. The fleet of trucks that came bringing his many large crates and boxes had a hard time finding it.

It was an inspiration to Melvin just to know so great a man lived now in town.

Narration/Dictation Exercise

From *The Furious Flycycle* by Jan Wahl

Name _____

Date _____

Dictation Exercise

From *Laura Ingalls Wilder, Young Pioneer*
by Beatrice Gormley

Earlier in this book, you read an excerpt from Farmer Boy *by Laura Ingalls Wilder. This is from a biography of Wilder—the true story of her life.* Laura Ingalls Wilder, Young Pioneer, *by Beatrice Gormley, tells how Laura started to write* Farmer Boy *with the help of her husband, Almanzo, and her daughter, Rose. She had to get help from Almanzo's big brother, Royal, and his sister Alice.*

Everyone loved *Little House in the Big Woods*, it seemed....Reviewers couldn't say enough good things about it: "Refreshingly genuine and lifelike"; "delightful and absorbing"; "treasurable." On top of that, Laura's first royalty check was five hundred dollars.

....Now that Laura had discovered how satisfying it was to write a book, she wasn't about to stop. Even before *Little House in the Big Woods* was published, she had started working on a second book. This one was about Almanzo's childhood in upstate New York. As she wrote, she checked facts with Almanzo, and she drew diagrams of the Wilder farmhouse and barns and fields. She tried to get her husband to talk about things that had happened to him as a boy.

Almanzo was good with facts, but almost no help with the stories. "I'm not much of a hand to tell a story," he protested.

"A hand!" retorted Laura. "No, you're certainly not a hand—you're more like an *oyster*, the way I have to pry every little thing out of you. Thank goodness that Royal told me about the time you fed taffy to your little pig, and she ran all over the farm with you chasing her. And that Alice told me about the time you threw the stove polish brush at her and made a big splotch on the parlor wall-paper, and you thought you'd get a whipping but Alice mended the wallpaper so your folks never knew."

Almanzo chuckled at the memories, but he still didn't say much....

Laura knew now that readers were eagerly waiting for as many books as she could turn out. Many children wrote letters to tell her so. In April 1933, a boy in Iowa wrote: "I wish this year would hurry so I could read your new book, *Farmer Boy*. I read *Little House in the Big Woods* twice. It helped us in our pioneer study a lot. We made butter like you did when you were a little girl."

Before *Farmer Boy* was published later in 1933, Laura had decided what her third book would be. She wanted to tell the story of the year the Ingalls family spent on the Kansas prairie, in Indian Territory. Because she'd been too young to remember that year, she made a special effort to research the facts for this book.

She and Rose even drove to Kansas to see if they could find the site of the log cabin Pa had built.

Laura wasn't able to find the exact place where the Ingalls house had stood on the Kansas prairie. But she learned a great deal about how much Kansas had changed. As Laura and Rose neared Independence, they were amazed to see oil wells on the horizon.

Oil wells, where once pioneers had homesteaded! This was another sign that Laura had better write down, as soon as she could, what life had been like for a pioneer girl. She needed to capture the scent of wild roses on the prairie, the taste of corn bread baked over a campfire, the thrill of meeting a wolf under the stars on a frozen lake.

Name _____

Narration Exercise

From *Laura Ingalls Wilder, Young Pioneer* by Beatrice Gormley

Name _____

Date _____

Dictation Exercise

From *Dr. Seuss, Young Author and Artist*
by Kathleen Kudlinski

This is from another biography, of another writer you are probably familiar with—Dr. Seuss, author of The Cat in the Hat, How the Grinch Stole Christmas, *and many other rhyming stories.*

Dr. Seuss's real name was Theodor Geisel, and his nickname was Ted. In this excerpt from Dr. Seuss, Young Author and Artist, *he takes his first real art class at Central High School, after years of drawing by himself just for fun.*

"We will draw this," the art teacher said, handing out charcoal and great white sheets of paper. Ted sat staring at a bunch of wilted daisies in an old milk bottle. His shoulders slumped. This was not what he had expected from his first high school art class. "What would a cow do?" he whispered to his classmates. "Eat the daisies or squirt milk on them?" Laughter rippled around him, as he knew it would.

"Silence," the art teacher said, and the giggles stopped.

Ted began sketching the daisies. He turned his paper around to sketch the milk bottle beneath them. With the drawing upside down, he could see that the shadows under the daisies needed to be darker. He was working on that when the teacher strolled by.

"Exactly what do you think you are doing?" she asked.

"Drawing," Ted said. He went on working as giggles spread again.

"Young man," the teacher said. "Turn your paper around this minute." Ted looked at her in disbelief. The new perspective had really helped his work. His still life was looking better than any of the other drawings in class. He went back to work.

"No, Theodor," the teacher said, loud enough that everyone in the classroom heard. "*Not* upside down! There are rules that every artist must abide by. You will never succeed if you break them."

Ted sat frozen. This was not fair. And it was not right. Rulebooks did not govern art. He waited until the hour was over before he went to the principal's office and signed out of the class. "I'll never take another art course," he said.

Other teachers at Central could work with Ted's wildly creative streak. "Ted, you have a gift," his English teacher said after class one day.

"Why? It's not my birthday!" Ted joked back.

"I don't mean your wit," Mr. Smith said. "I think you have what it takes to be a writer." His voice was so serious that Ted stopped teasing. He was startled and excited that an adult believed in his talent—and his future. Ted worked with Mr.

Smith on the newspaper and took every class he could with this dynamic teacher. Mr. Smith shared Ted's love of playful poetry. They recited funny poems together. Mr. Smith urged Ted to experiment with words in poetry. "Play with other kinds of writing, too."

"Call me Red," Mr. Smith said one day. That was a great leap in friendship at a time when students never called teachers by their first names....He encouraged Ted from the beginning. "Submit your work. This is good enough to be in the school newspaper." "Try something different." "Play with your words."

Sometimes Ted's work was rejected by the school paper. "I'm just not sure I'm good enough," he admitted.... "This happens to all writers," Red would say. "Remember, they didn't reject *you*. They just don't want this one piece of writing. Send them something else and keep sending until your work is accepted."

Ted learned this lesson well.

Narration/Dictation Exercise

From *Dr. Seuss, Young Author and Artist* by Kathleen Kudlinski

Date _____

Name _____

Dictation Exercise

From *Mrs. Piggle-Wiggle's Magic*

by Betty MacDonald

Mrs. Piggle-Wiggle is a little woman who can cure any bad habit that children have. In this story, she has to cure a brother and sister who are tattletales! The first excerpt describes just how bad the problem is. Wendy, who is nine, and Timmy, who is seven, have just come home from school—and their mother, Mrs. Hamilton, is about to find out just how bad the two children really are.

"And how was school?" she asked Wendy as she helped her off with her coat and leggings.

Wendy said, "Well, I hate everybody at school and everybody at school hates me."

Mrs. Hamilton was shocked. Wendy was nine years old. She had nice fat pigtails, shiny brown bangs, sparkling brown eyes and pink cheeks. Mrs. Hamilton didn't see how anyone could hate her. She said, "Why Wendy, that's dreadful, dear. Why does everyone hate you?"

Wendy said, "I don't know. They just do. And I don't care because I hate everybody." She sat down at the kitchen table and took a bite of sugar cookie.

Timmy, who was seven, was sitting on the floor taking off his leggings. His mother said, "Here, Timmy, let me help you."

Timmy said, "No thanks. I can do it myself. You want to know why everybody hates Wendy—it's because she's such an old tattletale. She tells the teacher on everybody. I hate her too."

Mrs. Hamilton said, "Why, Wendy Hamilton. Do you tell on people?"

Wendy said with evident pride, "Uh, huh. I tell Miss Worthington every time anybody whispers or cheats or writes notes. I even told her when Jimmy Murton sucked his paintbrush today. We're not supposed to suck our paintbrushes; we're supposed to use our fingers to make points." She took a little sip of her cocoa and wiped her lips daintily. Wendy was very pleased with herself.

Mrs. Hamilton wasn't pleased with her. She said, "Wendy Hamilton, I think that's horrid. Telling the teacher about a little thing like sucking a paintbrush."

Timmy said, "Oh, she's always in there tattling. She's so busy spying and tattling she doesn't even have time to play."

Wendy said, "You better be careful, Mr. Timothy Hamilton, or I'll tell Mother that you haven't brushed your teeth for five nights and you gave your liver to Spot last Wednesday and you spent some of your Sunday School money on candy and last night you read in bed with a flashlight."

Timmy said, "Yeah, and this morning you put the rest of your toast in the silverware drawer, you spilled Spot's water and didn't wipe it up and you ate half the candy I bought with my Sunday School money."

Wendy, quite red in the face, said, "Oh, bah, bah, bah, to you, you old crumpet."

"Bah, bah, bah, yourself, old Dog Eyes," Timmy said.

Wendy said, "Motherrrrrrrr, he calls me dog eyes all the time. He says only dogs have brown eyes."

Mrs. Hamilton said, "Wendy, change your school clothes and then go in and start your practicing. Timmy, change your school clothes and then go down in the basement and put away all of Daddy's tools that you got out last night. I must say, you're both so disagreeable I'm sorry you came home from school and spoiled my nice peaceful afternoon."

Narration Exercise

From *Mrs. Piggle-Wiggle's Magic* by Betty MacDonald

Name _____

Dictation Exercise

From *Mrs. Piggle-Wiggle's Magic*
by Betty MacDonald

Mrs. Hamilton gives Timmy and Wendy magic tattletale pills that Mrs. Piggle-Wiggle sends her. This tells what happens next! "Galoshes" is another name for rubber boots.

As Mrs. Hamilton took up her children's oatmeal and poured their milk, she glanced fearfully toward the back stairs. How would they look this time and what had the magic pills done to them? In no time at all she had her answer. First she heard shrill fighting voices, quick chasing footsteps, slaps and yelps and then racing down the stairs came the tattlers, each redfaced and anxious to tell first.

"Motherrrrrr," said Wendy as she slid through the kitchen door. "Motherrrrr, Timmy—" but instead of the long tattletale she intended, out of Wendy's mouth came a big puff of black smoke. The puff of smoke was shaped like a little black cloud except that hanging from the bottom of it were four little black tails. Little black tattletales. The black cloud rose to the ceiling and stuck—the four little tails swayed gently back and forth.

Timmy said, "My gosh, did you see that. Smoke came out of Wendy's mouth. Say, Mother, I bet ole Wendy's been—" but instead of saying "smoking" as he intended, a big puff of black smoke came out of his mouth. It too was a little black cloud but it had only one tail hanging from it because he had only intended to tattle about one thing. Timmy and Wendy stood with their mouths open staring at the ceiling.

Mrs. Hamilton said, "Well, I've always wondered what a tattletale looks like, now I know. Ugh, what ugly things!" Wendy and Timmy didn't say anything. They looked at the ceiling, then at each other and then back at the ceiling. Finally they sat down to breakfast.

After breakfast it was still snowing hard but Wendy and Timmy said they were going out to shovel the walks. They put on their leggings, coats, caps and mittens without a word but they couldn't decide whose galoshes were whose and they began jerking them back and forth and pushing and shoving and finally were just going to yell for Mrs. Hamilton to tattle when out of their open mouths came two huge rolls of black smoke each with a long black tattletale suspended from it. The two new tattletales soared slowly upwards and stuck to the ceiling not far from the first two.

Wendy said, "What if that happened in school?"

Timmy said, "Boy, the kids would sure be surprised. I can just hear ole Miss Harkness. She'd say, 'Timmy Hamilton, you have been SMOKING!'"

Wendy said, "I don't think I'd like to have that happen in school. All the children would laugh at me. Hey, these are your galoshes. I can tell because they are a teensy bit littler than mine."

They put on their galoshes and went quietly out to shovel the walks.

Narration/Dictation Exercise

From *Mrs. Piggle-Wiggle's Magic* by Betty MacDonald

Name _____

From *Money, Money, Money: Where It Comes From, How to Save It, Spend It and Make It*
by Eve Drobot

This excerpt from Money, Money, Money *will tell you more about the names we use for money.*

The word "money" comes from Latin, the language of the ancient Romans. Juno, one of their goddesses, was nicknamed Moneta, which means "the woman who warns." Juno was called that because one of her jobs was to warn people when they were doing wrong. She was an important goddess, and her temple was an important place. So it's not surprising that the ancient Romans made their coins right next to her temple. The coins themselves soon came to be called by the goddess's nickname.

Moneta is the word modern Italians still use to describe their coins. The Spanish call theirs *moneda* and the French say *monnaie*. The place where coins are made is called a "mint."

The first coins weren't all round—some were shaped like pie wedges. The Latin word for wedge, *cuneus*, gives us the English word "coin"....

The dollar is known from Australia to Zimbabwe, in 23 countries in all. The word "dollar" originally comes from the German word *thaler*. When a German emperor became the king of Spain in the 17th century, Spanish explorers and conquerors took the German word to the Americas, and from there it kept going until it reached all around the world.

No one is absolutely sure where the $ sign came from, but there are lots of interesting theories. One of the most accepted ones is that it is the initials U and S, for United States, stuck one on top of the other—people writing the symbol in a hurry just stopped using the bottom part of the U. Another idea is that it is a mangled form of the number 8, because the Spanish coins known as "pieces of eight" were the most common coins in North American 200 years ago.

We get the word "cash" from the ancient Chinese, who carried their coins in bundles on string. A bundle of a hundred coins was called one *cash*. But the Chinese didn't invent the word, either—they got it from the Portuguese, with whom they traded, and who called their coins *caixa* (pronounced "cash-a").

In every language there are slang terms for money—or the lack of it. If you had a dollar for every nickname money has, you'd be rich. Dollars are sometimes called "bucks," for the days when North American Native peoples used buckskins, or deerhides, for trade. A hundred years ago, you'd have heard North American money being called "saddle blankets" because the bank notes were very large—

large enough, people joked, to cover a horse's back. In Latin America, money is nicknamed "little paper." In France, money is "the ticket" or "the round stuff." In Germany it's known as "pinke-pinke," for the sound coins make as they jingle in your pocket.

Name _____

From *Money, Money, Money* by Eve Drobot

Name _____

Dictation Exercise

From *The Everything Kids' Money Book*
by Diane Mayr

Back in the days of Benjamin Franklin and Thomas Jefferson, the colonies did not have just one kind of money. Each colony had its own kind of coin and its own mint. Listen to what happened then. To "counterfeit" means to make a false coin.

In the early days of coins, with gold and silver being such soft metals, a dishonest person was able to shave off small pieces of the edge of a coin. This was called "clipping." After a while the dishonest person would have a collection of clipped pieces large enough to be melted down and sold....

In 1651, John Hull of the Massachusetts Bay Colony started a mint that produced very crude coins. The coins were stamped with NE for New England on one side and the denomination on the other. The simplicity of the coin led to trouble—it was easy to counterfeit and easy to clip. An improved design was necessary. From 1653 to 1674, Hull's mint produced redesigned coins that had a willow, oak, or pine tree on the obverse [the front of a coin] and the date...on the reverse [the back of the coin]. Hull's coins are usually referred to as "New England pine tree" coins.

There were different coins in each of the colonies. The values placed on the coins in each region also differed and often led to confusion....Imagine how confusing things got by the end of the eighteenth century when the British had been defeated and each of the states was minting its own coins! Take for example, Connecticut. During the years 1785 to 1788, more than three hundred different copper coins were made! Why so many? The state authorized private citizens to mint the coins for the state. Each developed its own design!

Individual states did not always find it easy to mint their own coins. In 1787 and 1788, when the state of Massachusetts began to make copper cents and half cents, it found that it cost two cents to make each cent, and one cent to make a half cent! Massachusetts only operated its mint for a short time.

By 1787 it was time for the United States to think about producing a national coin. James Jarvis was given a contract by Congress to produce three hundred tons of copper coins. Jarvis minted a coin known as the "Fugio" cent. The Fugio cent is the first official coin of the United States.

The cent had a sundial on the obverse and the Latin word *fugio* meaning "I fly," referring to the old saying, "time flies." Also on the obverse is the legend [saying] "mind your business." Mind your business refers to the citizens of the United States having to build up their businesses to make for a stronger country. It had nothing to do with nosiness!

The reverse of the Fugio cent had a chain with thirteen links representing the thirteen states, and the motto "We are one."

Narration/Dictation Exercise

From *The Everything Kids' Money Book* by Diane Mayr

Name _____

Date _____

Dictation Exercise

From *Babe: The Gallant Pig*
by Dick King-Smith

Babe *tells the story of a very unusual pig. When he is a little piglet, he is won at a fair by Farmer Hogget, who brings him back to the Hogget farm. There, the collie Fly and her four puppies meet the piglet for the first time. The puppies have never seen a pig before; they ask their mother if pigs are stupid, and Fly tells them yes.*

A "loose box" is a barn stall, used for horses or other livestock.

The floor of the stables had not rung to a horse's hoof for many years, but it was a useful place for storing things. The hens foraged about there, and sometimes laid their eggs in the old wooden mangers; the swallows built their nests against its roof beams with mud from the duck pond; and rats and mice lived happy lives in its shelter until the farm cats cut them short. At one end of the stables were two loose boxes with boarded sides topped by iron rails. One served as a kennel for Fly and her puppies. The other sometimes housed sick sheep. In there Farmer Hogget had put the piglet.

A convenient stack of straw bales allowed the dogs to look down into the box through the bars.

"It certainly looks stupid," said one of the puppies, yawning. At the sound of the words the piglet glanced up quickly. He put his head to one side and regarded the dogs with sharp eyes. Something about the sight of this very small animal standing all by itself in the middle of the roomy loose box touched Fly's soft heart. Already she was sorry that she had said that pigs were stupid, for this one certainly did not appear to be so. Also there was something dignified about the way it stood its ground, in a strange place, confronted with strange animals. How different from the silly sheep, who at the mere sight of a dog would run aimlessly about, crying "Wolf! Wolf!" in their empty-headed way.

"Hullo," she said. "Who are you?"

"I'm a Large White," said the piglet.

"Blimey!" said one of the puppies. "If that's a large white, what's a small one like?" And they all four sniggered.

"Be quiet!" snapped Fly. "Just remember that five minutes ago you didn't even know what a pig was." And to the piglet she said kindly, "I expect that's your breed, dear. I meant, what's your name?"

"I don't know," said the piglet.

"Well, what did your mother call you, to tell you apart from your brothers and sisters?" said Fly and then wished she hadn't, for at the mention of his family the piglet began to look distinctly unhappy. His little forehead wrinkled and he gulped and his voice trembled as he answered.

"She called us all the same."

"And what was that, dear?"

"Babe," said the piglet, and the puppies began to giggle until their mother silenced them with a growl.

"But that's a lovely name," she said. "Would you like us to call you that? It'll make you feel more at home."

At this last word the little pig's face fell even further.

"I want my mum," he said very quietly.

At that instant the collie made up her mind that she would foster this unhappy child.

"Go out in the yard and play," she said to the puppies, and she climbed to the top of the straw stack and jumped over the rail and down into the loose box beside the piglet.

"Listen, Babe," she said. "You've got to be a brave boy. Everyone has to leave their mother, it's all part of growing up. I did it, when I was your age, and my puppies will have to leave me quite soon. But I'll look after you. If you like." Then she licked his little snout with a warm rough tongue, her plumed tail wagging.

"There. Is that nice?" she said.

Narration Exercise

From *Babe: The Gallant Pig* by Dick King-Smith

Date _____

Name _____

Dictation Exercise

From *Babe: The Gallant Pig*

by Dick King-Smith

Fly's puppies grow up to be sheepdogs, and Babe asks his new mother why he can't be a sheep-pig. Fly agrees to teach Babe how to herd ducks—but she doesn't think that her foster child will ever be able to herd sheep properly. In this next part of the story, Babe meets a real sheep for the first time.

"Ewe" is the proper name for a female sheep. It is pronounced just like "you."

Farmer Hogget and Fly had been out around the flock, and when they returned Fly was driving before her an old lame ewe, which they penned in the loose box where the piglet had originally been shut. Then they went away up the hill again.

Babe made his way into the stables, curious to meet this, the first of the animals that he planned one day to work with, but he could not see into the box. He snuffled under the bottom of the door, and from inside there came a cough and the sharp stamp of a foot, and then the sound of a hoarse complaining voice. "Wolves! Wolves!" it said. "They never do leave a body alone. Nag, nag, nag all day long, go here, go there, do this, do that. What d'you want now? Can't you give us a bit of peace, wolf?"

"I'm not a wolf," said Babe under the door.

"Oh, I knows all that," said the sheep sourly. "Calls yourself a sheepdog, I knows that, but you don't fool none of us. You're a wolf like the rest of 'em, given half a chance. You looks at us, and you sees lamb chops. Go away, wolf."

"But I'm not a sheepdog either," said Babe, and he scrambled up the stack of straw bales and looked over the bars.

"You see?" he said.

"Well I'll be dipped," said the old sheep peering up at him. "No more you ain't. What are you?"

"Pig," said Babe. "Large White. What are you?"

"Ewe," said the sheep.

"No, not me, you—what are you?"

"I'm a ewe."

Mum was right, thought Babe, they certainly are stupid. But if I'm going to learn how to be a sheep-pig I must try to understand them, and this might be a good chance. Perhaps I could make a friend of this one.

"My name's Babe," he said in a jolly voice. "What's yours?"

"Maaaaa," said the sheep.

"That's a nice name," said Babe. "What's the matter with you, Ma?"

"Foot rot," said the sheep, holding up a foreleg. "And I've got a nasty cough." She coughed. "And I'm not as young as I was."

"You don't look very old to me," said Babe politely.

A look of pleasure came over the sheep's mournful face, and she lay down in the straw.

"Very civil of you to say so," she said. "First kind word I've had since I were a little lamb," and she belched loudly and began to chew a mouthful of cud.

Narration/Dictation Exercise

From *Babe: The Gallant Pig* by Dick King-Smith

Date _____

Name _____

Dictation Exercise

From *Hunting and Herding Dogs*
by Marie-Therese Miller

Fly and Babe are characters in a story, but farmers really do use collies (although not pigs!) to herd sheep. This selection describes how shepherds work with their dogs.

The handler and his black-and-white border collie enter the field. A flock of sheep stands grazing in the pasture. The handler holds a shepherd's crook, a long staff with a curve at the top, in his hand. He has a whistle tied around his neck. The handler whistles a command: "Away to me." The dog responds by running counterclockwise around the sheep. What happens next is a telltale sign that border collies are born to herd.

When the dog is behind the sheep, the handler tells it to lie down. The border collie stops in a crouch, with its shoulders down and its rear end up. The dog glares at the sheep. This stare is called "eye," and it helps convince the sheep to move away from the dog. "Walk up," the handler orders, and the dog slowly approaches the sheep. The sheep gather, as if following the dog's strict orders. The border collie collects the herd and walks the sheep directly to the handler.

The border collie has a natural instinct to gather stock and bring it toward the handler. With training that builds on this natural ability, the border collie can be an invaluable tool to sheep farmers.

Border collies are superb herding dogs that are known for their intelligence. By the time they are trained to herd, border collies understand nearly 20 different commands. Border collies also have the ability to work independently. On big farms, the dogs often herd out of sight of their handlers and must solve problems on their own.

This dog breed has lots of energy and loves to herd. The dog's shoulder-down stance and staring "eye" make it seem like a predator to the sheep. When a dog approaches the sheep herd like this, the group instinctively moves away. This is another reason border collies are successful at herding work....

In more advanced training, a border collie learns to move, or drive, the sheep herd away from the handler. Driving is difficult to teach a border collie because it goes against the breed's gathering instinct, to move the sheep toward the farmer. Driving is easier for the dog to learn if the sheep are placed in a narrow lane with fences on either side and with the handler and the dog behind the herd. This way, the dog cannot race around the sheep and gather them back to the handler. Soon, the dog will grasp the driving concept and the enclosed area will no longer be needed.

Name _____

Date _____

Narration Exercise

From *Hunting and Herding Dogs* by Marie-Therese Miller

Name _____

Dictation Exercise

From *A Dog's World*
edited by Christine Hunsicker

An American woman named Susan Allen Toth wrote this description of an English sheepdog trial. It is found in a book called A Dog's World, *which is a collection of essays and stories written by many different people. A woman named Christine Hunsicker had the job of putting all the essays and stories together into one book. We call her the book's "editor," and instead of saying that the book is "by Christine Hunsicker" (since so many other people wrote parts of it!), we say that the book is "edited by Christine Hunsicker."*

When a sheepdog leaves the post, he begins his *outrun,* the first phase of the trial. To avoid coming at the sheep head-on, and alarming or scattering them, the dog circles widely to the right or left....When the dog contacts the sheep, he has completed his second phase, the *lift.* Now he must drive the little flock back toward his handler.

Watching the eager border collies streak up the field, James and I could scarcely believe their speed. Crouching low, a black-and-white blur in the tall grass, a dog usually reached the end of the field in moments. "Oh yes," our neighbor assured us, "he can get up to forty miles an hour, can a good dog."

Speed is not the only consideration, however. In the third phase, the *fetch,* as the dog brings the sheep down the field, he is supposed to herd them in a straight line. But sheep do not like straight lines. They have their own ideas.

Nor do they have any desire to cooperate in the *drive,* the next phase, a triangular course that passes through two-gate obstacles. The dog is supposed to move, turn, and keep the sheep in line without upsetting them....Sheep have the irritating habit of bolting this way or that, separating from the flock without warning, or turning at the last possible moment to skirt a gate....

In the final two phases of the trial, the *shed* and *pen,* the dog has to perform even more intricate maneuvers. First, at a signal, the dog must identify two sheep specially marked by large collars and then cut them off from the flock. Finally, after again collecting the sheep, the dog is supposed to herd them into a pen. The sheep do not tend to file into the pen without a fuss. The handler, standing at the gate of the pen and holding it open, can wave his shepherd's staff and try to block the meandering sheep with his body, but he or she cannot let go of the gate.

Narration/Dictation Exercise

From *A Dog's World* edited by Christine Hunsicker

Outrun: leaving the post
Lift: making contact with the sheep
Fetch: bringing the sheep to the handler
Drive: herding the sheep through gates
Shed: cutting two particular sheep off from the rest of the flock
Pen: herding all of the sheep into a pen

Name _____

Dictation Exercise

From *Anne of Green Gables*
by Lucy Maud Montgomery

Marilla and Matthew Cuthbert are an elderly brother and sister who live together on Prince Edward Island, in Canada. They decide that they need help on their farm, so they send away to an orphanage in a nearby town, asking for a boy who can come live with them. Matthew Cuthbert goes to pick up the orphan at the train station—but when he gets there, he finds that they've sent a little girl instead. He doesn't know what to do, so he takes the little girl home.

Marilla came briskly forward as Matthew opened the door. But when her eyes fell on the odd little figure in the stiff, ugly dress, with the long braids of red hair and the eager, luminous eyes, she stopped short in amazement.

"Matthew Cuthbert, who's that?" she ejaculated. "Where is the boy?"

"There wasn't any boy," said Matthew wretchedly. "There was only HER."

He nodded at the child, remembering that he had never even asked her name.

"No boy! But there MUST have been a boy," insisted Marilla. "We sent word to Mrs. Spencer to bring a boy."

"Well, she didn't. She brought HER. I asked the station-master. And I had to bring her home. She couldn't be left there, no matter where the mistake had come in."

"Well, this is a pretty piece of business!" ejaculated Marilla.

During this dialogue the child had remained silent, her eyes roving from one to the other, all the animation fading out of her face. Suddenly she seemed to grasp the full meaning of what had been said. Dropping her precious carpet-bag she sprang forward a step and clasped her hands.

"You don't want me!" she cried. "You don't want me because I'm not a boy! I might have expected it. Nobody ever did want me. I might have known it was all too beautiful to last. I might have known nobody really did want me. Oh, what shall I do? I'm going to burst into tears!"

Burst into tears she did. Sitting down on a chair by the table, flinging her arms out upon it, and burying her face in them, she proceeded to cry stormily. Marilla and Matthew looked at each other deprecatingly across the stove. Neither of them knew what to say or do. Finally Marilla stepped lamely into the breach.

"Well, well, there's no need to cry so about it."

"Yes, there IS need!" The child raised her head quickly, revealing a tear-stained face and trembling lips. "YOU would cry, too, if you were an orphan and had come to a place you thought was going to be home and found that they didn't want you because you weren't a boy. Oh, this is the most TRAGICAL thing that ever happened to me!"

Something like a reluctant smile, rather rusty from long disuse, mellowed Marilla's grim expression.

"Well, don't cry any more. We're not going to turn you out-of-doors to-night. You'll have to stay here until we investigate this affair. What's your name?"

The child hesitated for a moment.

"Will you please call me Cordelia?" she said eagerly.

"CALL you Cordelia? Is that your name?"

"No-o-o, it's not exactly my name, but I would love to be called Cordelia. It's such a perfectly elegant name."

"I don't know what on earth you mean. If Cordelia isn't your name, what is?"

"Anne Shirley," reluctantly faltered forth the owner of that name, "but, oh, please do call me Cordelia. It can't matter much to you what you call me if I'm only going to be here a little while, can it? And Anne is such an unromantic name."

"Unromantic fiddlesticks!" said the unsympathetic Marilla. "Anne is a real good plain sensible name. You've no need to be ashamed of it."

Narration Exercise

From *Anne of Green Gables* by Lucy Maud Montgomery

Date _____

Name _____

Dictation Exercise

From *Pioneers in Canada*

by Harry Johnston

Pioneers in Canada is *a classic text about Canadian history written by Harry Johnston almost a hundred years ago. Johnston describes the journey that the French explorer Jacques Cartier made to the coast of North America in 1534. On this journey, Cartier came to Prince Edward Island, where* Anne of Green Gables *is set.*

Before you read, you should know that guillemots are birds related to the now-extinct great auk, which looked a little bit like a penguin. Gannets are seabirds that look something like seagulls, and eider ducks are sea ducks that live in cold areas. "Eiderdown," a kind of duck feather used to stuff mattresses, is named after the eider duck.

As he sailed northwards, past the deeply indented fiords and bays of eastern Newfoundland (the shores of which were still hugged by the winter ice), he and his men were much impressed with the incredible numbers of the sea fowl settled for nesting purposes on the rocky islands, especially on Funk Island. These birds were guillemots, puffins, great auks, gannets (called by Cartier *margaulx*), and probably gulls and eider duck. To his sailors—always hungry and partly fed on salted provisions, as seamen were down to a few years ago—this inexhaustible supply of fresh food was a source of great enjoyment. They were indifferent, no doubt, to the fishy flavour of the auks and the guillemots, and only noticed that they were splendidly fat. Moreover, the birds attracted polar bears "as large as cows and as white as swans." The bears would swim off from the shore to the islands (unless they could reach them by crossing the ice), and the sailors occasionally killed the bears and ate their flesh, which they compared in excellence and taste to veal.

Passing through the Straits of Belle Isle, Cartier's ships entered the Gulf of St. Lawrence. They had previously visited the adjoining coast of Labrador, and there had encountered their first natives, members of some Algonquin tribe from Canada, who had come north for seal fishing (Cartier is clever enough to notice and describe their birch-bark canoes). After examining the west coast of Newfoundland, Cartier's ships sailed on past the Magdalen Islands (stopping every now and then off some islet to collect supplies of sea birds, for the rocky ground was covered with them as thickly as a meadow with grass). On the shores of these islands they noticed "several great beasts like oxen, which have two tusks in the mouth similar to those of the elephant." These were walruses.

He reached the north coast of Prince Edward Island, and this lovely country received from him an enthusiastic description. The pine trees, the junipers, yews, elms, poplars, ash, and willows, the beeches and the maples, made the forest not only full of delicious and stimulating odours, but lovely in its varied tints of green. In the natural meadows and forest clearings there were red and white currants, gooseberries, strawberries, raspberries, a vetch which produced edible peas, and a grass with a grain like rye. The forest abounded in pigeons, and the climate was pleasant and warm.

Original Sentence Exercise

From *Pioneers in Canada* by Harry Johnston

Date _____

Name _____

Dictation Exercise

From *The Young Folks' History of England*
by Charlotte Yonge

This story about the Romans in Britain was written a hundred and fifty years ago.

Julius Caesar heard that a little way off there was a country nobody knew anything about, except that the people were very fierce and savage, and that a sort of pearl was found in the shells of mussels which lived in the rivers. He could not bear that there should be any place that his own people, the Romans, did not know and subdue. So he commanded the ships to be prepared, and he and his soldiers embarked, watching the white cliffs on the other side of the sea grow higher and higher as he came nearer and nearer.

When he came quite up to them, he found the savages were there in earnest. They were tall men, with long red streaming hair, and such clothes as they had were woollen, checked like plaid; but many had their arms and breasts naked, and painted all over in blue patterns. They yelled and brandished their darts, to make Julius Caesar and his Roman soldiers keep away; but he only went on to a place where the shore was not quite so steep, and there commanded his soldiers to land. The savages had run along the shore too, and there was a terrible fight; but at last the man who carried the eagle standard for Caesar jumped down into the middle of the natives, calling out to his fellows that they must come after him, or they would lose their eagle. They all came rushing and leaping down, and thus they managed to force back the savages, and make their way to the shore.

There was not much worth having when they had made their way there. Though they came again the next year, and forced their way a good deal farther into the country, they saw chiefly bare downs, or heaths, or thick woods. The few houses were little more than piles of stones, and the people were rough and wild, and could do very little. The men hunted wild boars, and wolves and stags, and the women dug the ground, and raised a little corn, which they ground to flour between two stones to make bread; and they spun the wool of their sheep, dyed it with bright colors, and wove it into dresses. They had some strong places in the woods, with trunks of trees, cut down to shut them in from the enemy, with all their flocks and cattle; but Caesar did not get into any of these. He only made the natives give him some of their pearls, and call the Romans their masters, and then he went back to his ships, and none of the set of savages who were alive when he came saw him or his Romans any more.

Do you know who these savages were who fought with Julius Caesar? They were called Britons. And the country he came to see? That was our very own island, England, only it was not called so then. And the place where Julius Caesar landed is called Deal, and, if you look at the map where England and France most nearly touch one another, I think you will see the name Deal, and remember it was there Julius Caesar landed, and fought with the Britons.

Name _____

Date _____

Narration Exercise

From *Young Folks' History of England* by Charlotte Yonge

Date _____

Name _____

Dictation Exercise

From *The Young Folks' History of England*
by Charlotte Yonge

This selection continues the story of the Romans in Britain.

It was nearly a hundred years before any more of the Romans came to Britain; but they were people who could not hear of a place without wanting to conquer it, and they never left off trying till they had done what they undertook.

The Romans made beautiful straight roads all over the country, and they built towns. Almost all the towns whose names end in *-chester* were begun by the Romans, and bits of their walls are to be seen still, built of very small bricks. Sometimes people dig up a bit of the beautiful pavement of colored tiles, in patterns, which used to be the floors of their houses, or a piece of their money, or one of their ornaments.

For the Romans held Britain for four hundred years, and tamed the wild people in the south, and taught them to speak and dress, and read and write like themselves, so that they could hardly be known from the Romans. Only the wild ones beyond the wall, and in the mountains, were as savage as ever, and, now and then, used to come and steal the cattle, and burn the houses of their neighbors who had learnt better.

Another set of wild people used to come over in boats across the North Sea and German Ocean. These people had their home in the country that is called Holstein and Jutland. They were tall men, and had blue eyes and fair hair, and they were very strong, and good-natured in a rough sort of way, though they were fierce to their enemies. There was a great deal more fighting than any one has told us about; but the end of it all was that the Roman soldiers were wanted at home, and though the great British chief we call King Arthur fought very bravely, he could not drive back the blue-eyed men in the ships; but more and more came, till, at last, they got all the country, and drove the Britons, some up into the north, some into the mountains that rise along the west of the island, and some into its west point.

The Britons used to call the blue-eyed men Saxons; but they called themselves Angles, and the country was called after them Angle-land. Don't you know what it is called now? England itself, and the people English. They spoke much the same language as we do.

As to the Britons, the English went on driving them back till they only kept their mountains. There they have gone on living ever since, and talking their own old language. The English called them Welsh, a name that meant strangers, and we call them Welsh still, and their country Wales. They made a great many grand stories about their last brave chief, Arthur, till, at last, they turned into a sort of fairy tale. It was said that, when King Arthur lay badly wounded after his last battle, he bade his friend fling his sword into the river, and that then three lovely ladies came in a boat, and carried him away to a secret island. The Welsh kept on saying, for years and years, that one day King Arthur would wake up again, and give them back all Britain, which used to be their own before the English got it for themselves; but the English have had England now for thirteen hundred years.

Name _____

Original Sentence Exercise

From *Young Folks' History of England* by Charlotte Yonge

Name _____

Dictation Exercise

From *The Black Stallion*

by Walter Farley

At the beginning of The Black Stallion, *young Alec Ramsay is sailing home on a steamship, the* Drake, *after visiting an uncle in India. He is fascinated by a horse which is also travelling on the* Drake; *the horse is a black stalllion, wild and hard to manage.*

The Drake *is in the middle of the ocean when a storm sweeps down on it, late one night, and the ship begins to sink.*

Immediately Alec thought of the Black. What was happening to him? Was he still in his stall? Alec fought his way out of line and toward the stern of the boat. If the stallion was alive, he was going to set him free and give him his chance to fight for life.

The stall was still standing. Alec heard a shrill whistle rise above the storm. He rushed to the door, lifted the heavy bar, and swung it open. For a second the mighty hoofs stopped pounding and there was silence. Alec backed slowly away.

Then he saw the Black, his head held high, his nostrils blown out with excitement. Suddenly he snorted and plunged straight for the rail and Alec. Alec was paralyzed. He couldn't move. One hand was on the rail, which was broken at this point, leaving nothing between him and the open water. The Black swerved as he came near him, and the boy realized that the stallion was making for the hole. The horse's shoulder grazed him as he swerved, and Alec went flying into space. He felt the water close over his head.

When he came up, his first thought was of the ship; then he heard an explosion, and he saw the *Drake* settling deep into the water. Frantically he looked around for a lifeboat, but there was none in sight. Then he saw the Black swimming not more than ten yeards away. Something swished by him—a rope, and it was attached to the Black's halter! The same rope that they had used to bring the stallion aboard the boat, and which they had never been able to get close enough to the horse to untie. Without stopping to think, Alec grabbed hold of it. Then he was pulled through the water, into the oncoming seas.

The waves were still large, but with the aid of his life jacket, Alec was able to stay on top. He was too tired now to give much thought to what he had done. He only knew that he had had his choice of remaining in the water alone or being pulled by the Black. If he was to die, he would rather die with the mighty stallion than alone. He took one last look behind and saw the *Drake* sink into the depths.

For hours Alec battled the waves. He had tied the rope securely around his waist. He could hardly hold his head up. Suddenly he felt the rope slacken. The

Black had stopped swimming! Alec anxiously waited; peering into the darkness he could just make out the head of the stallion. The Black's whistle pierced the air! After a few minutes, the rope became taut again. The horse had changed his direction. Another hour passed, then the storm diminished to high, rolling swells. The first streaks of dawn appeared on the horizon.

The Black had stopped four times during the night, and each time he had altered his course. Alec wondered whether the stallion's wild instinct was leading him to land. The sun rose and shone down brightly on the boy's head; the salt water he had swallowed during the night made him sick to his stomach. But when Alec felt that he could hold out no longer, he looked at the struggling, fighting animal in front of him, and new courage came to him.

Suddenly he realized that they were going with the waves, instead of against them. He shoook his head, trying to clear his mind. Yes, they were riding in; they must be approaching land!

Narration Exercise

From *The Black Stallion* by Walter Farley

Date _____

Name _____

Dictation Exercise

From *The Black Stallion*

by Walter Farley

Alec and the Black are marooned together on the island. It takes Alec a long time to make friends with the Black—and even longer before he dares to try and ride the stallion. The first time he mounts the Black, the horse throws him off immediately.

Alec waited for a few minutes—then once again led the stallion to the sand dune. His hand grasped the horse's mane. But this time he laid only the upper part of his body on the stallion's back, while he talked soothingly into his ear. The Black flirted his ears back and forth as he glanced backward with his dark eyes.

"See, I'm not going to hurt you," Alec murmured, knowing that it was he who might be hurt. After a few minutes, Alec cautiously slid onto his back. Once again, the stallion snorted and sent the boy flying through the air.

Alec picked himself up from the ground—slower this time. But when he had rested, he whistled for the Black again. The stallion moved toward him. Alec determinedly stepped on the sand dune and once again let the Black feel his weight. Gently he spoke into a large ear, "It's me. I'm not much to carry." He slid onto the stallion's back. One arm slipped around the Black's neck as he half-reared. Then, like a shot from a gun, the Black broke down the beach. His action shifted, and his huge strides seemed to make him fly through the air.

Alec clung to the stallion's mane for his life. The wind screamed by and he couldn't see! Suddenly the Black swerved and headed up the sand dune; he reached the top and then down. The spring was a blur as they whipped by. To the rocks he raced, and then the stallion made a wide circle—his speed never diminishing. Down through a long ravine he rushed. Alec's blurred vision made out a black object in front of them, and as a flash he remembered the deep gully that was there. He felt the stallion gather himself; instinctively he leaned forward and held the Black firm and steady with his hands and knees. Then they were in the air, sailing over the black hole. Alec almost lost his balance when they landed, but recovered himself in time to keep from falling off! Once again the stallion reached the beach, his hoofbeats regular and rhythmic on the white sand.

The jump had helped greatly in clearing Alec's mind. He leaned closer to the stallion's ear and kept repeating, "Easy, Black. Easy." The stallion seemed to glide over the sand and then his speed began to lessen. Alec kept talking to him. Slower and slower ran the Black. Gradually he came to a stop. The boy released his grip from the stallion's mane and his arms encircled the Black's neck. He was weak with exhaustion—in no condition for such a ride! Wearily he slipped to the ground. Never had he dreamed a horse could run so fast! The stallion looked at him, his head held high, his large body only slightly covered with sweat.

That night Alec lay wide awake, his body aching with pain, but his heart pounding with excitement. He had ridden the Black! He had conquered this wild, unbroken stallion with kindness. He felt sure that from that day on the Black was his—his alone! But for what—would they ever be rescued? Would he ever see his home again? Alec shook his head. He had promised himself he wouldn't think of that any more.

Original Sentence Exercise

From *The Black Stallion* by Walter Farley

Name _____

Date _____

Dictation Exercise

From *King Arthur and His Knights of the Round Table*
by Roger Lancelyn Green

This is from Roger Lancelyn Green's retelling of the legends about Arthur. The king of Britain who came before Arthur, Uther Pendragon, has just died without naming an heir, and Britain has fallen into disorder.

Then the land fell upon days more evil and wretched than any which had gone before. King Uther's knights fought amongst themselves, quarrelling as to who should rule; and the Saxons, seeing that there was no strong man to lead the Britons against them, conquered more and more of Britain.

Years of strife and misery went by, until the appointed time was at hand. Then Merlin, the good enchanter, came out from the deep, mysterious valleys of North Wales, which in those days was called Gwynedd, through Powys or South Wales, and passed on his way to London. And so great was his fame that neither Saxon nor Briton dared molest him.

Merlin came to London and spoke with the Archbishop; and a great gathering of knights was called for Christmas Day—so great that all of them could not find a place in the abbey church, so that some were forced to gather in the churchyard.

In the middle of the service, there arose suddenly a murmur of wonder outside the abbey: for there was seen, though no man saw it come, a great square slab of marble-stone in the churchyard, and on the stone an anvil of iron, and set point downwards a great, shining sword of steel thrust deeply into the anvil.

"Stir not till the service be done," commanded the Archbishop when this marvel was made known to him. "But pray the more unto God that we may find a remedy for the sore wounds of our land."

When the service was ended, the Archbishop and the lords and knights who had been within the abbey came out to see the wonder of the sword. Round about the anvil they found letters of gold set in the great stone, and the letters read thus:

WHOSO PULLETH OUT THIS SWORD FROM THIS STONE AND ANVIL IS THE TRUE-BORN KING OF ALL BRITAIN.

When they saw this, many and many a man tried to pull out the sword—but not one of them could stir it a hair's breadth.

"He is not here," said the Archbishop. "But doubt not that God will send us our King. Let messengers be sent through all the land to tell what is written on the stone: and upon New Year's Day we will hold a great tournament, and see whether our King is amongst those who come to joust. Until then, I counsel that we appoint ten knights to guard the stone, and set a rich pavilion over it."

All this was done, and upon New Year's Day a great host of knights met together. But none as yet could draw forth the sword out of the stone. Then they went all a little way off, and pitched tents, and held a tournament or sham-fight, trying their strength and skill at jousting with long lances of wood, or fighting with broad-swords.

Name _____

Date _____

Narration Exercise

From *King Arthur and His Knights of the Round Table* by Roger Lancelyn Green

Name _____

Date _____

Dictation Exercise

From *King Arthur and His Knights of the Round Table*

by Roger Lancelyn Green

The story of Arthur, continued.

It happened that among those who came was the good knight Sir Ector, and his son Kay, who had been made a knight not many months before; and with them came Arthur, Sir Kay's young brother, a youth of scarcely sixteen years of age.

Riding to the jousts, Sir Kay found suddenly that he had left his sword in his lodgings, and he asked Arthur to ride back and fetch it for him.

"Certainly I will," said Arthur, who was always ready to do anything for other people, and back he rode to the town. But Sir Kay's mother had locked the door, and gone out to see the tournament, so that Arthur could not get into the lodgings at all.

This troubled Arthur very much. "My brother Kay must have a sword," he thought, as he rode slowly back. "It will be a shame and a matter for unkind jests if so young a knight comes to the jousts without a sword. But where can I find him one?...I know! I saw one sticking in an anvil in the churchyard, I'll fetch that: it's doing no good there!"

So Arthur set spurs to his horse and came to the churchyard. Tying his horse to the stile, he ran to the tent which had been set over the stone—and found that all ten of the guardian knights had also gone to the tournament. Without stopping to read what was written on the stone, Arthur pulled out the sword at a touch, ran back to his horse, and in a few minutes had caught up with Sir Kay and handed it over to him.

Arthur knew nothing of what sword it was, but Kay had already tried to pull it from the anvil, and saw at a glance that it was the same one. Instantly he rode to his father Sir Ector and said:

"Sir! Look, here is the sword out of the stone! So you see I must be the true-born King of all Britain!"

But Sir Ector knew better than to believe Sir Kay too readily. Instead, he rode back with him to the church, and there made him swear a solemn oath with his hands on the Bible to say truly how he came by the sword.

"My brother Arthur brought it to me," said Kay, with a sigh.

"And how did *you* get the sword?" asked Sir Ector.

"Sir, I will tell you," said Arthur, fearing that he had done wrong. "Kay sent me to fetch his sword, but I could not come to it. Then I remembered having seen this sword sticking uselessly into an anvil in the churchyard. I thought it could be put to a better use in my brother's hand—so I fetched it."

"Did you find no knights guarding the sword?" asked Sir Ector.

"Never a one," said Arthur.

"Well, put the sword back into the anvil, and let us see you draw it out," commanded Sir Ector.

"That's easily done," said Arthur, puzzled by all this trouble over a sword, and he set it back easily into the anvil.

Then Sir Kay seized it by the hilt and pulled his hardest: but struggle and strain as he might, he could not move it by a hair's breadth. Sir Ector tried also, but with no better success.

"Pull it out," he said to Arthur.

And Arthur, more and more bewildered, put his hand to the hilt and drew forth the sword as if out of a well-greased scabbard.

"Now," said Sir Ector, kneeling before Arthur and bowing his head in reverence, "I understand that you and none other are the true-born King of this land."

Original Sentence Exercise

From *King Arthur and His Knights of the Round Table* by Roger Lancelyn Green

Date _____

Name _____

Dictation Exercise

"The Valiant Little Tailor"
by Jacob and Wilhelm Grimm

This story is found in the collection made by the brothers Jacob and Wilhelm Grimm.

One summer's morning a little tailor was sitting on his table by the window; he was in good spirits, and sewed with all his might. Then came a peasant woman down the street crying: "Good jams, cheap! Good jams, cheap!"

This rang pleasantly in the tailor's ears; he stretched his delicate head out of the window, and called: "Come up here, dear woman; here you will get rid of your goods." The woman came up the three steps to the tailor with her heavy basket, and he made her unpack all the pots for him. He inspected each one, lifted it up, put his nose to it, and at length said: "The jam seems to me to be good, so weigh me out four ounces, dear woman."

The woman who had hoped to find a good sale, gave him what he desired, but went away quite angry and grumbling. "Now, this jam shall be blessed by God," cried the little tailor, "and give me health and strength." So he brought the bread out of the cupboard, cut himself a piece right across the loaf and spread the jam over it.

Then he said, "I will just finish the jacket before I take a bite." He laid the bread near him, sewed on, and in his joy, made bigger and bigger stitches. In the meantime the smell of the sweet jam rose to where the flies were sitting in great numbers, and they were attracted and descended on it in hosts. "Hi! who invited you?" said the little tailor, and drove the unbidden guests away. The flies, however, would not be turned away, but came back again in ever-increasing companies.

The little tailor at last lost all patience, and drew a piece of cloth from the hole under his work-table, and saying: "Wait, and I will give it to you," struck it mercilessly on them. When he drew it away and counted, there lay before him no fewer than seven, dead and with legs stretched out.

He could not help admiring his own bravery. "The whole town shall know of this!" he said. And the little tailor hastened to cut himself a belt, stitched it, and embroidered on it in large letters: 'Seven at one stroke!' "What, the town!" he continued, "the whole world shall hear of it!" and his heart wagged with joy like a lamb's tail.

The tailor put on the belt, and resolved to go forth into the world, because he thought his workshop was too small for his valour. Before he went away, he sought about in the house to see if there was anything which he could take with him; however, he found nothing but an old cheese, and that he put in his pocket.

In front of the door he observed a bird which had caught itself in the thicket. It had to go into his pocket with the cheese. Now he took to the road boldly, and as he was light and nimble, he felt no fatigue.

Narration Exercise

From "The Valiant Little Tailor" by the Brothers Grimm

Date _____

Name _____

Dictation Exercise

"The Valiant Little Tailor"
by Jacob and Wilhelm Grimm

This is the continuation of the story of the little tailor.

The road led him up a mountain, and when he had reached the highest point of it, there sat a powerful giant looking peacefully about him. The little tailor went bravely up, spoke to him, and said: "Good day, comrade, so you are sitting there overlooking the wide-spread world! I am just on my way thither, and want to try my luck. Have you any inclination to go with me?"

The giant looked contemptuously at the tailor, and said: "You ragamuffin! You miserable creature!"

"Oh, indeed?" answered the little tailor, and unbuttoned his coat, and showed the giant the belt, "There may you read what kind of a man I am!" The giant read: "Seven at one stroke," and thought that they had been men whom the tailor had killed, and began to feel a little respect for the tiny fellow.

The giant took a stone in his hand and squeezed it together so that water dropped out of it. "Do that likewise," said the giant, "if you have strength."

"Is that all?" said the tailor, "That is child's play with us!" and put his hand into his pocket, brought out the soft cheese, and pressed it until the liquid ran out of it. "Faith," said he, "that was a little better, wasn't it?"

The giant did not know what to say, and could not believe it of the little man. Then the giant picked up a stone and threw it so high that the eye could scarcely follow it. "Now, little mite of a man, do that likewise," he said.

"Well thrown," said the tailor, "but after all the stone came down to earth again; I will throw you one which shall never come back at all," and he put his hand into his pocket, took out the bird, and threw it into the air. The bird, delighted with its liberty, rose, flew away and did not come back. "How does that shot please you, comrade?" asked the tailor.

"You can certainly throw," said the giant, "but now we will see if you are able to carry anything properly." He took the little tailor to a mighty oak tree which lay there felled on the ground, and said: "If you are strong enough, help me to carry the tree out of the forest."

"Readily," answered the little man. "Take you the trunk on your shoulders, and I will raise up the branches and twigs; after all, they are the heaviest." The giant took the trunk on his shoulder, but the tailor seated himself on a branch, and the giant, who could not look round, had to carry away the whole tree, and the little tailor into the bargain: he behind, was quite merry and happy, and whistled the song: "Three tailors rode forth from the gate," as if carrying the tree were child's play.

The giant, after he had dragged the heavy burden part of the way, could go no further, and cried: "Hark you, I shall have to let the tree fall!"

The tailor sprang nimbly down, seized the tree with both arms as if he had been carrying it, and said to the giant: "You are such a great fellow, and yet cannot even carry the tree!"

Original Sentence Exercise

From "The Valiant Little Tailor" by the Brothers Grimm

Date _____

Name _____

Dictation Exercise

From *Bambi: A Life in the Woods*
by Felix Salten

You may have seen the cartoon movie Bambi. *That movie was made from a wonderful book, written by Felix Salten. The book is much more interesting than the movie! It is called* Bambi: A Life in the Woods. *In this first selection, the newborn young deer is coming to the meadow with his mother for the first time.*

Presently he began to enjoy the meadow with his eyes also. Its wonders amazed him at every step he took. You could not see the tiniest speck of earth the way you could in the forest. Blade after blade of grass covered every inch of the ground. It tossed and waved luxuriantly. It bent softly aside under every footstep, only to rise up unharmed again. The broad green meadow was starred with white daisies, with the thick, round red and purple clover blossoms and bright golden dandelion heads.

"Look, look, Mother!" Bambi exclaimed. "There's a flower flying."

"That's not a flower," said his mother, "that's a butterfly."

Bambi stared at the butterfly entranced. It had darted lightly from a blade of grass and was fluttering about in its giddy way. Then Bambi saw that there were many butterflies flying in the air above the meadow. They seemed to be in a hurry and yet moved slowly, fluttering up and down in a sort of game that delighted him. They really did look like gay flying flowers that would not stay on their stems but had unfastened themselves in order to dance a little. They looked, too, like flowers that come to rest at sundown but have no fixed places and have to hunt for them, dropping down and vanishing as if they really had settled somewhere, yet always flying up again, a little way at first, then higher and higher, and always searching farther and farther because all the good places have already been taken.

Bambi gazed at them all. He would have loved to see one close by. He wanted to see one face to face but he could not. They flew in and out continually. The air was aflutter with them.

When he looked down at the ground again he was delighted with the thousands of living things he saw stirring under his hoofs. They ran and jumped in all directions. He would see a wild swarm of them, and the next moment they had disappeared in the grass again.

"Who are they, Mother?" he asked.

"Those are ants," his mother answered.

"Look," cried Bambi, "see that piece of grass jumping. Look how high it can jump!"

"That's not grass," his mother explained, "that's a nice grasshopper."

"Why does he jump that way?" asked Bambi.

"Because we're walking here," his mother answered; "he's afraid we'll step on him."

"Oh," said Bambi, turning to the grasshopper, who was sitting on a daisy; "oh," he said again politely, "you don't have to be afraid; we won't hurt you."

"I'm not afraid," the grasshopper replied in a quavering voice; "I was only frightened for a moment when I was talking to my wife."

"Excuse us for disturbing you," said Bambi shyly.

"Not at all," the grasshopper quavered. "Since it's you, its perfectly all right. But you never know who's coming and you have to be careful."

"This is the first time in my life that I've ever been on the meadow," Bambi explained; "my mother brought me..."

The grasshopper was sitting with his head lowered as though he were going to butt. He put on a serious face and murmured, "That doesn't interest me at all. I haven't time to stand here gossiping with you. I have to be looking for my wife. Hopp!" And he gave a jump.

"Hopp!" said Bambi in surprise at the high jump with which the grasshopper vanished.

Narration Exercise

From *Bambi: A Life in the Woods* by Felix Salten

Dictation Exercise

From *Bambi: A Life in the Woods*
by Felix Salten

One evening Bambi was roaming about the meadow again with his mother. He thought that he knew everything there was to see or hear there. But in reality it appeared that he did not know as much as he thought.

This time was just like the first. Bambi played tag with his mother. He ran around in circles, and the open space, the deep sky, the fresh air intoxicated him so that he grew perfectly wild. After a while he noticed that his mother was standing still. He stopped short in the middle of a leap so suddenly that his four legs spread far apart. To get his balance he bounded high into the air and then stood erect. His mother seemed to be talking to someone he couldn't make out through the tall grass. Bambi toddled up inquisitively.

Two long ears were moving in the tangled grass stems close to his mother. They were grayish brown and prettily marked with black stripes. Bambi stopped, but his mother said, "Come here. This is our friend, the Hare. Come here like a nice boy and let him see you."

Bambi went over. There sat the Hare looking like a very honest creature. At times his long spoonlike ears stood bolt upright. At others they fell back limply as though they had suddenly grown weak. Bambi became somewhat critical as he looked at the whiskers that stood out so stiff and straight on both sides of the Hare's mouth. But he noticed that the Hare had a very mild face and extremely good-natured features and that he cast timid glances at the world from out of his big round eyes. The Hare really did look friendly. Bambi's passing doubts vanished immediately. But oddly enough, he had lost all the respect he originally felt for the Hare.

"Good evening, young man," the Hare greeted him, with studied politeness.

Bambi merely nodded good evening. He didn't understand why, but he simply nodded. He was very friendly and civil, but a little condescending. He could not help himself. Perhaps he was born that way.

"What a charming young prince," said the Hare to Bambi's mother. He looked at Bambi attentively, raising first one spoonlike ear, then the other, and then both of them, and letting them fall again, suddenly and limply, which didn't please Bambi. The motion of the Hare's ears seemed to say, "He isn't worth bothering with."

Meanwhile the Hare continued to study Bambi with his big round eyes. His nose and his mouth with the handsome whiskers moved incessantly in the same way a man who is trying not to sneeze twitches his nose and lips. Bambi had to laugh.

The Hare laughed quickly, too, but his eyes grew more thoughtful. "I congratulate you," he said to Bambi's mother. "I sincerely congratulate you on your son. Yes, indeed, he'll make a splendid prince in time. Anyone can see that."

To Bambi's boundless surprise he suddenly sat straight on his hind legs. After he had spied all around with his ears stiffened and his nose constantly twitching, he sat down decently on all fours again. "Now if you good people will excuse me," he said at last, "I have all kinds of things to do tonight. If you'll be so good as to excuse me...." He turned away and hopped off with his ears back so that they touched his shoulders.

Original Sentence Exercise

From *Bambi: A Life in the Woods* by Felix Salten

Name _____

Date _____

Dictation Exercise

"Prince Wicked and the Grateful Animals"
from *More Jataka Tales*
by Ellen Babbitt

The Jataka Tales are traditional stories from India. This story was retold about a hundred years ago by Ellen Babbitt. You'll read the first half of the story today, and the rest of it later in the week.

Once upon a time a king had a son named Prince Wicked. He was fierce and cruel, and he spoke to nobody without abuse, or blows. Like grit in the eye, was Prince Wicked to every one, both in the palace and out of it.

His people said to one another, "If he acts this way while he is a prince, how will he act when he is king?"

One day when the prince was swimming in the river, suddenly a great storm came on, and it grew very dark.

In the darkness the servants who were with the prince swam from him, saying to themselves, "Let us leave him alone in the river, and he may drown."

When they reached the shore, some of the servants who had not gone into the river said, "Where is Prince Wicked?"

"Isn't he here?" they asked. "Perhaps he came out of the river in the darkness and went home." Then the servants all went back to the palace.

The king asked where his son was, and again the servants said: "Isn't he here, O King? A great storm came on soon after we went into the water. It grew very dark. When we came out of the water the prince was not with us."

At once the king had the gates thrown open. He and all his men searched up and down the banks of the river for the missing prince. But no trace of him could be found.

In the darkness the prince had been swept down the river. He was crying for fear he would drown when he came across a log. He climbed upon the log, and floated farther down the river.

When the great storm arose, the water rushed into the homes of a Rat and a Snake who lived on the river bank. The Rat and the Snake swam out into the river and found the same log the prince had found. The Snake climbed upon one end of the log, and the Rat climbed upon the other.

On the river's bank a cottonwood-tree grew, and a young Parrot lived in its branches. The storm pulled up this tree, and it fell into the river. The heavy rain beat down the Parrot when it tried to fly, and it could not go far. Looking down it saw the log and flew down to rest. Now there were four on the log floating down stream together.

Just around the bend in the river a certain poor man had built himself a hut. As he walked to and fro late at night listening to the storm, he heard the loud cries of the prince. The poor man said to himself: "I must get that man out of the water. I must save his life." So he shouted: "I will save you! I will save you!" as he swam out in the river.

Soon he reached the log, and pushing it by one end, he soon pushed it into the bank. The prince jumped up and down, he was so glad to be safe and sound on dry land.

Then the poor man saw the Snake, the Rat, and the Parrot, and carried them to his hut. He built a fire, putting the animals near it so they could get dry. He took care of them first, because they were the weaker, and afterwards he looked after the comfort of the prince.

Then the poor man brought food and set it before them, looking after the animals first and the prince afterwards. This made the young prince angry, and he said to himself: "This poor man does not treat me like a prince. He takes care of the animals before taking care of me." Then the prince began to hate the poor man.

A few days later, when the prince, and the Snake, the Rat, and the Parrot were rested, and the storm was all over, the Snake said good-by to the poor man with these words:

"Father, you have been very kind to me. I know where there is some buried gold. If ever you want gold, you have only to come to my home and call, 'Snake!' and I will show you the buried gold. It shall all be yours."

Next the Rat said good-by to the poor man. "If ever you want money," said the Rat, "come to my home, and call out, 'Rat!' and I will show you where a great deal of money is buried near my home. It shall all be yours."

Then the Parrot came, saying: "Father, silver and gold have I none, but if you ever want choice rice, come to where I live and call, 'Parrot!' and I will call all my family and friends together, and we will gather the choicest rice in the fields for you."

Last came the prince. In his heart he hated the poor man who had saved his life. But he pretended to be as thankful as the animals had been, saying, "Come to me when I am king, and I will give you great riches." So saying, he went away.

Narration Exercise

From "Prince Wicked and the Grateful Animals" by Ellen Babbitt

Dictation Exercise

"Prince Wicked and the Grateful Animals"
from *More Jataka Tales*
by Ellen Babbitt

Today we'll finish the story of Prince Wicked.

Not long after this the prince's father died, and Prince Wicked was made king. He was then very rich.

By and by the poor man said to himself: "Each of the four whose lives I saved made a promise to me. I will see if they will keep their promises."

First of all he went to the Snake, and standing near his hole, the poor man called out, "Snake!"

At once the Snake darted forth, and with every mark of respect he said: "Father, in this place there is much gold. Dig it up and take it all."

"Very well," said the poor man. "When I need it, I will not forget."

After visiting for a while, the poor man said good-by to the Snake, and went to where the Rat lived, calling out, "Rat!"

The Rat came at once, and did as the Snake had done, showing the poor man where the money was buried.

"When I need it, I will come for it," said the poor man.

Going next to the Parrot, he called out, "Parrot!" and the bird flew down from the tree-top as soon as he heard the call.

"O Father," said the Parrot, "shall I call together all my family and friends to gather choice rice for you?"

The poor man, seeing that the Parrot was willing and ready to keep his promise, said: "I do not need rice now. If ever I do, I will not forget your offer."

Last of all, the poor man went into the city where the king lived. The king, seated on his great white elephant, was riding through the city. The king saw the poor man, and said to himself: "That poor man has come to ask me for the great riches I promised to give him. I must have his head cut off before he can tell the people how he saved my life when I was the prince."

So the king called his servants to him and said: "You see that poor man over there? Seize him and bind him, beat him at every corner of the street as you march him out of the city, and then chop off his head."

The servants had to obey their king. So they seized and bound the poor man. They beat him at every corner of the street. The poor man did not cry out, but he said, over and over again, "It is better to save poor, weak animals than to save a prince."

At last some wise men among the crowds along the street asked the poor man what prince he had saved. Then the poor man told the whole story, ending with the words, "By saving your king, I brought all this pain upon myself."

The wise men and all the rest of the crowd cried out: "This poor man saved the life of our king, and now the king has ordered him to be killed. How can we be sure that he will not have any, or all, of us killed? Let us kill him." And in their anger they rushed from every side upon the king as he rode on his elephant, and with arrows and stones they killed him then and there.

Then they made the poor man king, and set him to rule over them.

Original Sentence Exercise

From "Prince Wicked and the Grateful Animals" by Ellen Babbitt

Date _____

Name _____

Dictation Exercise

From *The Jungle Book*
by Rudyard Kipling

This story from The Jungle Book *tells about Mowgli, a young boy being raised by a wolf family in the jungle. His tutors are Bagheera the panther and Baloo the brown bear. Baloo has told Mowgli not to play with the monkeys, who are known to the jungle folk as "the Bandar-log." But Mowgli has ignored the bear and has run off to play with the monkeys—who kidnap him and haul him away!*

They belonged to the tree-tops, and as beasts very seldom look up, there was no occasion for the monkeys and the Jungle People to cross one another's path. But whenever they found a sick wolf, or a wounded tiger or bear, the monkeys would torment him, and would throw sticks and nuts at any beast for fun and in the hope of being noticed. Then they would howl and shriek senseless songs, and invite the Jungle People to climb up their trees and fight them, or would start furious battles over nothing among themselves, and leave the dead monkeys where the Jungle People could see them.

They were always just going to have a leader and laws and customs of their own, but they never did, because their memories would not hold over from day to day, and so they settled things by making up a saying: "What the Bandar-log think now the Jungle will think later": and that comforted them a great deal. None of the beasts could reach them, but on the other hand none of the beasts would notice them, and that was why they were so pleased when Mowgli came to play with them, and when they heard how angry Baloo was.

They never meant to do any more—the Bandar-log never mean anything at all—but one of them invented what seemed to him a brilliant idea, and he told all the others that Mowgli would be a useful person to keep in the tribe, because he could weave sticks together for protection from the wind; so, if they caught him, they could make him teach them. Of course Mowgli, as a wood-cutter's child, inherited all sorts of instincts, and used to make little play-huts of fallen branches without thinking how he came to do it. The Monkey People, watching in the trees, considered these huts most wonderful. This time, they said, they were really going to have a leader and become the wisest people in the jungle—so wise that every one else would notice and envy them. Therefore they followed Baloo and Bagheera and Mowgli through the jungle very quietly till it was time for the midday nap, and Mowgli, who was very much ashamed of himself, slept between the panther and the bear, resolving to have no more to do with the Monkey People.

The next thing he remembered was feeling hands on his legs and arms—hard, strong little hands—and then a swash of branches in his face; and then he was staring down through the swaying boughs as Baloo woke the jungle with his deep cries and Bagheera bounded up the trunk with every tooth bared. The Bandar-log howled with triumph, and scuffled away to the upper branches where Bagheera dared not follow, shouting: "He has noticed us! Bagheera has noticed us! All the Jungle People admire us for our skill and our cunning!" Then they began their flight; and the flight of the Monkey People through treeland is one of the things nobody can describe. They have their regular roads and cross-roads, uphills and downhills, all laid out from fifty to seventy or a hundred feet aboveground, and by these they can travel even at night if necessary.

Two of the strongest monkeys caught Mowgli under the arms and swung off with him through the tree-tops, twenty feet at a bound. Had they been alone they could have gone twice as fast, but the boy's weight held them back. Sick and giddy as Mowgli was he could not help enjoying the wild rush, though the glimpses of earth far down below frightened him, and the terrible check and jerk at the end of the swing over nothing but empty air brought his heart between his teeth.

His escort would rush him up a tree till he felt the weak topmost branches crackle and bend under them, and, then, with a cough and a whoop, would fling themselves into the air outward and downward, and bring up hanging by their hands or their feet to the lower limbs of the next tree. Sometimes he could see for miles and miles over the still green jungle, as a man on the top of a mast can see for miles across the sea, and then the branches and leaves would lash him across the face, and he and his two guards would be almost down to earth again.

So bounding and crashing and whooping and yelling, the whole tribe of Bandar-log swept along the tree-roads with Mowgli their prisoner.

Narration Exercise

From *The Jungle Book* by Rudyard Kipling

Dictation Exercise

From *The Jungle Book*
by Rudyard Kipling

The monkeys have taken Mowgli to their headquarters, the Cold Lairs.

In the Cold Lairs the Monkey People were not thinking of Mowgli's friends at all. They had brought the boy to the Lost City, and were very pleased with themselves for the time. Mowgli had never seen an Indian city before, and though this was almost a heap of ruins it seemed very wonderful and splendid. Some king had built it long ago on a little hill. You could still trace the stone causeways that led up to the ruined gates where the last splinters of wood hung to the worn, rusted hinges. Trees had grown into and out of the walls; the battlements were tumbled down and decayed, and wild creepers hung out of the windows of the towers on the walls in bushy hanging clumps.

A great roofless palace crowned the hill, and the marble of the courtyards and the fountains was split and stained with red and green, and the very cobblestones in the courtyard where the king's elephants used to live had been thrust up and apart by grasses and young trees. From the palace you could see the rows and rows of roofless houses that made up the city, looking like empty honeycombs filled with blackness; the shapeless block of stone that had been an idol in the square where four roads met; the pits and dimples at street corners where the public wells once stood, and the shattered domes of temples with wild figs sprouting on their sides.

The monkeys called the place their city, and pretended to despise the Jungle People because they lived in the forest. And yet they never knew what the buildings were made for nor how to use them. They would sit in circles on the hall of the king's council-chamber, and scratch for fleas and pretend to be men; or they would run in and out of the roofless houses and collect pieces of plaster and old bricks in a corner, and forget where they had hidden them, and fight and cry in scuffling crowds, and then break off to play up and down the terraces of the king's garden, where they would shake the rose-trees and the oranges in sport to see the fruit and flowers fall. They explored all the passages and dark tunnels in the palace and the hundreds of little dark rooms; but they never remembered what they had seen and what they had not, and so drifted about in ones and twos or crowds, telling one another that they were doing as men did. They drank at the tanks and made the water all muddy, and then they fought over it, and then they would all rush together in mobs and shout: "There are none in the jungle so wise and good and clever and strong and gentle as the Bandar-log." Then all would begin again till they grew tired of the city and went back to the tree-tops, hoping the Jungle People would notice them.

Mowgli, who had been trained under the Law of the Jungle, did not like or understand this kind of life. The monkeys dragged him into the Cold Lairs late in the afternoon, and instead of going to sleep, as Mowgli would have done after a long journey, they joined hands and danced about and sang their foolish songs.

Original Sentence Exercise

From *The Jungle Book* by Rudyard Kipling

Dictation Exercise

From *Rabbit Hill*
by Robert Lawson

This book was first published in 1944. It is the story of the animals who live on a deserted farm called the Hill. One of these animals is Little Georgie, a young rabbit who lives with his family beneath the Hill. In this excerpt, Little Georgie is hopping past a neighbor's house, not really paying attention, when the neighbor's dog, the Old Hound, surprises him and begins to chase him.

You should know that "Porkey" is the name of Georgie's friend the woodchuck, an animal also called a "groundhog" in some parts of the country.

Instinctively Little Georgie made several wide springs that carried him temporarily out of harm's way. He paused a fraction of a second to tighten the knapsack strap and then set off at a good steady pace. "Don't waste speed on a plodder" was Father's rule. He tried a few checks and doubles and circlings, although he knew they were pretty useless. The great fields were too bare, and the Old Hound knew all the tricks. No matter how he turned and dodged, the Old Hound was always there, coming along at his heavy gallop. He looked for Woodchuck burrows, but there were none in sight. "Well, I guess I'll have to run it out," said Little Georgie.

He pulled the knapsack strap tighter, laced back his ears, put his stomach to the ground, and RAN. And *how* he ran!

The warm sun had loosened his muscles; the air was invigorating; Little Georgie's leaps grew longer and longer. Never had he felt so young and strong. His legs were like coiled springs of steel that released themselves of their own accord. He was hardly conscious of any effort, only of his hind feet pounding the ground, and each time they hit, those wonderful springs released and shot him through the air. He sailed over fences and stone walls as though they were mole runs. Why, this was almost like flying! Now he understood what Zip the Swallow had been driving at when he tried to describe what it was like. He glanced back at the Old Hound, far behind now, but still coming along at his plodding gallop. He was old and must be tiring, while he, Little Georgie, felt stronger and more vigorous at every leap. Why didn't the old fool give up and go home?

And then, as he shot over the brow of a slight rise, he suddenly knew. *He had forgotten Deadman's Brook!* There it lay before him, broad and deep, curving out in a great silvery loop. He, the son of Father, gentleman hunter from the Bluegrass, had been driven into a trap, a trap that even Porkey should have been able to avoid! Whether he turned to right or left the loop of the creek hemmed him in and the Old Hound could easily cut him off. There was nothing for it but to jump!

This sickening realization had not reduced his speed; now he redoubled it. The slope helped, and his soaring leaps became prodigious. The wind whistled through his laced-back ears. Still he kept his head, as Father would have wished him to. He picked a spot where the bank was high and firm; he spaced his jumps so they would come out exactly right.

The take-off was perfect. He put every ounce of leg muscle into that final kick and sailed out into space. Below him he could see the cream-puff clouds mirrored in the dark water, he could see the pebbles on the bottom and the silver flash of frightened minnows dashing away from his flying shadow. Then, with a breath-taking thump, he landed, turned seven somersaults, and came up sitting in a clump of soft lush grass.

He froze, motionless except for heaving sides, and watched the Old Hound come thundering down the slope, slide to a stop and, after eyeing the water disgustedly, take his way slowly homeward, his dripping tongue almost dragging the ground.

Original Sentence Evaluation

From *Rabbit Hill* by Robert Lawson

Dictation Evaluation

PERMISSIONS

Caxton Press: excerpts from Paul *Bunyan Swings His Axe*, by Dell McCormick. Copyright 1936, The Caxton Printers. Used by permission of Caxton Press, Caldwell, Idaho.

Scott Corbett: excerpts from *The Lemonade Trick*, by Scott Corbett, copyright 1960. Used by permission of Curtis Brown, Ltd.

Tom Doherty Associates, LLC: Excerpts from *The Furious Flycycle* by Jan Wahl, copyright 1968. Reprinted with permission of Tor Books, an imprint of Tom Doherty Associates, LLC.

William B. Eerdmans Publishing Company: Excerpts from *C.S. Lewis: The Man Behind Narnia*, by Beatrice Gormley. Copyright 1998 Beatrice Gormley. Used by permission of William B. Eerdmans Publishing Company.

Hachette Book Group: Excerpts from *Mr. Revere and I*, by Robert Lawson, copyright 1953/1981 Robert Lawson. Used with permission of Hachette Book Group.

Harcourt, Inc: excerpts from *The Moffats*, by Eleanor Estes, copyright 1941, 1969. Used by permission of Harcourt, Incorporated.

HarperCollins Publishers LLC: "Stegosaurus," from *Tyrannosaurus Was a Beast*, by Jack Prelutsky, copyright 1992, HarperCollins. Used by permission of HarperCollins.

HarperCollins Publishers LLC: Excerpts from *Farmer Boy* by Laura Ingalls Wilder. Copyright 1933, 1961 the Little House Trust. Used by permission of HarperCollins Publishers.

HarperCollins Publishers LLC: Excerpts from *Mrs. Piggle-Wiggle's Magic*, by Betty MacDonald. Copyright 1949, 1977. Used by permission of HarperCollins Publishers.

Henry Holt and Company, LLC: Excerpts from *Time Cat*, by Lloyd Alexander, copyright 1963. Reprinted with permission of Henry Holt and Company, LLC.

Henry Holt and Company, LLC: "Exploring" and "First Snowstorm" from *The Four-Story Mistake* by Elizabeth Enright. Copyright 1942 by Elizabeth Enright Gillham, c 1970 by Nicholas W. Gillham, Robert Gillham II and Oliver Gillham. Reprinted by arrangement with Henry Holt and Company, LLC

The C.S. Lewis Company, Ltd: Excerpts from The Lion, the Witch and the Wardrobe, by C.S. Lewis, copyright 1950; renewed 1978. Reprinted with permission of the C.S. Lewis Company Ltd.

Penguin Group USA: Excerpts from *And Then What Happened*, Paul Revere?, by Jean Fritz. Copyright 1973. Used by permission of The Penguin Group USA.

Penguin Group USA: Excerpts from *Homer Price*, by Robert McCloskey…copyright 1943, 1971. Used by permission of Penguin Group USA.

Penguin Group USA: Excerpts from *King Arthur and His Knights of the Round Table*, by Roger Lancelyn Green, copyright 1953. Used by permission of Penguin Group USA.

Penguin Group USA: *Rabbit Hill*, by Robert Lawson, copyright 1944 by Robert Lawson; renewed 1972 by John Boyd. Reprinted with permission of Penguin Group USA.

Random House, Inc: Excerpts from *The Black Stallion*, by Walter Farley, copyright 1941, renewed 1968 . Used by permission of Random House, Inc.

Random House, Inc: Excerpts from *Babe: the Gallant Pig*, by Dick King-Smith, copyright 1983. Used by permission of Random House, Inc.

Simon & Schuster: Excerpts from *Laura Ingalls Wilder: Young Pioneer* (Childhood of Famous Americans series) by Beatrice Gormley. Copyright 2001 Beatrice Gormley. Reprinted with the permission of Aladdin Paperbacks, an imprint of Simon and Schuster Children's Publishing Division.

Simon & Schuster: Excerpts from *Dr. Seuss: Young Author and Artist* (Childhood of Famous Americans series), by Kathleen Kudlinski. Copyright 2005 Kathleen Kudlinski. Reprinted with the permission of Aladdin Paperbacks, an imprint of Simon & Schuster Children's Publishing Division.